Available Through:
Quality Books Inc.
1003 W. Pines Rd.
Oregon IL 61061
1-800-323-4241

A Bedtime Companion

Dedication

I would like to dedicate this book to my wife Martha who has patiently put up with my ways for many years and has always been supportive of my activities.

I would also like to express my deep appreciation to Jacque Cordle for her encouragement and her help in editing and proofreading of the text. Her help and encouragement have been instrumental in this book being completed. If not for her urging and that of another friend, Carolyn Huntley, I probably would never have finished, and if not for the help of another old and dear friend, Iona Kargel, I probably would still be wondering what to do with it.

Play up! Play up for the big prizes! Ten, ten, nine — twenty-nine points. 'Ard lines, Sir. If you'd thirty you'd have won a gold watch. M'ria, give the gentleman a bag o' nuts.

This cartoon by F. H. Townsend appeared in *Punch* in 1910. How little times have changed. The favorite gamble today is not the dart board but the lottery. Far less chance of winning. The lottery is a tax on people who cannot add.

Gambling: The sure way of getting nothing for something.

Wilson Mizner

A Bedtime Companion

Compiled and edited by
Robert E. Bell

Penrith Publications
Mechanicsville, Virginia

Published by Penrith Publications
          Mechanicsville, Virginia
Printed and bound in the United States of America.

Library of Congress Control Number: 2001130789

The Library of Congress cataloging in Publication Data:
A bedtime companion: a non-habit forming aid to peaceful
    slumber / compiled and edited by Robert E. Bell. -- 1st
    ed.
        p. cm.
        ISBN: 0-9710519-5-X

    1. American wit and humor.   I. Bell, Robert E.,
    1924-

    PN6162.B44 2001   818'.602
                                     QBI01-700818

Table of Contents

Cover picture by Charles Dana Gibson, ca.1898

Introduction

Friends and relatives who have read some booklets that I have produced have told me that they keep the booklets beside their beds. They have found that reading the booklets at bedtime puts them right to sleep. That doesn't bother me because I intended to put together material that could be picked up and read almost anywhere without needing to refer to anywhere else in the book. Likewise, the book can be put down anytime without the reader feeling that something must be completed before stopping or that you are missing something important.

The items are short and complete in themselves. This book is intended to entertain or amuse without selling anything or espousing any creed or belief. If you like the sort of thing that I as the compiler found entertaining, you'll like this book; if you want something more profound, you won't like it.

This book is an anthology of quips, quotations, cartoons, memoirs, and amusing stories, in fact almost anything that I found amusing, enlightening, or inspiring over the past fifty years or so. There are lots of pictures also for people who prefer them. It includes cartoon ideas, interesting quotations, experiences that I have had, disasters that have happened to others I have known, inspiring thoughts, humorous situations I have learned about, sometimes first hand, and miscellaneous things that I have found interesting.

The setting for many of the anecdotes I have written is Stoney Creek, the small Ohio community where I grew up. Stoney Creek is not the real name, but to protect the guilty and prevent possible libel suits, that is the name I have used. Those readers who grew up in the same community will be able to identify without much trouble the places and characters described even though I have changed the names.

You may find it amusing. I certainly hope so. It was written to entertain, as a hobby rather than to make money. Writing and publishing has been more or less of a hobby with me. That is, if you define hobby as something one does for fun but doesn't make any money at it. I hope that nothing in this book hurts anyone's feelings.

"Thank you so much for the gift of your latest book. I'll waste no time reading it." I have heard this quote attributed to several different people and it possibly could be attributed to Moses Hadas, Thomas Macauley, Oscar Wilde, G. B. Shaw, et. al. In any case, I hope you waste no time in reading my book.

Robert E. Bell
October 2001

Acknowledgments

Every writer owes a lot to other people if only for putting up with his moods and lack of attention. In this case, I owe nearly everything to other people for that and also for many of the ideas for amusing and inspiring items.

Specifically I would like to thank some of the people by name, although the list will be far from comprehensive. They are listed basically alphabetically to help them find their names.

Amy Able	Evan Jellicoe
D. V. Aight	M. P. Kunious
Horace Bach	Carol Liner
Myrtle Bush	Lana Lynn
Virginia Creeper	Harley Quinn
Ernie Doczy	Horace Ryder
Eileen Dover	Ernest Lee St. Cyr
Al Dunn	Avery Thyme
Della Gaight	Noah Vale
Ann Jellick	Rhoda Waye

Like Klick and Klack, the automotive consultants, in legal affairs we are represented by the law firm of Dewey, Cheatham, and Howe.

Musical accompaniment is by the British music group, Dicky Hart and the Pacemakers.

Travel arrangements are by Juan der Luste.

Any anthologist or compiler of quips, quotes, etc., has the problem of feeling somewhat of a parasite, living on the hard work of others. Most of the quotations and remarks printed in this book have been printed in a large number of other publications, I am confident. I know that I have heard them many times but I can't remember where in most cases. The ones where I don't remember the source are quoted to the best of my memory; like most people I do not keep very good notes. As a result, they may not be completely accurate and I apologize for that.

The ideas used in some of the cartoons have also been shamelessly stolen from my favorite cartoonists and humorists over the past fifty years or so. The fact that ideas are not copyrighted accompanied by the fact that they stole the ideas from earlier artists, doesn't help my conscience much, but in most cases I don't even remember whose idea it was to begin with.

When I knew the source of the work, I requested and received permission to use the material; I only hope that others who recognize their ideas will be forgiving enough to overlook the use.

The pundit Wilson Mizner, who is one of my favorite cynics, once said :
Copy from one, it's plagiarism; copy from two, it's research.

A Brief Word about Pictures and Quotes

Every effort has been made to trace and contact all copyright holders but if any have been inadvertently overlooked, the editor and publisher will be pleased to make the necessary arrangement at the first opportunity.

A compiler of any anthology like this uses many sources, often other anthologies. A number of the quotations in this book are from the *Wit* series of books compiled by Des McHale and published by Mercier Press, Ireland. All are quoted with permission.

The pictures in this book come from several sources inasmuch as I am not much good at drawing. Most of the photographs are ones that I took myself or they are from *Art Explosion 250,000* or *Art Explosion 750,000,* two collections of graphics from Nova Development, Calabasas, California. Some of the drawings are cartoons done by my parents, Ray and Caroline Bell, and first published in several farm magazines in the 1930's and 1940's. Most of the others are composites that I have done using parts of drawings that are about a hundred years or so old and are copyright-free or are reprinted with permission. The principal sources of these drawings are:

Women, a Pictorial Archive from Nineteenth Century Sources, Selected by Jim Harter.

Men, a Pictorial Archive from Nineteenth Century Sources, Selected by Jim Harter.

Harter's Picture Archives for Collage and Illustration, Edited by Jim Harter.

Gibson Girl Illustrations, Selected and Arranged by Carol Belanger Grafton.

Old-Fashioned Eating and Drinking Illustrations, Designed by Carol Belanger Grafton.

Trades and Occupations, A Pictorial Archive from Early Sources, Selected and Arranged by Carol Belanger Grafton.

The above books were published by Dover Publications, Inc., New York.

The Gibson Book by Charles Dana Gibson, published by Charles Scribner's Sons, New York

Art Explosion 250,000 by Nova Development, Calabasas, California

Art Explosion 750,000 by Nova Development, Calabasas, California

The definitions of southern words listed in Southern Exposure come from a column published by Jim Henderson in the *Norfolk Virginian Pilot* some years ago and is reprinted with permission.

The portions of *The Lord of the Rings*, by J.R.R. Tolkien, are reprinted with permission of Houghton Mifflin Co., Boston, MA.

The July, 1998, news item from the *Richmond Times Dispatch* is reprinted with permission from the Associated Press.

The picture on page 298 of the girl holding a sign for Grandpa is reprinted with permission from GNResound, manufacturers of digital hearing aids.

The portions of *Alice in Wonderland* and *Through the Looking Glass* are reprinted from *The Annotated Alice* by Martin Gardner, published by Wings Books.

The picture and caption on page 122 are reprinted with permission from *Spotlight,* the program guide of WCVE, the PBS station in Richmond, Virginia.

The several cartoons and portions of other cartoons by F. H. Townsend are taken from *Punch Drawings* by F. H. Townsend, published by Cassell and Company, Ltd, London, New York, Toronto, and Melbourne, in 1921. I found the book in an antique store in Scotland several years ago and I have searched diligently for Cassell and Company unsuccessfully. In as much as the drawings were made between 1908 and 1920 by an artist who died over eighty years ago and also because presumably Cassell and Company no longer exists, I believe I am free to reprint some of the drawings and cartoons. If I am guilty of infringement, I hope that Cassell and Company is forgiving enough to permit the use because I do not see how such use can be of harm to them.

Below is a picture of the artist and editor himself. Photograper and date unknown. This picture appears in the book described above.

Two men were sitting on the porch visiting when the host's dog came strolling up to them and lay down.

"What's the dog's name?" the visitor asked.

"Well, you'll have to help me with that," the host said. "What's the name of them purty flowers with the real soft petals and the thorns on the stems?"

"Why, them's roses," the visitor replied.

"That's it! That's it!" the man said. Then he called through the open door to his wife in the house, "**Rose! Rosie!** What the devil is that dog's name?"

Book One
Olla Podrida

olla podrida: 1. A stew of highly seasoned meat and vegetables.   2. An assorted mixture, miscellany. [Sp. *olla*: an earthenware pot + *podrida*: rotten]

The second meaning is the one I prefer. It better describes what this book is meant to be. I hope it is spicy enough to be interesting but not so much as to spoil your enjoyment.

God has always been hard on the poor.

Jean Paul Marat (1743-1793)

Speaking of coincidences: Would you believe it? Forty years ago, Mrs. Betty Lomax of Pugh Street, Ponders End*, while sunbathing in her garden, lost her engagement ring. Yesterday, while digging up the very same garden, her son Wilfred ruptured himself.

Anonymous

   * I'm not sure about Ponders End, but Loose Chippings and Hidden Summit must be the names of towns in England. I have never seen either of them, but I have seen signposts along the roads in several places indicating that they are just ahead. Some other towns within a ten mile radius in Suffolk are Maggot's End, Roast Green, Green Tye, Ugley, Ugley Green, Pale Green, Starlings Green, and End Green, so Ponders End sounds about right.

   Welcome aboard the *Viking Adventures* luxury cruise, gentlemen. We are heading for three exotic destinations, France, England, and Wales. In France we will find the best wine and food in the world, but I must caution you to keep one hand on your pocketbook and one eye on your belongings at all times. In England you will see the most beautiful women in the world but I must caution you to beware of the men, who are belligerent and unfriendly to Norsemen. In Wales are the best singing voices in the world but there is not much there worth stealing so don't waste time in looting. Now, we are off to a delightful time of wine, women, and song.

               Eric Plunder (914 - 951) Viking tour director

   An honest politician is one who does not lie, cheat, or steal more than is necessary. A statesman is an honest politician who didn't get caught.

               Unknown

Ernie Doczy's comment on Murphy's Law: Beauty is only skin deep but ugly is to the bone.

Ernie Doczy

We see what we want to see.

REB

Mirror, mirror, on the wall, …

What a strange illusion it is to suppose that beauty is goodness.

Leo Tolstoy

Do not insult the mother alligator until after you have crossed the river.

Haitian proverb

Tell the truth and run.

Yugoslavian proverb

I want a girl just like the girl that married dear old Dad.

Lyrics by Oedipus Rex

Never engage in a battle of wits with an unarmed person.

Unknown

Providence protects children and idiots. I know, because I have tested it.

Mark Twain

I do not want people to be agreeable, as it saves me the trouble of liking them.

Jane Austen

I'm careful of the words I say,
To keep them soft and sweet.
I never know from day to day
Which ones I'll have to eat.

Anonymous

Cannibals aren't vegetarians, they're humanitarians.

Unknown

He that justifieth the wicked, and he that condemneth the just, even they both are an abomination to the Lord.

Proverbs 17:15

Caution: This full bodied whiskey should be sipped gently as you would a fine liqueur. You should not gulp it like water. If you do you will lose the delicate aroma and subtle flavor. You may also lose consciousness.

Warning on a whiskey bottle label

Swallow a toad in the morning if you want to encounter nothing more disgusting the rest of the day.*

Nicolas Chanfort (1741-1794)

* Actually, you'll be dead.

At the office today, about the middle of the morning, well more like early morning between 8:30 and 9:00, say 8:45 give or take a couple of minutes, I pushed back from my desk. I have a new chair, one of those molded fiberglass chairs, much more comfortable than the old wooden chairs. It really has excellent strength to weight ration, not like titanium would have of course, but then titanium would be overkill in a desk chair. Anyway, I overheard one of the secretaries, well, not a secretary exactly, more like a clerk actually — works over in production planning keeping track of orders — telling one of her friends just how boring she thought engineers were.

Having spent most of my working career as an engineer, I can sympathize as well as empathize with the poor fellow in the picture above. Many engineers, myself included, are boring because they have an obsession with being very precise in their description of anything. Engineers don't like to be inaccurate, even in things that don't matter a lick. I'm sorry if that is boring, but that's just the way it is.

1. I wonder if it was something I said.
2. Maybe if I asked for an upgrade from Tourist to Business class.
3. I can't believe I forgot to have children.

Choose the caption you like.

"I can't believe *that*!" said Alice.

"Can't you?" the [White] Queen said in a pitying tone. "Try again: draw a long breath, and shut your eyes."

Alice laughed. "There's no use trying," she said: "one *can't* believe impossible things."

"I daresay you haven't had much practice," said the Queen. "When I was your age, I always did it for half-an-hour a day. Why sometimes I've believed as many as six impossible things before breakfast."

Lewis Carroll in *"Through the Looking Glass"*

I don't know half of you half as well as I should like, and I like less than half of you half as well as you deserve.
Bilbo Baggins at his farewell party
(J. R. R. Tolkien in *The Lord of the Rings*)
[The guests spent the next few minutes trying to figure out if this were complimentary.]

In April 1975, several newspapers and periodicals reported that scientists believed that the earth was cooling down drastically and that we would soon be experiencing a new ice age which would destroy agriculture as we know it.

In June 1992, the same newspapers and periodicals reported that the same scientists were now warning that the atmosphere was fast approaching its limit to absorb carbon dioxide and the earth would soon experience the greenhouse effect in which temperatures would rise to the point that the ice caps would soon melt and inundate all the earth's coastal areas to the depth of about two hundred feet.

New Ice Age! Global Warming! Who cares! Run for your life! The sky is falling! The sky is falling!

The first item appeared over twenty five years ago, and the media are still at it with about the same amount of evidence.

Your criticism of this product shows that you have an unsound technical background.

Unknown

Gravity isn't easy, but it's the law.

Unknown

I read the other day about the insomniac who was an agnostic and also dyslexic. He lay awake all night worrying about whether there really is a Dog.

Unknown

An economist was walking in Scotland and came upon a shepherd and a large flock of sheep. The economist said to the shepherd, "If I can guess the exact number of sheep in your flock, will you give me one." The shepherd agreed so the economist looked over the flock and said, "289." "That's right," said the shepherd, "Pick out any sheep you want." The economist looked over the flock again and finally picked up an animal and started to walk away. The shepherd stopped him and said, "Wait a minute. If I can guess your profession exactly, will you give me back the animal." The economist agreed so the shepherd said, "You're an economist." "That's right," said the economist, "How did you guess so quickly?" The shepherd replied, "Easy. That's my dog you're carrying."

Lost in the Wilds of New Jersey

Some years ago when I was a young engineer working for Bell Telephone Laboratories in North Carolina, I had to make frequent business trips to the Bell Labs location in Whippany, New Jersey. On one of the first trips I made there, I had the terrifying experience of being lost in a storm.

I had arrived at the Newark Airport one mid-November evening and rented a car to drive to Whippany, about 20 miles west of Newark where I stayed the night. The following day I had an early morning appointment with some colleagues at the Whippany Lab, so I drove over there to eat breakfast at the Lab cafeteria which was the best place in the area to eat. It was still dark when I arrived at the Lab.

Whippany is a large location and the parking area had about a dozen guard gates open during the early morning hours. I parked in line with one of them and walked in toward the cafeteria. I neglected to check which gate number I used; bad mistake.

After a good breakfast, I went to the conference room where I was scheduled to meet with some other engineers. They expressed surprise at seeing me saying, "We thought you would stay home. Have you seen the weather report? The worst blizzard in years is coming this way and due to reach here about noon. If you expect to get home, you had better head for the airport."

So I did. I found that the weather had become a bit nasty while I was at breakfast; it was now blowing a gale with mixed rain and snow. When I got to the parking area, I discovered to my surprise that only one gate was open. The question now occurred to me, "Which gate did I come in?" My car was in line with that particular gate about twenty or so cars away. I also remembered that I had never seen the car in the daylight and wasn't really sure what color it was. Not that it mattered, the cars now all had a layer of wet snow and all were white. I did remember that it was a new Mercury Cougar, which narrowed the search a bit.

So I now had to check for a Mercury which was about twenty cars or so out in line with every gate in the lot. After searching only about three lines of cars I found it, opened the door and got in. As I did, I thought, "The instrument panel looks different somehow." It was more elaborate than the one I remembered in the rental car, but I tried the key anyway.

No luck, the key wouldn't turn. So I got out, wiped the snow off the licence and compared it to the tag on the key chain. It was not my rental car. So back to the search. My feet were getting a bit wet and cold by now and the snow was getting heavier.

Finally I found it, got in and started for the airport. It was a real relief to listen to the radio and hear how much trouble the storm was causing others, now that I was in a warm car and headed for home. Of course, I still had to get to the airport and check in the car, all the while hoping the planes were still flying out. Ah well, never mind, look on the bright side. At least I was headed home in the sunny south.

On the radio the announcer was telling about commuters from Staten Island to Manhattan Island who were now stranded on ferry boats in the harbor because the waves and wind in the harbor had made it too rough to dock the ferry boats. The boats were pitching pretty badly in the water. The announcer had made radio contact with the captain of one ferry and was asking him, "Now that the passengers have been on the ferry for three hours, how are they making it?" I could imagine how they were making it.

"Oh," the captain replied cheerily, "They're just fine. They're all regulars on the ferry and they don't mind this at all. They are all getting along fine. No complaints so far."

Sure. I know I was glad to get on the airplane and get out of the area. I got home a few hours earlier than I had originally planned and was mighty glad to see familiar territory and get some dry shoes.

Insults and Curses by Experts

The art of insult and curse has largely been lost in the present generation. Now it seems that all the insulter can think of is a dirty name for the insultee. In earlier generations, the insulter had more imagination. Consider these gems.

May the curse of Mary Malone and her nine blind illegitimate children chase you so far over the hills of Damnation that the Lord himself can't find you with a telescope.

Old Irish curse

Here is one of my favorites about modern "classical" music:

I love Wagner, but the music I prefer is that of a cat hung by its tail outside a window and trying to stick to the panes of glass with its claws.

Charles Baudelaire (1821-1867)

This is essentially the way I feel about the "music" of Scriabin or Bartok.

His imagination resembled the wings of an ostrich. It enabled him to run, though not to soar.

Thomas Babington Macaulay (1800-1859)

What was all that shouting about back there?

Customer: Gentle disposition! Why he wants to bite the head off every dog he meets. I've been swindled!

Shopkeeper: You didn't ought to keep dogs at all, Mister. The animals you ought to keep wiv your temperament is silkworms!

F. H. Townsend in *Punch* 1910

Health Tip

How to keep from growing old:

Get plenty of exercise in the fresh air.

A Mysterious Event

Saturday October 21,1996, was not quiet. Marty and I took the dogs around the block and went to bed about 9:30. So far, all was quiet.

A few minutes later the cordless phone in the study across the hall from our bedroom made a strange buzzing, so I got up to investigate. It seemed to have a dial tone when I picked it up, but it didn't sound quite right. Marty listened to the regular phone by our bed and it had nothing but lots of static. I disconnected the cordless phone and that seemed to have no effect. So we went back to bed.

A few minutes later the regular phone clicked loudly. When I picked it up it was completely dead, not a sound. I hung it up, planning to deal with it in the morning and rolled over to go to sleep. Before I closed my eyes however I noticed that there were lots of lights shining on the tree tops behind the house, lights that were moving around and flashing on and off. This did not appear to me to be normal so I looked out back to see what was happening.

I could see 20 or so flashlights moving around in the woods behind our house, but these were not shining into the tree tops. Then I looked out the front windows where I could see an ambulance in front of our house with the lights flashing and a big fire engine behind the ambulance with all of its lights flashing. No sirens at all. Next to our driveway there was a white truck with lots of lights flashing and three more fire engines behind that. In addition, several other vehicles and a police car were parked further up the street and around the corner. All had their emergency lights flashing. It looked like the group that brings Santa Claus around for the kids at Christmas.

There seemed to be no activity except for some of the firemen leisurely putting on their gear. So I went out to see what the excitement was about. The ambulance left about that time but I asked one of the fireman what was happening. He wouldn't tell me anything; didn't seem to know himself except that the Browns who live next door had called 911. About that time Robbie Brown, who was then about 15, came over to our house and rang the door bell. (Of course the dogs made a big commotion. Every time a door bell rings, they go bonkers.) To add to their confusion, we have an alarm across the driveway which rings the door bell when any vehicle drives in. It was ringing every time anyone walked through the beam, which this evening was often.

Robbie told me that the power to half of their house went off and he had gone down to the basement to check the breaker box. He got a shock when he touched it. He then noticed that the ground wire from the phone cable to the plumbing was red hot and smoking. So his mother called 911 on the cellular phone — their regular phone was out of service. Somehow the phone cable and the power cable had become crossed and 110 volt power was coming in on the phone line. It also had affected our phone line but to a lesser extent. Our phone line was just dead.

The firemen checked Brown's house, cut the telephone ground wire, looked all over the woods behind our houses for where the cables could have gotten crossed, checked our house and garage, and found no problems, except that the phones were out of service and half of the power circuits in Brown's house were dead.

The firemen got the power company and the phone company crews out and then stayed around to be sure that there was no more hazard. We went on back to bed after checking to see that our TV cable seemed to be OK and was bringing in a good signal as though nothing was happening.

One of the fire engines was still there three hours later. We have a volunteer group and I thought that was remarkable dedication.

It turned out that the TV cable people had been working on their cables for several days and at some time had nicked one or more of the power cables and phone cables. The moisture in the ground had eventually caused a short circuit which killed the phone lines and caused the power outage at Brown's. The problems were corrected the next day and all was well.

I figured out how half the power could be out at the Brown's, but I'm guessing — no one confirmed the guess.

The power line into the house has three wires, A, B, and C. The voltage between A and B is 110V, between C and B is 110V and between A and C is 220V. About half the circuits in the house are from wires A and B and the other half from C and B. The stove and dryer and other heat units are from A and C. If either A or C were cut and the others were not, it would kill only half the 110V circuits in the house and, of course, all the 220V circuits. That's the only explanation I can think of.

A Second Mystery — Solved

We had another mystery the following day. There was a scorched smell in the house that seemed to be coming from the kitchen. Marty found a small bit of food that had gotten into one of the burners of the stove so she cleaned that out, but the smell only gradually disappeared. The following day the smell came back stronger than ever and I finally traced it down to the outlet and plug for the clothes dryer. A wisp of smoke was coming from behind the outlet box on the baseboard in the laundry and the box itself was smoking. It of course was phenolic and I then recognized the strange odor, burning phenolic. (I used to work with plastics molding, and the smells of the various plastics are distinct and unforgettable, but it had been almost 30 years since I had smelled scorched phenolic.)

I tripped the breaker to turn off the power, and we had an electrician come and replace the outlet box. The wood behind it was blackened and the box itself was pretty well burned. I'm glad we were home when it happened. The smoke detectors had not gone off yet, but they would have soon.

Picturesque Speech

A few years ago I worked for an engineering supervisor at Western Electric who prided himself on his picturesque speech. During one all-day meeting he chaired in the late summer of 1979 I took notes and this collection of pithy remarks and analogies is the result. All are quotations: the explanations in italics are my translations of the quotes where translations are needed.

At the lunch break, he complimented me on my diligence in taking notes during the course of the meeting. I thanked him for the compliment, but did not offer to show him my notes. As Winston Churchill once said of Clement Atlee, his successor as Prime Minister, "He packs a minimum of thought into a maximum of words."

Here are some of his comments:
1. Make an intelligent decision, maybe by flipping a coin.
2. He's done something behind the scenes that you can touch base on at this juncture.
3. We're between a rock and a hard place on this bag of worms.
4. That thing is stumbling our toe.
5. As the situation matured during the day …
6. Sweep one more under your blanket. *[Add one more item to your list of activities.]*
7. Take that ball and run with it. *[Assume the responsibility for that task.]*
8. Some of those balls are in your court. *[You are responsible for some of those problems.]*
9. Pushing the boulders off the road. *[Not as you might think, making the job easier by removing some of the obstacles. Rather, ignore details and look only at the superficial problems.]*
10. Be sure to document that, even if it is only orally. *[A neat trick and I was hoping he would explain how one can document something orally.]*
11. Carry on an ongoing dialogue with those guys. *[He never understood that dialogue is a conversation between two persons. He meant "Keep in touch with those guys".]*
12. Have a thumbnail conference with those guys. *[Have a small caucus with them.]*
13. Keep everything in prospective. *[He never really understood the difference between "perspective" and "prospective".]*
14. Bring everyone up to speed. *[Inform everyone.]*
15. These events are engraved on your memory drum, but keep a running track of them and later on we'll compare belly buttons on it. *[I'm not really sure, but I **think** he meant, "You have a vivid memory of these events, but let's not discuss it now. Remember them well and later on we'll discuss them."]*
16. It doesn't pay to fiddle while Rome is burning when the tigers are nipping at our heels. *[Stop trying to solve the problems on this project and devote your time to preparing a status report which is due in the near future.]*

17. From time to time one must divorce yourself from the heat of battle, drop back ten, and count your marbles. *[Honest, this is exactly what he said, including the "one" and "yourself". He meant to take time out from the engineering work and write a status report. It is just another way of saying the same thing as he did in item 16.]*

18. Create a miracle and raise the fence a few strands higher. *[Find a quick temporary fix for the problem.]*

19. Have a settee with those guys. *[He thought "settee" and "set-to" were synonymous, but he didn't really mean to have a fight with those guys. He just meant for us to discuss it with them.]*

20. Don't put a hole in the boat. *[Don't upset anyone by disagreeing with them.]*

Some of this man's favorite expressions include "early on", "bite the bullet", "deepening dialogue", in-depth discussion", and "where the rubber meets the road". *[By these he means, "early", "accept the facts" (he would say "true facts"), "detailed discussion", "further discussion", and "the results". Today, he would say "bottom line" for the last expression.]*

But maybe he's not walking backward. Maybe you've put the leash on the wrong end.

A Spanish Fable

A man was packing his bag and his neighbors said, "Where are you going?"
"I'm going to Madrid," he replied.

"Oh, you mean you are going to Madrid, God willing," they said.

"No," the man said emphatically, "I'm going to Madrid".

God heard the man and was angry so he turned the man into a frog and sent him down into the pasture to a frog pond. The man stayed there for seven years and God finally had pity on him and turned him back into a man. The first thing the man did when he got home was start packing his bag. His neighbors said, "Where are you going?"

"I'm going to Madrid," he replied.

"Oh, you mean you are going to Madrid, God willing," they said.

"No," the man replied, "I'm going to Madrid or back to that damn frog pond".

(Doesn't that remind you of the song that Sinatra made popular some years ago when he could still sing, *I Did It My Way*? That song always impressed me at its arrogance.)

This is Pentre Ifan, supposed to be a burial place for an important person some 4000 years ago. The capstone is estimated to weigh about 20 tons and is supported by just three upright stones, and the points are pretty darn small. The stones are from the nearby Presely Hills in Wales, from whence came the bluestones for Stonehenge in England.

Marty is not standing directly under the capstone; it doesn't look safe to be under. I personally think that the whole thing was put together by some stone age hunter who just wanted to get out of the rain, considering where it is located.

Patron: I'd like to call my sister Lois.
Waiter: Certainly sir. Shall I bring you the phone?

Patron: What on earth for?

Waiter: So you can call your sister Lois.

Patron: My sister's name is Charlotte. I would just like to call her Lois.

I'm Very Well Thank You

There is nothing the matter with me.
I'm as healthy as I can be.
I have arthritis in both my knees,
And when I talk — I talk with a wheeze.
My pulse is weak, and my blood is thin.
But — I'm awfully well for the shape I'm in.

Arch supports I have for my feet,
Or I wouldn't be able to be out on the street.
Sleep is denied me night after night,
But every morning I find I'm all right.
My memory is failing, my head's in a spin.
But — I'm awfully well for the shape I'm in.

The moral is this — as my tale I unfold,
That for you and me who are getting old,
It's better to say, "I'm fine" with a grin
Than to let folks know the shape we are in.

How do I know that my youth is all spent?
Well, my get up and go has got up and went.
But I really don't mind when I think with a grin
Of all the grand places my got up has been.

Old age is golden I've heard it said,
But sometimes I wonder as I get into bed
With my ears in the drawer, my teeth in a cup,
And my specs on the table until I get up.
Ere sleep overtakes me I say to myself,
Is there anything else I could lay on the shelf?

When I was young my slippers were red.
I could kick my heels right over my head.

When I was older my slippers were blue,
But still I could dance the whole night through.

Now I am old and my slippers are black.
I walk to the shop and I puff my way back.
I get up each morning and dust off my wits,
And pick up the paper to read the obits.

If my name is still missing I know
I'm not dead,
And so I have breakfast and go back
to bed.

Author Unknown

Your Horoscope

Aquarius (January 21- February 18)

You have an imaginative mind and are inclined to fantasize. You lie a lot. On the other hand, you are careless and impractical and you make the same mistakes again and again. People think you are incompetent.

Pisces (February 19 - March 20)

You have a minor influence over your associates at the office, and tend to flaunt your power. You lack self confidence and are easily bullied. You are very paranoid and believe you are being followed by the KGB, the CIA and the FBI. Pisces people do horrible things to small animals and children.

Aries (March 21 - April 19)

You are arrogant and flaunt what little power you have. You are contemptuous of other people. You are quick tempered, impatient, and heedless of advice. You are not a nice person at all. Most swindlers are Aries people.

Taurus (April 20 - May 20)

You are   persistent but impractical. You work like hell trying to force others to do what they don't want to do. People see you as stubborn and bull headed. You are a Liberal.

Gemini (May 21 - June 20)

You believe that you are a quick and intelligent thinker. People don't like you because you have loose morals and no principles. On the other hand, you are expect too much for too little. This just means that you are cheap. Geminis are often shoplifters.

Cancer (June 21 - July 22)

You are very sympathetic and understanding of other people's problems but you are gullible and fall for any confidence game. Others think you are a sucker. You are always postponing things and that is why you'll never make anything of yourself. Welfare recipients are usually Cancer people.

Leo (July 23 - August 22)

You overestimate yourself and believe you are a born leader. Others just consider you pushy. Leo people are most often bullies. You hate criticism, are extremely vain, and your arrogance is disgusting and unfounded. Leo people are almost always thieves.

Virgo (August 23 - September 22)

You are very logical and hate disorder. This leads you to nitpicking which sickens your friends. You are cold and unemotional and frequently fall asleep while making love. Virgos make excellent bus drivers and editors.

Libra (September 23 - October 22)

You are artistic and have a very difficult time distinguishing reality from fantasy. You are wishy-washy and will agree with anyone at all. Chances for employment and monetary gain are excellent. Libras will do or say anything for money.

Scorpio (October 23 - November 21)

You are shrewd in politics and totally without ethics. You will likely achieve the pinnacle of success because of your total lack of morals, probably even become President. Scorpio people are often murdered.

Sagittarius (November 22 - December 21)

You are optimistic, enthusiastic and have a reckless tendency to rely on luck because of your lack of talent. Most Sagittarians are either drunks or dope fiends or both. People are always laughing at you.

Capricorn (December 22 - January 20)

You are ultraconservative and afraid of taking any risk. You are too lazy to do much of anything constructive. Because of this there has never been a Capricorn of any importance at all. Capricorns are careful not to attract attention and often make good burglars.

Astrology is not an art, it is a disease
Maimonides (1135-1204)

Personnel Manager: *Wow! Look at this applicant's credentials! PhD in both physics and electronics from MIT, six years at Bell Labs, fourteen patents, two Nobel prizes! I wonder what his sign is.*

Boy! From now on I'm gonna read the fine print in those
bargain air fare tickets

Hospitality
Yankee

Friends of ours from England were visiting New York City recently and became somewhat lost. They saw a policeman on a corner and stopped him to ask how to get to a particular intersection. He listened politely to their request and gave a simple answer which they never forgot: "Buy a map!"

French

In constrast to that warm response, another couple of our friends from England were visiting a small village in southern France. They had heard about the interesting organ that was in the old church in the village and, being an organist himself, the husband wanted to see it. There was a notice on the church door that the key could be obtained from the caretaker who lived in the house next door to the church, so they knocked on the door to ask for the key. The woman listened politely as they explained that they wanted to see the inside of the church and especially the organ and asked if they could have the key. Then she said, "No." and firmly closed the door in their faces.

The following is a wedding invitation from the Lake District of England about 1750:

We are sending out an invitation to each and every location.
From Whitehaven, Workington, Harrington, Dean,
Hail, Ponsonby, Blaing, and all places between,
From Egremont, Cockermouth, Barton, St. Bees,
Cint, Kinnyside, Calder, and parts such as these.

Such sports there will be as have seldom been seen,
Such wrestling, and fencing, and dancing between,
And races for prizes, for frolic, and fun,
By horses, and asses, and dogs will be run,
That you'll all go home happy as sure as a gun,
In a word, such a wedding can ne'er fail to please,
For the sports of Olympus were trifles to these.

"Would you tell me, please, which way I should go from here?" asked Alice.
"That depends a good deal on where you want to go," said the [Cheshire] Cat.
"I don't much care where —" said Alice.
"Then it doesn't matter which way you go," said the Cat
                    Lewis Carroll in *Alice in Wonderland*

Citizens listening to the promises of a politician before election.

Citizens learning what the politician did after election.

Painesville, Ohio, Railroad Bridge

This picture was taken sometime in the 1860's by an unknown photographer. [He was probably known at the time, but we don't remember his name.] This was the first bridge of the Cleveland, Painesville, and Ashtabula Railroad just east of Painesville. The CP&A railroad later became the LS&MS [whatever that is] and

later still became the New York Central. The covered highway bridge later was replaced by a more modern bridge as the road became US 20. The river is the Grand River which flows into Lake Erie at Fairport Harbor. In this picture, the river is flowing away from the photographer who is looking essentially north.

British Workman (to German Comrade): "My poor friend, I hear that under your fiscal system you are reduced to eating black bread!"

German Workman: "My dear fellow, my heart bleeds for you. I hear that under your fiscal system you have to put up with white!"

When F. H. Townsend drew this cartoon in 1910, he titled it *The Colour Question* and was referring to the political propaganda that was being put out in Europe at that time.

Tornado Alert

Harold and Heidi Gage lived next door to Marty and me when I was a junior at Purdue. Harold was a junior in the Aeronautical Engineering School, and he worked part-time at one of the businesses in Lafayette, Indiana. He and Heidi had been married for about six or seven years, long enough to have four children.

They had had one fight in all that time. It started on their honeymoon and had continued with only brief intermissions ever since. At first, I felt sorry for Harold, but as I got to know them better I began to feel sorry for Heidi. Later still, I no longer felt sorry for either of them; they deserved each other, but I did feel sorry for the kids.

When we first moved to campus housing at Purdue, Marty and I had a one-bedroom apartment in one of the old prefabricated barracks that had been converted to make housing for married students. We lived there for one year. When graduating seniors left some of the two-bedroom apartments open, we obtained permission to move into one of them. Our son Fred was about a month old and his brother Steve was two years old when we got the two-bedroom barracks apartment.

We had until September to move out of the one-bedroom place because Purdue was not renting the one-bedroom places to anyone else. The bull-dozers were coming in to destroy them after we moved. Purdue was building new modern steel and masonry apartment buildings to replace these barrack apartments, and my class was the last to occupy the old buildings. It suited us fine because these apartments were a bit small but they were warm and comfortable and all on the ground floor. Not only that, they were cheap and that counted for a lot when most students were on tight budgets. The one bedroom places were $43 a month, the two bedroom places were $54 a month, while the new places were $88 a month. Included in that were electricity, gas, and water.

Because we had three months to move into the two bedroom place, we decided to redecorate it to suit our tastes and make a few changes in the place, such as install a gas line to the space where we wanted our gas clothes dryer. Purdue very generously allowed students to make changes in the apartments and even supplied lumber for shelves and paint for the walls and woodwork, so we painted all the rooms before moving in.

One day, when I was taking a break from painting and sitting on the little front porch, Harold stepped out of the front door of his next door apartment and looked up and down the courtyard between our building and those nearby. I had briefly met Harold and Heidi earlier that day.

When he saw me, Harold came over and said,"Have you seen Heidi in the last few minutes?"

I had not and Harold then said,"Well she's gone off to the neighbors somewhere. She's left a pie in the oven and it's burning."

I said, "Why don't you take it out?"

"Oh no!" Harold replied. "If she's so dumb as to leave a pie in the oven and go off somewhere, let the damn thing burn! The hell with 'er!"

I began to feel sorry for Heidi.

One evening shortly after we moved in, I was studying at the desk which was in our bedroom right next to the wall between our apartment and the Gages' living room. The walls were not very soundproof, and I could hear quite well what was going on next door. I tended to tune out the noise of the children playing when I was studying, so that never bothered me. This particular evening, Harold was right on time coming home from his part-time job. Often he was a few minutes early or as much as an hour late, but he demanded that supper be ready and on the table when he walked in or there would be a row. I was still feeling sorry for Heidi.

This time, as he walked in and asked if supper was ready, Heidi said, "Yes, sit down."

Harold walked to the table, took a look, and shouted, "What! Bacon and eggs for supper?!"

Heidi replied, "Well you didn't leave me enough money to get anything else" and the evening went downhill from there.

Whenever Harold had any studying to do, that is, every night, he found it virtually impossible to get anything done at home. When Heidi wasn't screaming at the kids, who weren't all that bad, she was screaming at Harold. He found it a bit difficult to concentrate at home so he often went down to the campus library to study. He was having a rough time with his classes anyway, and what with working 20 or 25 hours a week to supplement the family income, he really needed time to study. Heidi never gave him that time at home, and after listening to her communicate with Harold and the children when I was trying to study at my desk, I began to feel sorry for Harold.

While we were at Purdue, the Weather Bureau was starting their tornado warning system on the radio and TV. They had two types of alerts. "Tornado warning" meant that a tornado had been sighted and touched down somewhere close and we married students should get to the Student Union building on campus as quickly as possible and go down to the lower level where the cafeterias and game rooms were. "Tornado alert" simply meant that the conditions were right for a tornado to form, and we should stayed tuned to radio or TV for further information. Marty and I had grown up in Ohio and knew that the chances of a tornado hitting anywhere close by were remote, even in the so-called "tornado alley". Harold and Heidi on the other hand had come to Indiana from Buffalo, NY, and were terrified of tornadoes or anything that even looked like a heavy thunderstorm.

One evening I arrived home from my part time job a few minutes after five, my usual time. I noted that the sky was really black with the ominous cloud formations that could turn into a tornado but usually meant only a heavy thunderstorm any second now. I parked behind the apartment building and hurried into our apartment, thankful to reach it before the rain started.

I was greeted with relief by Marty and my son Steve because shortly before I got home, Steve had caught a part of a small toy between his lower front teeth and couldn't get it loose. Marty had tried and couldn't get it out either. Both of them had the misplaced confidence that "Daddy will know how to get it out." I couldn't get it loose either without damaging Steve's teeth; he was about 2 1/2 years old at the time, so I called the dentist, hoping that he would still be in his office a little after five.

He was just leaving but agreed to wait until we could get over there so he could remove the toy without damaging Steve's teeth. I grabbed Steve and Marty grabbed Fred, who was a couple of months old, and we hurried to the car before the rain started. It began to pour before we got to the dentist's office, and we got plenty wet going from the car to his door, but he was still waiting for us.

"Now, take the toy out of your mouth so I can see what the trouble is," he asked Steve when Steve was in the dentist chair. The dentist hadn't understood what the problem was, obviously.

"That **is** the trouble," I explained.

The dentist removed the toy without much difficulty and we thanked him properly and headed for home. When we got home, we were greeted by a very irate Harold Gage.

It seemed that Harold had gotten home a few minutes before I had, and both he and Heidi had been nervously watching out the window to see what the storm would do. There was a "tornado alert" out but Marty and I had gotten tired of listening to them; there seemed to always be a tornado alert whenever there were clouds on the horizon.

Then as Harold and Heidi watched, I came home and only a few minutes later, Marty and I came hurrying out of the apartment carrying the boys and headed quickly down the street in the car. It was obvious to them that Marty and I knew something they didn't know. To their minds, that could mean just one thing: *there was a tornado on the way and they had better get to the Student Union building as quickly as possible.*

They hurried their children into their car and went racing along the street to the main campus. It started pouring rain as they were going along. As they reached the Student Union building, they parked the car and went rushing into the building and down the stairs. They were drenched and water was streaming off of them as they got down to one of the cafeterias where early diners were just sitting down to eat. Harold and Heidi felt very self conscious as everyone turned to stare at the spectacle of two terrified and drenched adults with four small soaking wet children standing against one of the walls.

Harold and Heidi finally realized that there was no tornado and only a very heavy rain, so they sheepishly gathered the children back into the car and went home. Then they decided that Marty and I had been playing a trick on them and Harold was pretty angry about it. I don't think he ever accepted my story about the toy caught in Steve's teeth.

Their youngest child would be about 45 years old at the time of this writing. I wonder what became of them, and if they stuck together long enough for the children to grow up.

Albert and the Lion

There's a famous seaside place called Blackpool that's noted for fresh air and fun
And Mr. and Mrs. Ramsbottom went there with young Albert, their son.
A grand little lad was young Albert, all dressed in his best, quite a swell,
With a stick with an 'orse's 'ead 'andle, the finest that Woolworth's could sell.
They didn't think much to the ocean, the waves they was piddling and small.
There wasn't no wrecks and nobody drownded, 'fact nothing to laugh at at all.
So seeking for further amusement, they paid and went into the zoo,
Where they'd lions and tigers and camels, and old ale and sandwiches too.
There was one great big lion called Wallace, his nose was all covered with scars.
He lay in a sombulent posture, with the side of his face on the bars.
Now Albert 'ad 'eard about lions, 'ow they was ferocious and wild.
To see Wallace lying so peaceful, why it didn't seem right to the child.
So straightway the brave little fellow, not showing a morsel of fear,
Took 'is stick with the 'orse's 'ead 'andle, and shoved it in Wallace's ear.
You could see that the lion didn't like it, for giving a kind of a roll,
He pulled Albert inside the cage with 'im, and swallowed the little lad 'ole.
Then Pa, who had seen the occurrence, and didn't know what to do next,
Said, "Mother, yon lion's et Albert," and Mother said, "Eee, I am vexed."
Then Mr. and Mrs. Ramsbottom, quite rightly when all's said and done,
Complained to the animal keeper that the lion 'ad eaten their son.
The keeper was quite nice about it, 'e said "What a nasty mis'ap,
Are ye sure that it's your boy that 'e's eaten?" and Pa said, "Am I sure? There's
'is cap".
The manager had to be sent for; he came and said, "What's to do?"
Pa said, "Yon lion's et Albert, and 'im in 'is Sunday clothes too."
Then Mother said, "Right's right, young feller, I think it's a shame and a sin
For a lion to go and eat Albert, and after we've paid to come in."
The manager wanted no trouble. 'e took out 'is purse right away,
Saying, "'ow much to settle the matter?" Pa said, "What do you usually pay?"
But Mother 'ad turned a bit awkward, when she thought where 'er Albert 'ad
gone,
She said, "No, someone's got to be summons'd," so that was decided upon.
Then off they went to the Police Station, in front of the magistrate chap.
They told 'im what 'appened to Albert, and proved it by showing 'is cap.
The magistrate gave 'is opinion, that no one was really to blame,
And 'e said that 'e 'oped the Ramsbottoms would have further sons to their
name.
At that Mother got proper blazing, and "Thank you kindly!" said she,
"What, waste all our lives raising children, to feed ruddy lions, not me!"

Albert Stages a Comeback

You've 'eard 'ow young Albert Ramsbottom, in the zoo up at Blackpool one year,
With a stick with an 'orse's 'ead 'andle, gave a lion a poke in the ear.
The name of the lion was Wallace. The poke in the ear made 'im wild,
And before you could say, "Bob's your uncle", 'e'd up and 'e'd swallowed the child.
'e were sorry the moment 'e'd done it, with children 'e'd always been chums,
And besides 'e'd no teeth in 'is noddle, and 'e couldn't chew Albert on gums.
'e could feel the lad moving inside 'im, as he lay on 'is bed of dried ferns,
And it might 'ave been the little lad's birthday, 'e wished 'im such happy returns.
But Albert kept kicking and biting, 'til Wallace arose feeling bad,
And felt it were time that 'e started to stage a comeback for the lad.
So with 'is 'ead down in a corner, on 'is front paws 'e started to walk,
And 'e coughed and 'e sneezed and 'e gargled, 'til Albert shot out like a cork.
Old Wallace felt better directly, and 'is figure once more became lean,
But the only difference with Albert was 'is face and 'is 'ands was quite clean.
Meanwhile, Mr. and Mrs. Ramsbottom 'ad gone to their tay feeling blue.
Ma says, "I feel down in the mouth like", and Pa says, "Aye, I'll bet Albert does too."
Says Ma, "It just goes to show you, that the future is never revealed,
If I'd thought we were going to lose 'im, I'd 'ave not got 'is boots soled and 'eeled."
"Let's look on the bright side," said Father, "What can't be 'elped must be endured,
Every cloud 'as a silvery lining, and we did 'ave young Albert insured."
A knock on the door came that moment, as Father these kind words did speak.
'Twas the man from Prudential; 'e'd called for their tuppence per person per week.
When Father saw 'oo 'ad been knocking, 'e laughed and 'e kept laughing so,
That the young man said, "What's there to laugh at?" Pa said, "You'll laugh an'
all when you know."
"Excuse 'im for laughing," says Mother, "But really things 'appen so strange,
Our Albert's been et by a lion; you've got to pay us for a change."
Said the young fellow from the Prudential, "Now come, come, let's understand this,
You don't mean to say that you've lost 'im", Ma says, "Oh no, we know where 'e is."
When the young lad 'ad 'eard all the details, a bag from 'is pocket he drew,
And 'e paid them with interest and bonus, the sum of nine pounds, four and two.
Pa 'ad scarce got 'is 'and on the money, when a face at the window they see,
And Mother says "Eee, look it's Albert." and Father says, "Aye, it would be."
Young Albert came in all excited, and started 'is story to give,
And Pa says, "I'll never trust lions again, no, not ever as long as I live."
The feller from the Prudential to pick up the money began,
And Pa says, "Eee, just a moment, don't be in a 'urry young man."
And giving young Albert a shilling, he said, "Pop off back to the zoo.
" 'ere's your stick with the 'orse's 'ead 'andle. Go see what the tigers can do."

On the previous two pages are two British music hall monologues, the author(s) of which I have no idea. I have heard them recited by several different people on several occasions and none of the ones reciting them gave any credit to an author. I assume they are in the public domain and if they are not, someone will let me know, I am sure.

Your dinner fell on the floor. You still want it?

Traveler's Tales

Monkeys at Longleat

On a vacation trip to England a few years ago, Marty and I had an adventure that made the trip memorable, one that we don't want to ever experience again. Of course, we remember that adventure more than any others on that trip.

We rented a car when we arrived at Gatwick airport and stayed overnight nearby. The next day we planned to drive over to Glastonbury for our next overnight stay, stopping at Longleat to visit the stately home there on the way. Longleat has, in addition to the stately home, a park and an animal park as well. The animal park has various exotic animals and can be visited by taking a bus tour through the compounds where the animals are running free, or one can drive one's own car through at a lower cost.

We chose to drive though with our virtually new rental VW. That was the first mistake.

I got out and took some closeup pictures of giraffes and zebras and things looked pretty good in the first compound. Then, just as we were approaching the gate to the second compound, we noticed a large signboard which said something to the effect: "The monkeys in this compound can be destructive to automobiles with soft tops. Enter at your own risk". I assumed that "soft top" meant convertible top and since we had an ordinary metal roof and could close the windows, we continued on our way. That was the second mistake.

In the monkey compound, several monkeys jumped onto the hood of the car and on up to the roof. Then we heard strange popping noises from above us. Then we saw one of the monkeys lay the weatherstrip on the hood of the car. These strips run the length of the car from the base of the windshield to the back of the roof at the hinge of the hatchback on either side of the car. The monkeys ripped both of the strips out and put them on the hood of the car. We left before they could do any more damage. We learned later that we got off easy. The monkeys often rip windshield wiper arms off; plastic trim strips from the sides of cars are easily torn off; most modern cars have plastic bumper covers that can be torn off by monkeys too. Even the big cats such as lions and tigers in their enclosure have been known to jump on the hoods and tops of cars and leave great scratches in the finish that require repainting the whole vehicle.

We put the strips back as best we could which was not very well at all because there is a formed aluminum channel inside the rubber strip which cannot be reshaped satisfactorily. But we continued on our way, listening to the new whistles that the air made in the deformed weather strips.

When we arrived at our overnight B&B, we asked the hostess if there was a VW dealer in Glastonbury where we could get our car fixed. She informed us that there was not a VW dealer but that her husband was the Renault dealer in town and he had a body shop. She called to get someone to stay past their quitting time and we drove in to see him. He informed us that he did not have the parts needed to fix the damage, but he could get them a few days later. This was Friday evening a little after five o'clock and everything would be closed until Monday morning.

We had planned to go on down to Devon for a few days and come back to Glastonbury later anyway to spend a few more days in the area so this didn't change our plans much.

When we returned, the body shop replaced the strips in about 15 minutes and we were on our way. It cost a bit more than we had allowed for in our travel budget, but it was less than the car rental place would have asked us to pay if we hadn't had it done on our own. But we won't go in animal parks again, at least we won't drive through on our own.

Slurry Is Great on the Road

The treatment often used on asphalt roads is a slurry of cement, sand, and tar, put down by special machines which leave a thin coating which hardens rapidly to a tough, long wearing surface. It is great on the road.

Marty and I were traveling with a rental car on an unclassified road along the Welsh/English border a few years ago. As we drove round a curve in the road we came suddenly upon a slurry paving machine which took up all of the left side (our lane) of the road. There were no warning signs or flagmen to let us know to look out for road work, nor was anyone near the machine. There was no traffic coming, so I quickly turned out to the right and went past the machine. Just as I got past and swung back to the proper (left) side of the road, I realized that the pavement in front of that machine had a strange color. It also had a very strange feel as we entered it too; it was wet and sloppy. I very quickly swerved back into the right side lane and onto dry pavement. Just then, as we topped a slight rise, I saw the work crew a few hundred feet down the road with some more equipment.

One of the workmen grabbed a squeegee and started back toward us to repair the damage I had done to the new pavement. I stopped and apologized for the damage. He said, "I'm not concerned about the damage to the pavement. That is easily remedied. I'm more concerned about your car. That stuff sets up hard and should be removed as soon as possible."

We stopped a little way down the road and inspected the car. The slurry had splashed on the wheels and along the lower sides of the car, more on the left side than the right. It was mostly gray with flecks of black tar in it and was the consistency of wet mud. We were miles from any car wash or hose; this area of the borders has very few farms or villages. But we did have a fresh bottle of glass cleaner and several rolls of paper towels which we always buy as soon as we arrive in England to clean the glass each morning before we start out.

Did you ever try to wash a car, even just the lower part of a small car, using only paper towels and glass cleaner solution? It can be done, but don't expect to stay clean doing it. The tar in the slurry got on our shoes, our sleeves, our hands, and our trouser legs. But we did get it off the car.

We also found out what will dissolve it and a number of things that won't dissolve it. Fingernail polish remover (acetone) is useless on it. We stopped in the first village we came to and bought some because my fingers were sticking together and that made it difficult to drive. No good. Water, even with soap, won't touch it.

Gasoline helps a little but smells terrible and it's not all that great anyway. The only thing that cut it was WD40 which we bought at a small filling station.

That did a pretty good job on our shoes and trousers and a fair job on Marty's white silk sweater. It cleaned trousers and my shirt well enough that the next time they were washed they looked as good as new. The shoes were alright too, but Marty's sweater was too great a challenge for the WD40. I eventually got it clean after we returned home to the States but it took a lot of naphtha and elbow grease to do a decent job.

Driving to Mull of Galloway

On a visit to Scotland one year, we wanted to go down to the Mull of Galloway, the southernmost point of Scotland where the waters of the Irish Sea and Luce Bay come together with great turbulence and conflicting currents when the tide is running either in or out. If there is any swell or surf at all it is supposed to be quite spectacular. So away we went.

On the way, as we stopped for gasoline at Stranraer, a port for ferries to Ireland, we had the car washed because it was getting pretty dirty after having been driven over a lot of country for three weeks or so. Then we headed south, over classified roads (two lane) for a while, then unclassified roads (mostly single track with passing places) until we arrived at Drummore which has the southernmost post office in Scotland. From there, we had to drive about three miles further over a single track road and then another two miles or so through a farmer's pasture field over a single track, but paved, road to get to the Mull of Galloway. There we found a light house and a car park; no people or cars but plenty of space to park.

However, on the way through the pasture, the cattle had been crossing the track. They were off to one side now, but they had very recently been crossing the road and they had obviously had plenty of lush new grass to graze on. The road was a mess, and now our nice clean car was also a mess, fresh wet manure having splashed at one time or another within inches of the open sun-roof and all over the lower sides of the car.

The clashing currents must have been turned off that day too. The water was as still as a millpond, hardly a ripple on it. The weather was mild though, and we wandered around a bit looking at the scenery. As we were doing that, another vehicle made its way carefully into the car park, a Good Humor man, or the Scottish equivalent of a Good Humor man. He pulled up, parked, and began putting small hand made cardboard signs in the windows of the little van advertising his wares. I went over and said, "You're expecting a coach load of school children maybe?" He never cracked a smile and simply said, "No". He obviously didn't want to chat, so we went on our way back to Drummore.

We stopped at the post office to mail a couple of boxes back to the States and to enquire about a car wash. The postmaster and his wife laughed at our request and wondered why we would be wanting to wash a rental car. We explained that for the five weeks that we rented that car, we regarded it as ours and wanted it clean. Besides, it didn't smell very good at the moment. They laughed again at our problem and said that the nearest car wash would be in Stranraer, right where we had gotten it washed that morning.

They laughed at us again when we were listing the articles in the boxes that were going to the States. Included in one of the boxes was a small hand carved wooden owl I had purchased. When I listed "one owl", the postmaster's wife said, "Stuffed, I presume."

The lady at the car wash laughed at us too when she saw us for the second time that day. (People laugh at us a lot. We spread joy and hilarity wherever we travel.) It took a couple of tokens in the washing machine to get enough time with the wand to get the car cleaned, especially under the fenders and along the lower side. But the car smelled a lot better when we were done.

Sheep at Fat Lips Castle

We had read about a castle near Jedburgh in the Scottish Borders District named Fat Lips and wanted to see it. We were going to be going within a couple of miles of it one morning so we turned off the main road and went down to a village named Denholm and then went out of the village onto an unclassified road that went past Fat Lips Castle.

We left the village and drove up the road a couple of miles before we saw Fat Lips Castle up on a crag a few hundred feet from the highway. It doesn't look like much and it is not open to the public so a picture from a distance was the best I could get. It didn't look like it was worth the climb to get up to see it closer. With nearly every town of any size having its own castle and many castles out in the

✓ This is it!

country, you can't expect every one to be a fairy tale perfect image of a castle, the way Walt Disney would have us believe.

When I got out of the car to take the picture of the castle, I heard a strange clicking noise coming down the road. I turned to look and was surprised to see a flock of perhaps 200 sheep or so coming along the road, filling the road from verge to verge. Behind the sheep were

two dogs trotting along quietly, and behind the dogs, a man on a tractor idling along very quietly. The whole entourage was so quiet that the only sound was the clicking of the sheep's hooves on the pavement. As one of the dogs came past where I was standing, it stopped and looked surprised to see someone standing there. It then went trotting on to catch up with the rest of the group.

Marty and I were staying at a motel in Ripley, West Virginia, one summer night. We had been out for the evening and came to our room about ten o'clock. We had just nicely gotten to sleep when a heavy thud overhead woke us. It was 11:15 and the thuds continued. They came in bursts like someone walking but carrying something very heavy and nearly falling every step. They shook the walls.

When the thuds continued until midnight, I called the room above and asked what they were doing.

"Nuthin', we're just watching TV," was the reply.

"Then what is the heavy thudding noise we hear?" I asked.

"Oh, that must be Jane," was the reply, "She just went to the bathroom. She does walk kinda heavy."

"Please ask her to sit down to watch TV," I requested.

The noise stopped and we went to sleep again. The next sound we heard was a heavy pounding on the door and a voice shouting, "Open the door! Police!" repeatedly. We quickly determined that it was the door to the adjoining room. The time was now 4:05 a.m.

The pounding and shouting continued for five minutes. If they expected to find any contraband, there was plenty of time to put it down the drain. Apparently it was just a policeman calling on a friend who slept soundly. We went back to sleep.

At five forty-five, Jane got up to go to the bathroom again. We got up, sighed, dressed, checked out and headed down the highway. We started driving at six fifteen in the morning with no breakfast until farther down the road.

PRECEPT AND EXAMPLE.

This cartoon by F. H. Townsend appeared in *Punch* in 1907

The Homewrecker

Howard Clay was a homewrecker, not the kind that breaks up marriages, but the kind that breaks up houses. That wasn't his vocation, just his avocation. By trade Howard was a bookkeeper for one of the manufacturing firms in Mount Pleasant, but in his spare time he remodeled houses. Well, one house anyway.

Howard often expounded on his theory that they didn't build houses the way they used to. By this he meant that the way they used to build houses was far superior to the way they were built today. He was right that they don't build them now the way that they used to, but not necessarily right that the way they built them years ago was better.

Marty always said that Howard's name, Clay, was descriptive of his head, solid clay. She maintained that Howard took "stupid pills" because no one could be that stupid naturally. Dr. Samuel Johnson referring to Thomas Sheridan once said: "Why, Sir, Sherry is dull, naturally dull; but it must have taken him a great deal of pains to become what we now see him. Such excess of stupidity, Sir, is not in nature." This describes Howard Clay very well. He was much like Johnson's view of Thomas Sheridan.

I always maintained that Howard's wife Eleanor must be as stupid as Howard or else she would have hidden or sold his tool box and all his tools.

Howard bought an old house, one that had been built in about 1880 or so. It was a nice old house with a large front porch, an inviting back porch all across the width of the house, a good-sized living room, dining room, study, and kitchen downstairs with three large bedrooms and a bath upstairs. There was a full basement with a gas furnace that had at one time been coal-fired but had been converted. All in all, a satisfactory house that was in good repair. It just suited Howard who said, "They don't build 'em like this anymore. Just wait till I get through modernizing it. It will be great!"

The first thing Howard did after he and Eleanor moved in was to enlarge the living room. The kitchen was big enough in Howard's view to use for a dining area and he wanted to combine the living room and dining room into one big room. So he got out his sledge hammer one evening and removed the partition between the rooms. Unfortunately, the partition was a load-bearing wall and just as Howard took out the last remaining studs, the upstairs floor sagged about eighteen inches, cracking plaster all over the house.

Howard and Eleanor slept on the couch in the living room that night because both were afraid to trust the stairs which leaned at a peculiar angle now.

The next day, Howard got the Sawyer brothers, who were pretty good carpenters and general handymen, to come in and fix the house properly. Times were a little tight and the Sawyers didn't charge Howard a whole lot for their time; it actually didn't cost him a whole lot more than if he had gotten the Sawyers to do it right in the beginning.

They jacked up the upstairs floor and put in a supporting beam and columns to support it. The columns and beams formed a nice-looking arch in the center of the new living room. After the Sawyers finished patching plaster over the whole house, it looked great and Howard began to be right proud of his handiwork and ideas in remodeling an old house. "Just wait till I've finished," he boasted at his office the next day.

The next project was a fairly simple one. Howard didn't like the effect of having a chandelier in one end of the living room where the dining room had been and blank ceiling in the other end. He wanted to remove the old chandelier and replace it with an ornamental cover like an inverted dome that would hide the old electrical box which held the chandelier.

This time Howard thought it all out ahead of time and he turned off the power to the light fixture before he removed it. He got out his stepladder and removed the chandelier and got a surprise. When the house was built, it was supplied with gas light and when electricity came along later, the gas lines were left in place and the wiring was placed beside the pipes. The base of the chandelier was deep and had concealed the 1/4 inch steel pipe that stuck out of the ceiling about six inches through the electrical box. The pipe was neatly capped but it was too long to allow Howard to cover it with the ornamental dome he had bought. It obviously must be removed.

Howard was still thinking and before he removed the pipe he traced it out to determine if there was gas still in the line. He discovered that the only gas that came into the house now went to the furnace, the water heater, and the kitchen stove. All the other lines in the house had been disconnected and now hung empty and open in the basement. So it was safe to remove the pipe in the living room ceiling.

Howard got his trusty pipe-wrench and went back up the stepladder. The ceilings in this house were ten feet from the floor; high ceilings were the style when this house was built. He put the wrench to the pipe and gave a gentle push; nothing happened. He gave a stronger push; again nothing happened. That pipe had been in place for many years and was almost as strong as if it had been welded. So Howard gave a really strong push and felt the stepladder begin to lean away from him. So he got a very good grip on the wrench and as the ladder tilted completely away from him, he hung tightly to the wrench. The wrench in turn gripped the pipe tighter than ever and the pipe came out of the ceiling.

When the pipe had been installed the builders had never expected any great force to be exerted on it so there was only a small clip holding it to the ceiling joists. The pipe ripped through the light laths that held the plaster all the way across the ceiling to the wall and all the way down the wall to the floor, letting Howard fall and covering him with bits of broken plaster and lath.

Howard wasn't hurt much and soon cleaned up the mess. Then he called the Sawyer brothers again and had them come in to repair the damage to the wall and ceiling. They did a good job and when they were through, no one could tell that there had ever been a ceiling fixture in the room at all. Howard boasted to his colleagues at the office the next day that the room looked so much better than it would have with a chandelier or a tacky upside down dome in the ceiling. The Sawyer brothers didn't charge him a whole lot either; they were beginning to look on Howard as a regular customer.

Now that the living room was completed, Howard decided that the house needed a recreation room in the basement. There was only a crawl space put in when the house was built and later, when the furnace was installed, the basement had been dug out and a concrete floor put in. It was quite spacious and the old, no longer needed, coal bin could be enlarged and would make a recreation room large enough for a pool table, something dear to Howard's heart.

The furnace would need to be moved from one side of the chimney to the other but that presented no problem. It was summer so the heat could be off for however long the job took and, with minor rerouting of the duct work and gas lines, the job should be easy. So Howard started in.

The first obstacle was the chimney. The chimney ran up one inside wall of the living room and, when the house was built, rested on a foundation in the crawl space. When the basement had been dug out, the base of the chimney had been supported by a thick steel plate which rested on two large flanged pipe supports which rested on the concrete basement floor. When Howard started to move the furnace he discovered that one of the pipe flanges interfered with the movement of the furnace. So Howard removed that pipe.

As he moved the furnace still further, he discovered that the other pipe flange also interfered with the movement of the furnace. So he removed it too.

Eleanor had been sitting in the living room reading while Howard was working in the basement. She heard a loud crack and looked up just in time to see the chimney sliding straight down the living room wall. The chimney was made of old fashioned soft brick and when it hit the basement floor it began to break up into small pieces. When all the crashing and banging had stopped and the dust cleared, there was a pile of rubble on the floor and Howard could look up through the hole in the basement ceiling and see the stars through the hole in the roof where the chimney had been.

The Sawyer brothers did a very good job of building a new chimney, much better and safer than the old one, as Howard was quick to point out to his colleagues. They also fixed the plaster in the living room and the bedroom above it and repainted the walls to hide any evidence of the disaster. The place really looked nice when they were done. They also completed the job of moving the furnace, putting in partitions and doors in the basement and making a very attractive recreation room. The old house was beginning to look quite modern, inside at least.

Howard still was not satisfied with the bathroom though. It had one of those old fashioned freestanding tubs with the funny feet and looked as though it had come with the house. Howard wanted a nice modern, more built-in looking, tub so he got out his tool box again.

He removed the old tub and fastened the new tub in place without incident. He had turned off the water to the tub so there was no problem there. Where the problem arose was when he started to reroute the pipes to the new tub. The connections were at the opposite end of the tub from the old one so it was necessary to extend the lines.

The old pipes had been against one of the inside walls where they were protected from freezing in the winter and to extend them to the other end of the tub necessitated crossing several floor joists. Howard knew better than to try to remove the joists because they were the only things holding up the new tub; he had removed the floor boards under the tub because when he finished with the job, that part of the floor would be hidden anyway. Howard pondered the problem for a short time and then decided to simply cut away a small section of each floor joist to allow the pipe to pass through. So he did.

He got the pipe installed, connected, and ready to use. He then finished the floor in the rest of the bathroom and put in a nice cabinet and basin and a new toilet. When he had finished, the bathroom really looked good. Howard could do very nice looking work when he tried.

Then, Eleanor filled the tub to take a bath. The extra weight of water in the tub was a bit too much for the weakened floor joists and they began to creak loudly and the tub began to tilt. Eleanor left the bathroom hurriedly and watched from the doorway as the tub sank slowly through the ceiling below, tilting away from the wall it was mounted against. The floor in the rest of the bathroom sagged and tilted toward the tub and the water in the tub began to pour over one side. When enough water had poured out, the sagging ceased and only part of the tub extended into the ceiling of the kitchen below. There was quite a lot of water on the kitchen floor below however.

The Sawyer brothers came out the next day and began to fix the damage. They did a very good job of it and when all was done, the bathroom and kitchen both looked very modern and new. It really was a big improvement over the old style cabinets and fixtures that had come with the house.

The inside of the house now was very nice. As Howard proudly showed his friends around, he commented that they didn't build houses like this any more. Now all that was left was to improve the outside a bit. The old open back porch needed to be closed in to make it habitable in winter as well as summer.

Howard had a good plan for fixing the porch. He would put in a concrete footer along the periphery of the porch and lay concrete blocks to support the new walls. Then he would cover the blocks with bricks to make it pretty, install windows the full length of the porch except for a modern storm door at the steps.

He began by digging the trench to pour the footer. As he came to the first column holding up the porch roof he discovered that when the house was built, the builders had put in some field rocks to hold the boards under each column. Howard had to dig around those rocks to make his trench for the footer. He did so and continued on along the porch.

As he neared the end of the porch, a job that took longer than Howard had expected, he failed to notice that the rocks he had dug around at first had begun to shift a little and the porch floor had started to sag slightly. The rocks had not had any mortar applied and when the dirt was removed from three sides, they begin to move a little under the load of the porch roof. It wasn't sudden or catastrophic, just a gradual slipping of the rocks into the open space of the new trench.

Howard had finished the trench and stepped back to admire his handiwork when he first noticed that the end of the porch where he had started seemed to be sagging a bit. He began to look more closely and suddenly decided to go see the

Sawyer brothers and try to get them to come and put in some shoring to raise the roof back up to where it should be. Howard would have done it himself, but the job required some large jacks which Howard didn't have.

As he left he turned to look back just in time to see the porch floor slide into the trench along the full length of the porch and the roof pull away from the house. The whole roof tilted, still supported partially by the columns, and it gracefully slid away from the house and landed with a crash on the porch floor and in the lawn behind the house.

When the Sawyer brothers finished building a new closed-in back porch it improved the appearance of the house a great deal. It also provided a pleasant, light airy dining room, something that was lacking after the living room had been remodeled. The new roof didn't leak either, something that had been a bit of a problem before. Howard was very proud of his home and many times told friends and colleagues that, "They just don't build 'em like this anymore."

Bathroom styles have changed a bit in the past sixty years.

There's no shame in being poor, but there's no great honor either.

Jewish proverb

"Take what you want," God said, "And pay for it."

Spanish proverb

I've met only four perfect people in my life and I didn't like any of them.

Unknown

There are no pockets in shrouds.

Audrey Gill

PRIDE OF COUNTRY.

French Socialist: "Does it not make your blood boil, my friend, to see all these rich people?"

Bill (down on his luck): "Frenchman, ain't yer?"

Socialist: "Yes"

Bill: "You ain't got 'orses like that in Paris, I bet."

This cartoon by F. H. Townsend appeared in *Punch* in 1907. Bill's attitude toward the French was and still is shared by many British people. In most cases the antipathy is well earned and is reciprocated.

Igor Stravinsky once said that he thought that too many pieces of music finish too long after the end. I feel that way about most of Stravinsky's music. He always passed up too many good stopping places.

REB

Blasted Basement

After Howard Clay had finished remodeling his house and the Sawyer brothers had to find other carpentry work to do to make a living, things were peaceful in the Clay household. Howard found that his wife was much easier to live with as long as he kept his tool box closed. Times were getting a bit better as the 1930's were coming to a close and the Sawyer brothers were finding other work too instead of correcting Howard's blunders.

Howard, by virtue of his white collar job in town, considered himself an authority on any subject. He lacked one thing that he really deserved though, an inferiority complex. The several fiascoes he had in remodeling the house had not shaken his self confidence.

Howard began to make plans to enlarge the basement of his house. A good share of the house which had been built around 1870 had been constucted over a crawl space and Howard believed he needed a work shop. He actually needed it about as much as he needed a third left hand, but once he had made up his mind, it took a lot to make him change it, past experience notwithstanding.

Howard consulted the Sawyer brothers before he started work and they advised him to set some beams and posts under the floor of the house as he went forward with excavation so that the house wouldn't fall on top of him. Howard laughed and said that any fool would know that, the thought not having occurred to him before.

Howard got along fine setting beams and posts next to the old field-stone wall where the basement ended and the crawl space began. He had no trouble knocking the old wall out either, but when he started digging the dirt out of the crawl space, the job lost some of its appeal.

After a week of evening work in addition to spending all day on his regular job, Howard began to tire of pick, shovel, wheelbarrow, and sweat. He wished he could quit now and forget the whole thing, but he had broadcast his intentions to the neighborhood and he had too much pride to admit he'd made a mistake.

At the end of the second week of digging it became obvious that this job was going to take all summer. The ground was clay mixed with lots of gravel; this part of Ohio was moraine from the last glacial period. It had been under the kitchen of the old house for 60 years and was dry and hard as brick. Two weeks of work had removed about a foot and a half with twelve or thirteen feet to go.

Then Howard had an inspiration. When miners needed to enlarge their tunnels or when highway construction workers had a lot of excavation to do, what did they do? Why, use dynamite, of course! Howard was just upset that he hadn't thought of it sooner.

This time, sad experience had made Howard more cautious and he determined that he would study up on how to do it before he started using explosives. At lunchtime one day he went over to the public library and found some books about explosives. Unfortunately, the books weren't very specific about how to use them, but they referred to drilling holes and setting small charges. Howard decided that this was enough research; his lunch hour was over anyway.

That afternoon, Howard slipped out of his office and went to talk to the foreman in the constuction office. The firm that Howard worked for built bridges, and the foreman was supposed to know all manner of construction methods. They even had some explosives in a small storeroom at the back of the property for occasional use on a job.

The foreman was cordial until Howard told him what he'd been planning to do.

"Goodbye, Howard," he said, "You play with dynamite all you want, but I don't want to have anything to do with it. I got enough problems without having your blood on my hands."

"What would you use then?" Howard asked.

"Nothing stronger than black powder. That has enough power to do what you want but you ain't likely to kill yourself with it." The foreman went on to explain that it could be obtained in sticks of a gray waxy material something like dirty looking brown sugar wrapped in a wax paper tube. You could cut it to small lengths for the amount of blast you wanted and it didn't blow up unless you set fire to it. He explained how to set a fuse in it and told Howard to try a little bit to see how much he needed. He gave Howard a small stick from the supply room to try out and told him where he could buy as much as he needed.

On his way home that evening, Howard stopped at Sam Harris's place. Sam had a gravel pit on his farm which supplied the county with gravel for the roads and Sam with enough liquid refreshment to keep him in a good humor. The arrangement worked to everyone's advantage. Sam was quite agreeable to Howard's trying out a little black powder in the gravel pit. Sam even went along to watch.

Sam had been drinking a little but he knew better than to get too close when Howard was setting the fuse. Sam sat down on one of the gravel loaders a distance away from where Howard was setting his first charge of powder in a bank of gravel.

The first charge that Howard set off had a more powerful effect than Howard had anticipated and made his ears ring. There was a big cloud of gray smoke and dust in the air and a fair amount of gravel had been loosened from the wall of the pit.

Sam called from his vantage point, "That was a good 'un Howard. Fire another 'un."

Howard wasn't quite so enthusiastic. He rather wished he hadn't started this, but he remembered how much digging it was going to save him, so he decided to set off a smaller charge this time and see what it did. The resulting explosion was more to his liking so he decided that he had learned enough about black powder and had better get on home. He thought that maybe the idea was pretty good after all.

The following day, Howard went by the dealer and filled out the necessary forms and bought a small case of the powder. The dealer pointed out that the powder was not sensitive to being handled but to keep all fire away from it and keep it dry. He showed Howard how to measure the length of fuse to give him time to get a little distance away before the charge blew. Howard felt pretty confident as he drove home.

Howard waited until his wife Eleanor was doing dishes after supper before he slipped the box of powder out of the car and down into the basement. He wasn't sure just how Eleanor would look on this project. He didn't know how to silence the explosions but maybe when she saw that no damage had been done, Eleanor wouldn't feel too irritated with him.

Howard drilled a hole about a foot deep into the dirt on the side of his excavation by pounding a pipe into the dirt with a sledge hammer. Then he loosened the pipe and after quite a struggle managed to free it. He then pushed a small charge of powder with a fuse attached into the hole. Then he packed in dirt to fill the hole. He lit the fuse and retired behind the furnace on the other side of the basement to watch.

The blast, even behind all the dirt, was considerably louder than Howard expected. His ears were ringing again and the basement air was full of smoke and dust when Eleanor came pounding down the basement stairs. She groped her way through the cloud of dust to where Howard was inspecting with satisfaction the pile of loose dirt that would need only to be hauled away.

"Hey, look at this!" Howard said with a big grin. "It sure beats usin' a pick to loosen all that dirt."

"It beats washin' dishes too!" his wife yelled. "We'll just buy new ones every time you do that!"

"Oh, no!" Howard exclaimed, his elation waning, "It broke all the dishes?"

"No, not all of 'em", Eleanor yelled, "Just the stack I had in my hands. I threw 'em against the ceilin' when I jumped. Next time you're gonna do some wild stunt, let me know so's I can be somewhere else."

The use of the black powder helped the progress of the excavation enormously. After the neighbors got used to the sound of muffled explosions from time to time, they began coming by to admire the size of the hole. Howard proudly explained to anyone who would listen the great amount of skill required and cautioned them not to try it.

Eleanor too became accustomed to the occasional boom from below and because there was no more loose plaster or broken dishes, her fears began to subside a little. She had learned to live with Howard, and her nerves could stand almost anything.

As the excavation neared completion, Howard became impatient with his progress and began to use a little larger charges. No damage resulted and his confidence began to increase again. Eleanor hadn't said anything, so either she hadn't noticed or didn't care.

When the work was nearly done Howard made the charge just a little bigger so that he could get the last of the dirt loose in one shot. Again, the results were beyond his expectations. He had become accustomed to the noise of the blasts but this one was greater than any that had gone before. He was accustomed to a cloud of dust and smoke after a blast but this time everything was pitch black.

"Oh, damn!" Howard exclaimed, "I musta blowed a fuse."

Howard heard a familiar shouting and his wife's feet pounding down the basement stairs. He saw the gleam of a flashlight faintly through the smoke and through the ringing in his ears he made out what Eleanor was saying.

"Every window's broken! An' every dish, an' all the plaster's cracked! An' all the light bulbs are broken, an' you better do somethin' quick or I'm gonna kill you right now!"

Howard could still hear Eleanor shouting as he made his way down the street toward the Sawyer brothers' house. They would probably do a pretty good job of it, and Howard was tired of working on the basement anyway. Maybe they could use the rest of the black powder somewhere too. There wasn't much of it left anyway.

Howard wrote to the manufacturers of the black powder to complain that there was insufficient instruction provided on how to use it. Specifically, he wanted to know how to tell when he had enough to loosen the soil without making a lot of commotion.

WOMAN——EVER UNREASONABLE.

"Hands up ! or I fire ! !"

Now there is a nice reasonable request. This cartoon by F. H. Townsend appeared in *Punch* in 1904. Notice that the poor burglar's feet are at the top of the window on the floor below where the lady is.

Spray Paint

About 1950 when aerosol paint cans came on the market, Bill Payne and his bride of a few months were living with her parents until they could get a place of their own. The place was large enough and Bill got along well with his in-laws, so that wasn't a problem; Bill's lack of judgment was the problem.

For example, Bill built a birdhouse at the workbench in his father-in-law's garage and bought a aerosol can of white paint to finish it with. Aerosol cans of paint were new on the market at the time and Bill had never used one. He also had the common failing among humans of never reading the instructions until after he was in trouble.

Bill lived close enough to his work that he usually went home for lunch and often had some spare time after lunch before he had to return to work. After lunch one day, Bill went into the garage to paint that bird house. He didn't bother to shake the can well first so the nozzle clogged before he had done much painting. Not having had much experience with aerosol paint cans and not having read the label, Bill pulled the tip of the nozzle from the can and used a hammer and nail to open the valve in the cap of the can.

The paint came out in a generous stream and Bill grabbed a bucket and pointed the stream into the bucket.. The stream hit the bottom of the bucket and splashed back all over Bill's face and also all over the front of the new Plymouth sedan his father-in-law had just purchased. White paint on a black car does tend to show and Bill wiped some of it off as soon as he could see, but it still looked pretty bad.

Bill got back to work a little late that afternoon. His eyebrows and hair were flecked with patches of white. His hair was black so the white spots tended to be noticeable. He had used paint thinner and gotten most of it off his skin but the clothes he had been wearing were a total loss. The car had to be repainted professionally before it looked right. Bill decided then that he would not use aerosol paint anymore.

But Bill didn't give up painting. He just quit using aerosol cans. After he and his wife found a house of their own, they needed to redecorate and paint the walls on the inside of the house. They got along fine until they got to the kitchen.

"What color shall we paint the kitchen?" Bill asked

"Blue", replied his wife.

"Oh no", said Bill, "Blue is depressing. Let's paint it yellow."

"I don't like yellow." said his wife. "Paint it blue!"

"Yellow!" said Bill.

"Blue!" said his wife.

The result was that for several days the kitchen walls remained the dull dirty white that they had been when the Payne's moved in.

Then one day when Bill went home for lunch he discovered that his wife had gone to the store and bought paint herself and had the job about half done. She had chosen blue, dark blue at that. The kitchen was a little gloomy looking already.

It was considerably darker after Bill grabbed the paint brush and finished the job by painting everything in sight blue, including the inside of the glass of the windows. He was right, blue was depressing.

It stayed that way for a few days but on Saturday Bill spent the better part of the morning scraping the paint off the glass with a razor blade. After a few years, Bill's wife decided that Bill had been right after all, and they repainted the kitchen yellow.

If you don't have a good reason for doing something, you have one good reason for not doing it.   Unknown

Pressure cooker

After Bill Payne and his wife Mary had been settled in their house a few weeks they asked me to have dinner with them. Mary had bought a new pressure cooker and was eager to try it out with a special recipe for Hungarian goulash and the recipe called for too much for just two people. I accepted because I was fond of goulash.

The pressure cooker was a new design that was sold for a brief time about 1950. The design was dropped soon after because of a fault that appeared after it was on the market. The lid was a curved flexible stainless steel disk with a handle fastened in the middle. When it was free, the curve permitted it to be placed inside the opening of the pot. The lip of the pot curved inward and the seal was on the underside of the lip. When the lid was inside the pot one pressed the lid handle down to the pot handle and latched them together. This forced the lid against the underside of the pot lip and made the seal. The more pressure inside the pot, the tighter the seal. Safety was provided by a hole in the lid with a small rubber plug in it that theoretically would blow out and release the pressure before it could it reach dangerous levels.

Mary had not used the cooker yet and we were all interested in how quickly it would make goulash. All the ingredients were put in the pot and the cooker was placed on the stove. Soon it was obvious from the bubbling sounds inside the pot that the goulash was cooking. We watched the clock to make sure that we didn't let it overcook.

Suddenly the small rubber plug came out of the hole in the lid and bounced here and there on the ceiling and walls of the kitchen. I don't think the Paynes ever did find it. Immediately the goulash in the pot also came out of the hole in the lid in a steady stream, hitting the ceiling and spraying all over the kitchen. When everything had settled down, we discovered that the pot was completely empty and its inside was the only thing in the kitchen not covered with goulash.

We all cleaned up the mess a bit and I went home to change my clothes. I stopped at the local restaurant and got a bite to eat later and found the Paynes had just finished having their supper there too. I don't think they ever used that pressure cooker again.

More Pressure Cooker Adventures

When I was small, my mother had an old-fashioned cast aluminum pressure cooker, and I loved the bean soup she would make in it sometimes. It would sit on the wood stove and simmer at a low pressure all afternoon. It smelled so good when Mama would open the vent valve to let some of the pressure out. (The automatic safety valve had long since quit working, and one had to watch the pressure gauge pretty carefully to prevent it from getting too high. When the gauge got too high, one could open the little petcock on the top and vent some of the pressure.)

I was about 15 or 16 when the pressure cooker was used last. It was a Sunday morning and I had a little cold, not enough to be much of a bother but enough that I could beg off going to church and Sunday school. Mama put a pot roast in the pressure cooker and cautioned me to be sure to watch it closely so that the pressure wouldn't get too high. I assured her that I was capable of watching an old pressure cooker.

However, watching a pressure gauge from time to time is boring and my Jessie dog was only about a year old and full of play. I was lying on the kitchen floor playing with the dog and paying less and less attention to the cooker. The last time I had looked, the pressure was well within the safe range, but it probably had been 15 or 20 minutes since I had looked. Suddenly it sounded like a cannon went off in the kitchen.

Jessie hit the screen door which was not latched and went to the barn in about 1/10 of a second. I doubt that the lid was more than 6 inches above the pressure cooker before she was gone! The lid broke into three pieces, one of which went straight up through the ceiling and put a dent in the underside of the wooden floor upstairs. The roast hit the ceiling about a foot north of the hole the lid made; it was easy to see where it hit. Then the roast fell to the floor and rolled along it a few feet. I don't remember where the other two pieces of lid went, but the vegetables and juices from the roast were turned into a fine mist which deposited itself as a greasy, nearly uniform, layer on everything in the room, including me. (I don't think the dog got anything on her; she left pretty fast.)

I looked out the door to see my parents turning into the driveway. If that stupid pressure cooker had waited just a few more minutes, Mama would have opened the vent in time and we would have had pot roast for dinner. I don't remember what we had, but it wasn't pot roast. Mama and Dad were so thankful that I wasn't hurt that they didn't bawl me out, but I lied and said that I had just looked at that pressure gauge. I suspect now that they knew the truth. It was quite a mess, and Mama never used any pressure cooker again that I can recall.

It really wasn't a very safe design anyway. The top was held with thumbscrews and the only safety relief was a spring-loaded safety valve which had long since plugged up and quit working. The modern cookers use a weight sitting over a normally open vent. The weight holds the pressure to any one of three levels, and anything above that pressure simply lifts the weight enough to vent the excess pressure. The disadvantage of that is that some water is lost during the cooking, so enough must be put in to begin with to allow for the loss. You can burn food in a modern pressure cooker, but you couldn't in one of the old ones. However, the old ones had a certain entertainment value that the new ones lack.

Traveling the South Pacific

The following is taken from *Traveling the South Pacific, Without Reservations*, by Evangeline Brunes (rhymes with Tunis). The book is the story of a woman in her sixties, traveling alone through the islands in the South Pacific, without reservations and on a very limited budget.. Here is the excerpt:

From the crest of the hill I saw a scene that epitomizes every man's dream of the South Seas. It was all there. The deep blue of the sea beyond the foaming white line of breakers at the reef, a placid lagoon, a curve of white sand reaching to far distant rocky headlands. Coconut palms sheltered thatched roof fales [open huts] by the sea. And there was not a soul in sight. Which posed a problem. To whom should I give Tagaloa's letter? I was not expected.

There was nothing else to do. I walked to the beach and then along the lagoon. Sitting in the shade of a thatched shelter, far down the beach, I saw a bearded young man leaning against his backpack. I sat down beside him on the sand. He was so like a hundred other young backpackers I had met throughout the Pacific.

"I have a letter. Do you know who I should give it to?

"I had a letter too, but mine didn't work," he teased.

He had been discharged from the Israeli army six months before and had been traveling since then.

"I will probably be out another year and a half," he said. "I don't think I can stop traveling..." then, growing serious, he added, "...but when does the lonesomeness end?"

It was not a casual question. He meant for me to answer it.

I told him that when I was 34 I had come into Faith and that had wiped away the nagging soul-deep sense of loneliness forever.

He looked bewildered and asked me to explain, so there on a deserted beach half the world away from both our homes, I told this young Jewish stranger the whole story.

"I was pregnant with my sixth child and going through the inevitable search for Truth, a quest we all make at some time in our lives. I longed for Truth...tears dripping into the dishpan as I thought about it, searching endlessly for answers to questions still too vague for me to formulate."

He still seemed interested, so I continued, "My neighbor Martha had four children and a live-in [semi-invalid] mother-in-law [not to mention a large dog and four or five cats]. Yet, she always seemed at peace above the family turmoil. She began telling me about Bible Study classes she and her husband attended. But I thought, if I had a baby sitter I'd do something FUN! She had an intangible something I needed and one night I went to Bible Study with her. I found a taste of unconditional loving acceptance in their midst that I had never known and was drawn into it without questions."

By then I felt compelled to continue. "The night my baby was born a most extraordinary thing happened that to this day I cannot explain. I only know that it changed my life forever. I was up and outside myself and as I was suspended there somewhere between the bed and ceiling, I was surrounded by beings that were loving me so tenderly and completely that no human language could describe it. I did not see or hear them with my normal senses, I perceived them through some other sense. From that experience I knew that Truth was tangible and that I had touched it. I still did not understand the nature of this Truth. I just knew that it embodied Love. From then on, I have never been lonely or afraid of dying."

I hesitated and he asked me to tell him more.

"I wasn't a Christian then. I'd say that I was more of an agnostic. I still didn't equate this Truth that I had found with God until one evening at a church meeting a circle of women were praying. I had gone to the meeting to see slides of India that a missionary was showing. While they were praying, I thought *What a lot of theological double talk, this Father, Son, and Holy Ghost!* As quickly as I thought it God spoke within me, 'Why should it not be so? Man was made in God's image.'"

"In that moment I understood the reality of the Trinity. For each of us is a triune being...body, mind, and spirit. I knew then that God, the great mind and Creator; Jesus, who walked the earth for 33 years (or 80 as we might); and the Holy Spirit, that part of us that is eternal and exists before we were born and after we die, are ONE. For the first time, God had become real to me."

A young woman came to speak to him. The young man told me that I should give Tagaloa's letter to her. She took it and went down the path into the bush.

"Did you know there is no food here?" *he asked.*

I told him that I always travel with a little bag with my toothbrush and a change of clothes in case the unexpected happens, but that I had brought no food. I had simply not anticipated an overnight stay.

He opened his backpack and took out a handful of uncooked spaghetti and a package of instant sauce, insisting that I take them.

"There's a small store in the village about three miles away." *He showed me some of the treasures in his backpack including an intricately carved, museum-quality war club that he had purchased in the village.*

When the girl returned, she said, "I'll show you to your home for tonight."

She took me to one of the enclosed fales and unlocked the door. The young Israeli was staying with her family in the village.

He came in to sit with me until she was ready to leave. When we were alone he said, "Please tell me the story again."

For some, life's journey is a straight path; for others a strangely convoluted trail punctuated by brief, improbable, but deeply meaningful encounters.

Book Two
Stoney Creek

October's Smoky Weather

    This cartoon and others like it were drawn by Ray and Caroline Bell, the compiler's parents, in the late 1930's and all through the 1940's. They were published mostly in *Country Gentleman*, a farm magazine by Curtis Publishing Co. The magazine and artists are now deceased, sad to say.

Stoney Creek

Stoney Creek is a place you won't find on even a very detailed map of Ohio. It is real however and it exists today with very few changes from when I grew up near there during the Great Depression of the thirties. The people who live there now look a bit more prosperous than those who lived there in the thirties.

Some of the people in these stories still live there, and if they read this book and study the map carefully, they probably will be able to recognize themselves or people they know, even though I changed the names. If they do, I hope they think as kindly of me as I do of them. I have no intention of ridiculing anyone and I have used fictitious names for nearly all of the characters.

The map that shows where these characters lived is fictitious. Someone who is familiar with the area will be able to figure out exactly where it is, where the various characters lived, and what their real names are, but no one who is not well acquainted with that part of Ohio will be able to identify it.

Stoney Creek is a small community surrounded by farms. It lies in the gently rolling countryside of Ohio between the eastern hills and the western flat plains. Towns in the area have names like Brandon, Pagetown, Fargo, Sparta, Centerburg, Mount Gilead, Mount Liberty, Mount Vernon, Pataskala, Croton, Sunbury, Delaware, Killbuck, Bangs, and Chesterville.

The farms now are mechanized and all have electricity. At the time of these stories, only a few farmers had tractors and most used horses or mules to plow the land and harvest the crops. Kerosene lamps lit the houses and the only lights in the barns were kerosene lanterns.

Living standards were never very high in Stoney Creek, and the depression didn't help much. Farm prices were low and times were hard, but most farmers raised a lot of their own food so they got by. The typical farm had six or eight cows, a dozen or so pigs, two horses for work, a small flock of chickens, maybe a few geese or ducks, perhaps some sheep, and always a dog or two and a bunch of cats. Corn, oats, wheat, and hay were the principal crops and these were rotated to conserve the soil.

Every farm had a garden and the women would spend many hours every summer preserving food for the winter months, mostly by canning. Many farms had a woods lot and, because sugar maples were common in that area, many farmers tapped the trees and made maple syrup in the late winter, mainly for the family's own use.

The stories told here are mostly true. That is, they are true to the best of my memory. I may have embellished them a bit, but none are made up completely; I don't have that good an imagination. I hope that any added details only improve a good story and don't embarrass anyone.

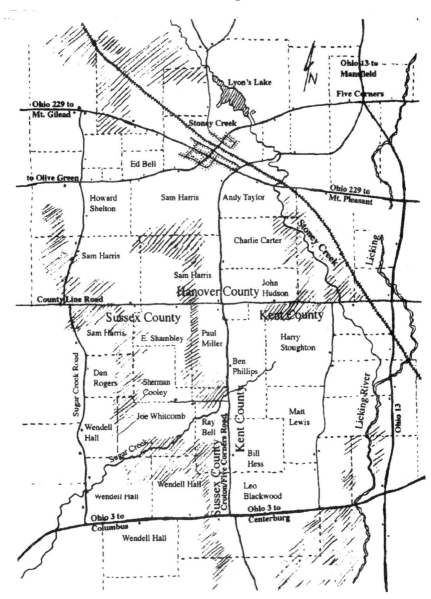

Stoney Creek Country

Don't bother to look for it on a map of Ohio. This is a completely false, well, almost completely false, map. Some of the towns mentioned exist, but not where this map indicates that they are. The counties shown do not exist in Ohio. However, those familiar with the community where the author grew up will recognize some of the farms shown.

The Family Reunion.

Family reunions were traditional summer activities in Stoney Creek.

The Winds of March Blow Hot and Cold!

March in Ohio is not only the beginning of spring, but it also is still the end of winter and can alternate between the two seasons.

Between the April Showers

April is always a busy time for Ohio farmers.

"... what is so rare as a day in June?"

June in Ohio is the real beginning of summer.

Summer is Over

August is the end of summer and the "tourist season".

A Basket of Eggs

Lois Burton was a big strapping woman with muscular arms, a round red face and a suspicious mind. She did more hard physical work than a lot of men, but she could always find time to pick a quarrel with a neighbor. Her favorite antagonist was Tiny Crawford who was almost as big as Lois and nearly as belligerent. The women had lived next door to each other since World War I and had carried on their own private war for over sixteen years.

Lois raised a few chickens. At that time most people in Stoney Creek raised a few chickens and those who didn't could sometimes lift a few from those who did. Lois was careful to keep a pretty close count on hers. Some of her neighbors suspected that she kept a pretty close count on her neighbors' chickens too, but no one ever caught her at it.

Broody hens don't hold with people fooling around with their chicks.

One day in spring, one of Lois's hens had been missing for a couple of weeks and Lois discussed it with Tom as he ate breakfast that morning.

"I bet that ole hen is settin' in Tiny's brush pile" Lois said.

Tom didn't look up from his plate of fried eggs, fried potatoes, sausage and pancakes. "Aw now, why would Tiny be settin' in the brush pile?" He poured some more syrup over his pancakes. "Where's m' coffee?"

Tom was known in Stoney Creek as a man with an appetite. He was only a little over five feet six inches tall but he weighed over two hundred pounds. He was about fifty years old and had made his living for over thirty years as a blacksmith's helper.

"Not Tiny! My broody hen that's been missin' for a coupla weeks." Lois set a steaming cup of coffee in front of Tom and sat down to her own breakfast which was just like his. "I think I'll go look around over there after breakfast."

"You go foolin' around in Crawford's back yard and Tiny'll run you out with a broom."

"She better not try er I'll snatch her bald-headed." Lois set her cup down firmly. "I'm a good mind to do it anyways, so she better not start nuthin' ".

After Tom left for work at the blacksmith shop in Centerburg, Lois went out to the fence between the Burton's and Crawford's back yards. She looked toward the

Crawford house but could see no activity. Early in the morning Moose Crawford had walked up the road toward the farm where he was working at the time, and the neighbors knew that Tiny had probably gone back to bed as usual.

Lois climbed the board fence and went snooping in Crawford's back yard. She found her hen, or at least *a* hen, setting on a clutch of eggs back in the weeds by the brush pile. Lois could tell that it was her hen because it was red and most, but not all, of the Crawford's chickens were black and white. Lois climbed the fence again back into her own yard, got a basket, and returned to the Crawford's yard to gather up the eggs and the hen.

But on this particular morning, Tiny had not gone back to bed. Earlier in the year, Moose and Tiny had managed to borrow enough money to buy a small plot of land just up the road from Stoney Creek. On this morning, Moose had arranged to borrow a team of horses from his employer and he had left early to plow the field for a crop of his own. Before he left, he had suggested that Tiny and their fifteen-year-old daughter Emma could get the household chores done early and come help gather rocks off the field as he plowed. (In that part of Ohio, the last glacier had left lots of rocks in the ground and a regular chore when plowing was to gather the rocks and put them in the corner of the field.) So the Crawford ladies were finishing cleaning up the kitchen as Lois climbed over the fence with her basket.

When Tiny saw Lois gathering up the clutch of eggs in the Crawford back yard, she reached for a broom and called to her daughter. "Hey Emma! That ole Lois Burton is stealin' our eggs. Come and fetch yer broom!"

The broom was the weapon of choice among the ladies of Stoney Creek. It was used for all purposes, sweeping among them. It was a convenient implement to shoo dogs and cats out of the house, chase chickens out of the garden, and in any dispute, the broom was the ultimate weapon. The first lady to grab a broom won the argument.

"Hey! Whatcha doin' in my back yard, Lois Burton?" Tiny called as she came out of the house carrying a broom.

"Yeah! Whatcha doin' in our back yard?" echoed Emma, following closely behind her mother with another broom.

"Shut up, Emma!" said Tiny. "Well, Lois?"

"I'm jist gittin' my broody hen. She stole a nest over here." Lois's eyes darted from the Crawford women around the yard looking for a suitable weapon. Both Tiny and Emma were carrying brooms at the ready and they held the immediate advantage, but Lois was a little bigger than Tiny and Emma wasn't a grown woman yet, so if Lois could find a club or other suitable weapon soon enough, there was still a chance. She had to watch out for Emma though; Emma wasn't big but she was quick.

"Whatta you mean, **your** broody hen? That's **my** broody hen!" Tiny challenged.

"**Your** hen? You **never** had no Plymouth Rocks!"

"Well I have now!" Tiny smiled and shook the broom suggestively. "Yer standin' on my property, Lois Burton, an' I don't wantcha here."

"Hit 'er, ma!" yelled Emma, jumping around and waving her broom.

"Shut up, Emma," said Tiny. "Now git fer home, Lois Burton, an' stay outa my yard!"

Lois backed away cautiously toward the line fence which she had already climbed three times that morning. She was still looking around for a rock or a stick with which to even up the odds against her, but the Crawford ladies were watching and following closely. By this time several of the neighbors had noticed the commotion and were watching avidly. Stoney Creek was normally a pretty quiet community and nothing brightens a dull day like a little controversy.

Lois finally was backed up against the fence. She had left the basket by the nest and the hen seemed to be trying to decide whether the eggs in the basket or those left in the nest were the ones most needing to be covered. Lois seemed almost as undecided herself as she faced the two ladies with the brooms. If she turned her back to climb the fence, one or both of those brooms was likely to be put to use.

It is virtually impossible to climb over a fence backwards, so Lois was forced to turn her back momentarily. As she put one leg over the top board of the fence, Tiny swung the broom with all her strength and connected with Lois's ample rear, hastening her exit into the Burton's back yard.

"You ain't heared the last of this!" Lois roared as she reached her own yard.

"Hit 'er agin, ma!" Emma yelled.

"Shut up, Emma," Tiny shook the broom at Lois. "Jist you stay outa my yard, Lois!"

Lois didn't stop at her house. She went next door to her son Harry's house and woke him up. Harry worked nights in Mt. Pleasant, and was a little annoyed at being wakened. Lois insisted that Harry get up and drive her to Centerburg to the blacksmith shop where Tom was at work.

Tom was fitting shoes on a farmer's horse as Lois entered the shop. The horse's owner was sitting on a bench near the forge waiting for the job to be completed, so he watched and listened with interest as Lois walked up to Tom.

"Tom, you gotta go beat up Moose Crawford." Lois opened the conversation.

"What the hell fer this time?" Tom didn't miss a beat on the horse shoe he was shaping on the anvil.

Lois explained the whole situation to Tom. "Cuz that hussy of his stole my hen and won't give it back! That's what fer!"

Tom had never beaten up Moose Crawford. Lois had often asked him to but something had always come up to prevent it. The two men got along quite well together, often sharing a few bottles of beer on Sunday afternoons. The last time that Lois had asked Tom to beat up Moose was a windy October day when Lois was raking and burning leaves. The smoke was blowing onto Tiny's freshly laundered clothes and Tiny had asked Lois to put out the fire. Lois had offered a counter proposal, suggesting something that Tiny could do with the clothes. Tiny found that suggestion offensive. Tiny had retaliated by carrying a bucket of water into the Burton's back yard and dousing the fire herself. Lois in turn had chased Tiny with the rake. The dispute had ended in the alley back of their properties with several of the neighbors separating the two who were scratching and pulling each other's hair.

On that occasion too, Lois had hurried in the house to Tom, who happened to be home that day, and insisted that he go beat up Moose. During the fracas in the back yard, several of the neighbors had seen Moose Crawford, who had been sick in bed with a cold, scoot out of the front door and head up the street to the Stoney Creek store. When Tom found him, Moose was sitting on a bench in the store sniffling and trying to look invisible. The Stoney Creek code of ethics prevented a man from punching a nose with a cold in it, so Tom had settled for beating Moose three out of seven games of checkers.

During the heated discussion which followed Lois' insisting that Tom do something to Moose, Tom punctuated his protests with the clang of his hammer on the horse shoe he was continuing to shape. The spectators listened to Lois explain that it wouldn't be proper for Tom to beat up Tiny, but it was up to him to do something if he expected to have any supper that evening.

On another occasion, Lois had used the same argument to get Tom to go give Moose a beating. That was the time when Tiny and Lois had gotten into a shouting and hair-pulling contest over what Lois considered an insulting reference to her weight that Tiny had made at a Ladies Auxiliary lunch at the Perfect Love Holiness Church where they were both active members. Tiny had called everyone's attention to Lois's heaped up plate as they were both getting dessert. Lois had turned the full plate upside down over Tiny's head and relations sort of went down hill from there.

That time Tom had been unable to find Moose all afternoon, mainly because he didn't go looking for him at Wendell Hall's where he was told that Moose was working that day. Tom had gone home at suppertime and explained that he couldn't find Moose, but he sure would have beaten him up if he could have found him. After supper, he postponed the battle until the next day, by which time, the situation had cooled a little.

This time it looked like Tom was stuck. Everyone, including Lois, knew where Moose was and Lois made it clear that this time Tom had better go through with it.

After Lois left with their son Harry, Tom's boss, Joe Baird, brought out a bottle he kept in a space behind some scrap iron. Joe bought it from a man over near Pagetown who made it himself, and it was guaranteed to make anybody mad unless he was used to it. Tom had used it before when preparing for battle. It was well known locally as an inspiration for great deeds of courage.

After fortifying himself with several sips from the bottle, Tom drove home and walked up the road toward where Moose was plowing. One of the local farmers, Howard Shelton, was standing by the fence visiting with Moose who was resting the horses at the end of a round. They watched as Tom approached. Tom raised his fist and shouted something as he saw the two men watching him. They couldn't hear what Tom shouted but they could tell by the way that he walked that he was

mad about something. Tom always stomped when he was mad, and since he was bowlegged, it made for a very distinctive walk.

"Now what's he mad at?" Moose asked. "I bet he's been at Joe's bottle agin."

As he approached the two men, Tom began swearing at the top of his voice. They could pick out only a few words now and again from the roar. Tom tended to become incoherent when he got mad, particularly if he had had a drink or two. The occasional understandable words like "hen", "women", and "broom" weren't much help to the men in figuring out what was troubling Tom. Moose leaned casually against the fence, still in his own field.

"Don't you set foot on my property, Tom," Moose warned.

Community custom forbade anyone from violating such a warning. Property rights were such that no one would trespass on another's personal property.

"You come out here in the road an' I'll beat the hell outa you!" Tom shouted. They were about six feet apart, but Tom was up to full volume. He could be heard half a mile away, but he couldn't be understood any better from that distance than he could up close.

"Don't git me mad, Tom, or I jist might come out there," Moose said calmly. Moose and Howard had noticed that Tiny and Emma were approaching carrying a basket between them.

"What's all the fuss about anyway?" Moose asked Tom, taking care not to call Tom's attention to the two approaching women.

"Never you mind what it's about!" yelled Tom. "I'm gonna give you a thrashin'."

"Aw, Tom, I ain't mad at you. Why you wanta stir things up? 'Sides, you never could lick me. You been drinkin'?"

Before Tom could answer, an egg whizzed past his nose. Emma's aim was poor.

Tom jumped backwards, whirled to face the two women, fell over his own feet, and sat down abruptly in the road. Before he could get to his feet, Tiny turned the basket upside down over Tom's head and jammed it down around his ears.

"Here, take your ole eggs an' leave my man alone!" Tiny said. The eggs **were** old all right; they had been incubated for a couple of weeks and those that weren't nearly ready to hatch were rotten. Tom sat in the road for a few minutes with the remains of the eggs running down over him. He then picked himself up and walked back toward home carrying the basket.

By the time Tom got home, the hen, having no more eggs to incubate, had also gone home. Tom stomped in the back door, slammed the basket into the corner of the kitchen, filled a wash basin with warm water from the cook stove reservoir, and started washing up at the kitchen sink. Lois watched a few minutes and then went on getting the noon meal ready.

"The hen's come home," she said.

There was no reply as Tom continued washing.

"I guess we showed them Crawfords they can't steal **my** hen and get away with it."

"Yep," Tom replied. "Now git my food on the table, woman. I gotta git back to work an' I'm hungry."

Lois grinned and started filling the plates.

We had a preacher one time who couldn't tell a joke, but he thought he needed to in order to keep his parishioners awake during his sermons. He had heard the old joke about the man who said, "The best years of my life were spent in the arms of a woman who was not my wife." After a short hesitation, the man would explain, "She was my mother."

Our preacher thought that would be an amusing and appropriate joke to liven up his Mother's Day sermon so he included it. However, he worded it a little differently. He said, "The best years of my life were spent in the arms of a woman who was not my wife." After a short hesitation, he added, "But I can't remember who she was."

Free Man

Enos* Myers was a free man, the only really free man in the community of Stoney Creek. He didn't usually have a dime to rub in his fingers and he really should have been born a couple of hundred years earlier, but he was free from any worries. Nobody told him what to do, and nobody ever told him he ought to stop doing whatever he was doing at the time. That's free.

Enos lived in Wendell Hall's old sugar house back in the woods behind my dad's farm about half a mile from the nearest road. No one seemed to know why Wendell let Enos live in the old sugar house rent-free, especially when everyone knew Wendell was a bit on the tight side. Maybe it was because Enos kept an eye on Wendell's sheep which were kept in the woods lot during the summer and Wendell figured it was a small price to pay. Besides, Wendell didn't make maple syrup anymore anyway so the old sugar house would just have rotted into the ground. At any rate, there Enos was and there he stayed.

* The name Enos was pronounced to rhyme with "tennis" by Stoney Creek people.

Enos had fixed up the old sugar house a bit. He had battened over the cracks between the boards and had lined the inside walls with tar-paper to keep out the winter winds. There was a small window in one wall and a small glass pane in the door to let in some light. An old beat-up wood cook stove provided heat and cooked his meals. The floor was dirt but it was packed hard and smooth and drainage around the house was good, so the floor was dry most of the time. Enos always wore knee-length rubber boots year-round so it didn't matter anyway.

The sugar house was in a fair sized patch of woods, about 30 acres or so. It was about as far as anyone could get from one road or another around there so it suited Enos. If he had been born two hundred years earlier he would have lived in a similar manner. His neighbors wouldn't have considered it so strange then and there would have been considerably more distance between them.

Most of the people around Stoney Creek in the 1930's were poor. That is, by the commonly understood meaning of the word they were poor because they didn't have all the things they needed. By this definition however, Enos was not poor. He never had any money to speak of and he had the lowest standard of living in the community, which certainly wasn't high for anyone. But he didn't want or need much that money would buy. For meat he depended on wild game he could trap or shoot, for vegetables and fruit he picked wild greens, roots, berries, and nuts in season and did without the rest of the year. When he wanted some money to buy a little corn meal, beans, salt, tobacco, or ammunition for his gun, Enos would walk over to one of the neighbors to do a little work for cash. Enos didn't beg.

He almost never went to the house. Women and houses made him nervous and because he made most of the women in the community nervous too, they didn't make him feel too welcome around their houses. Enos would choose a time when the farmer was around the barn or out in the fields away from the house.

Enos would move quietly up to wherever the farmer was working and stand close by until the farmer noticed and greeted him. He always carried an old 12-gauge shotgun or a .22 calibre rifle and he always had a dog or two along. Stray pups often found a home with Enos.

"You gotta tree blew down in the woods," Enos would mumble after he was greeted. Enos never spoke first; he always waited until someone spoke to him before he said anything.

"That so, Enos?" would be the reply.

"Yeah, that old hollow oak in the south end o' the woods," Enos would say. Enos always spoke softly and he had a speech impediment that made him slur his words. This made him hard to understand, and only by listening closely could one follow the conversation.

"You need any firewood?" Enos would ask next.

The answer was always affirmative because everyone used wood for fuel back then, and most farmers had trouble finding time to cut enough wood to meet the household needs. More often than not they would go looking for Enos to get him to cut wood before he was needing any money. This was usually fruitless because Enos worked only when he was completely out of shells for his guns or he had used up the last of his chewing tobacco. Not when he was almost out, but when one or both was completely gone.

Enos never cut a tree down, not even a dead tree. He thought they were better left standing as shelter for wildlife. That was meat on the table for Enos. He was always roaming the woods and when he found a tree that had not survived a windstorm, he would tell the farmer about it when he saw him. These windfalls were the logs that Enos cut into firewood.

Enos had a one-man crosscut saw and a good ax. He never worked rapidly but he did a good job. The farmer would furnish him with a stick of the size needed so Enos could mark the log for cutting to the right length sections. Dad always cut about a half inch from the end of the sample because of the way Enos always marked the log. He would lay the sample down, whack the log with his ax at the end of the sample, move the sample to the mark and repeat the process all the way down the log. He didn't have a yardstick to measure the logs and wouldn't have known how to use one if he had it. All the sticks would be the size of the sample except that they would all be about a half inch longer because of the thickness of Enos's ax when he was marking for the saw cuts.

After he had sawed the log and split it to size, he would gather all the brush and pile it so that it would serve as shelter for small woods creatures. Then he would hunt up the farmer to collect his fee. No one ever paid Enos in advance more than once, because he wouldn't do the job until he needed money again.

Enos helped keep the woods clear of deadfalls for several neighbors. This was a big help in sugar making season and it meant just that much less effort to keep wood in the stove. The farmer had to haul it himself because Enos didn't care to drive horses. He couldn't be trusted to stay out of trouble with a sled or wagon anyway.

Most of the farmers kept sheep. During the summer when the sheep were in the woods pasture, it was a comfort to know that Enos traveled the woods so much. He saw everything and would tell the farmer if there was a hole in a fence where a sheep could get out. He would also notice if any of the sheep were limping or if one had died for some reason. When a sheep died, Enos would skin it and with the farmer's permission would sell the hide. I never knew how much he got for a sheepskin or even who would buy one, but Enos knew.

Enos couldn't read nor write, not even his own name, and he had difficulty counting. When a farmer paid him for a service, or whenever Enos made a purchase, no one ever cheated him badly. Not many people can cheat a child, and in many ways Enos was childlike. He was trusting and good-natured, he worked only when absolutely necessary, and he never seemed to worry about tomorrow. He derived pleasure from simple things such as sitting quietly under a tree for hours watching a vixen preparing a den under the roots of a big elm, and no one ever knew him to steal anything. Why should he steal? He could satisfy his wants by a few hours of cutting wood when he needed something he couldn't find in the woods.

Enos was out in all kinds of weather. He came by the barn when my Dad and I were cleaning stalls one winter Saturday afternoon along toward dark. It was cold and a strong northeast wind was driving a few flakes of snow out of a leaden sky. Enos's shack was about a mile from our barn and his face was red with cold when he stepped into the barn. A small drop of moisture hung from the tip of his nose. As usual, Enos had about a week's growth of beard. He must have shaved from time to time because he never seemed to have more or less beard than will grow in a week. The dog that accompanied Enos sniffed noses with our dog and they renewed old acquaintance by chasing each other around the barn floor.

Enos was wearing a ragged sheepskin coat that had been brown at one time but was now nearly black with age and dirt. He had an old plaid hunting cap on his head with the ear flaps tied under his chin, and his bib overalls were stuffed into the tops of his knee-length rubber boots. He wore a ragged mitten on his left hand in which he was carrying an ax head with a broken handle sticking out. His right hand was shoved deep into his coat pocket and the rifle rested in the crook of his right arm.

It was warmer in the barn out of the wind. Enos set the gun down, wiped his nose on his sleeve, and slowly unbuttoned his coat.

"Aren't you cold after that walk from your place?" Dad asked.

"Ain't come fum my place," Enos mumbled.

"Where you been then?"

"Been up on the hill behind Whitcomb's sheep barn since 'bout sun-up" Enos said slowly.

"What were you doin' up there?" I asked.

"Cut some wood fer a while 'fore I busted m' ax. Then I set up there to see if a ole possum I know 'bout was fool enough to come out in the daylight 'n' git shot."

He wasn't carrying any dead possum, so we knew his wait had been futile. We also knew that he didn't have any money or he wouldn't have been cutting wood. "You had anything to eat today, Enos?" Dad asked.

"Naw. Ain't got nuthin' to home."

"Go see what your mom can scare up," Dad told me, so I headed for the house. I came back a little later with a package of food that Mom had fixed for Enos to take with him. We knew that he wouldn't eat at our place. Mom had wrapped up some leftover roast beef and corn bread that we had had at dinner and she had added a big piece of liver for Enos to fix the next day. Then she had gone down into the cellar and filled a paper bag with apples. Enos never got much fruit in winter and Mom worried about people getting scurvy from not eating enough fruit. She didn't realize that Enos got plenty of vitamin C from the meat diet he was accustomed to.

When I got back to the barn, Dad was examining the ax-head that Enos had broken off. This ax was Enos's only source of money so it was very important to him. The edge was razor sharp and the metal was in good shape. Enos was handy with an ax so Dad and I were surprised that he'd broken a handle.

"M' foot slipped when I was trimmin' limbs off'n the log," Enos mumbled when Dad asked how it happened.

"You got another handle?"

"Naw," Enos scuffed the barn floor with one foot and slipped the package of food into the left coat pocket without looking at it and picked up the bag of apples. "Guess I better be goin'."

We didn't expect Enos to thank us for the food. He took favors of one kind or another for granted. He didn't expect anyone to thank him for letting them know how things were in the woods or for any small service he might perform; neither did he thank anyone verbally for things like the food package.

"Leave that ax-head here." Dad told him. "You can come by in a day or two and get it."

Enos nodded and strolled out into the cold wind again, slowly buttoning his coat. The dog stopped playing with our dog and followed him. Enos knew that when he came back for the ax it would have a new handle. That was why he came by in the first place; the food was just incidental.

During the spring and summer, Enos shot groundhogs for his meat supply. In the fall he usually had rabbits or squirrels, and in the winter he would have coon or possum when he could shoot or trap one. Farmers around Stoney Creek would often supplement his meat supply which was pretty slim in the winter by giving him the less desirable portions of meat when they butchered a hog or beef. We always gave him the head and kidneys when we butchered an animal.

Enos never had much in the way of material goods, so he never worried about anything being stolen. He had a .22 rifle and a 12-gauge shotgun, but one or the other was always with him. He also had a good ax and a one-man crosscut saw. These things, along with the clothes he had on were about the extent of his worldly possessions.

Enos did a little trapping in the winter, but more for food than for profit in fur. Even my Dad and my uncle Ben gave him permission to trap on their land, although they granted that privilege to no one else. One reason was that Enos set only a few traps and he visited each one every morning, a chore that some of the other trappers in the community would neglect when the weather was bad. Enos would leave a trap sprung empty when he had meat to eat rather than try to catch more than he could use. His choice of meat was whatever he found, and he dined on game of one kind or another the year round, regardless of season. If the game warden was aware of Enos's activities, he conveniently turned his back.

Some folks said that Enos was part Indian, but maybe that was because of the life that he led. He walked the way an Indian is supposed to walk, silently and gracefully even in rubber boots. Also, he was completely at home in the woods. Some of the women in the community were afraid of him, perhaps because of his sudden and silent arrival when he wanted to see their menfolks. They needn't have feared. Enos was as nervous as a wild creature around women and he avoided their houses.

Enos would have felt perfectly at home in frontier Ohio a couple of centuries earlier, but civilization didn't bother him too much. Stoney Creek's people were tolerant of eccentricities and Enos used only such modern conveniences as he wanted to, such as firearms and tobacco.

When the government passed the Social Security act it had almost no effect on Stoney Creek. The people were all either self-employed or unemployed. Wendell Hall quietly put Enos on his company payroll and paid the taxes so that Enos would be eligible for benefits when he reached sixty-five. In the 1930's when I was growing up I thought of Enos as ancient, but he must have been in his middle thirties.

The last time I saw Enos was in August 1971 or 72. He was sitting on a shady bench in Centerburg's park across from the old town hall. A small dog was sitting at his feet and he looked as old as I remembered him from childhood with the same week's stubble on his face. Neighbors told me that he stopped cutting wood on his 65th birthday, or as near to it as the Social Security people could figure it out. It is a good thing too. Farmers had long since quit using wood cook stoves and only a few used wood to heat their houses. Enos had had pretty slim pickings for a few years I expect.

Inheritance

Sam Harris owned about seven hundred acres in three farms on the County Line Road that ran past Ernest Shambley's place. There were three sets of houses and barns on the place and on the main farm where Sam lived there was a big gravel pit. Sam had retired from farming and gone to his second career of drinking before I was old enough to remember, but he had the good judgment to choose competent and honest tenant farmers to run the places and enough sense to treat his tenants fairly. He may have been a bit eccentric but he was no dummy.

Sam was a friendly man and was on good terms with all of his neighbors, but he did have some unusual habits. He had lived alone for years but every morning he would step out on his front porch and shout "Breakfast!" three or four times, loudly enough that his nearest neighbors could hear him. Then he would go back in his house.

Neighbors had an infallible way of knowing how much alcohol Sam had in him whenever they saw him drive his Model A Ford down the road. If he was moving along about forty mph and looking straight ahead, he was sober. If he were going about twenty and waving at people he saw as he passed, he had been drinking a bit, not drunk, just feeling good. If he was driving about five or ten mph in low gear, in and out of the ditch, and waving at horses and cows in the fields, people tried to stay out of sight. When he had been drinking that much, he wouldn't wave as he passed by. He wouldn't pass by if he saw someone. In that condition he would want to stop and visit a while — a long while.

The state and county governments were spending a lot of money at that time improving the roads for the farmers. Automobiles and trucks were coming into common usage through the 1920's and 1930's and road improvement was imperative. To do this, they bought a lot of gravel and Sam's pit had a good supply of high quality gravel. It probably originally came from the bottom of Lake Erie, scraped up by the last glacier and dumped in central Ohio when the glacier finally retreated. This area is moraine, and though it looks like the foothills of the Appalachians a few miles to the east, it would be more like the flat plains of western Ohio if it weren't for the moraine left by the last glacier.

The gravel pit brought Sam more money than he could drink, and even if the farms had not been prosperous, which they were, he would have had more money than he could use. Always when someone has more money than others think he should have, there is someone else who wants to help him take care of it. In Sam's case it was his two daughters.

Hattie Crandall and her sister Martha Ridenour were his two daughters. They had left Sam along with their mother long before I was born and had very little to do with their dad until late in his life when he took in John Hudson to keep house for him. Sam was getting up into his late seventies by that time, and the two girls, who had been content to wait until Sam died to inherit his property, in the view of the neighbors, began to be worried that he would do something foolish and leave some of it to John Hudson, who was a bachelor in his mid sixties by this time.

Both of the women began to visit Sam pretty regularly about then, and Sam seemed to find it a bit amusing. He used to needle them and apparently took delight in getting one or both of them upset.

He often hired one or another of the local boys to do some odd jobs around the place, such as cutting weeds in the barn lot or mowing the grass in his yard. Sam was inconsistent in these chores; on alternate years he would let the front yard grow up to grass and weeds, letting newspapers blow into the fence along the road, and leaving his long underwear hang over the front porch rail. He would sit in the rocking chair on the front porch in warm weather and wave at passersby, sipping on his bottle from time to time. Sam bought his supplies from a man in Pagetown who made it himself. It was a lot less costly than stuff with taxes on it but it did leave something to be desired in smoothness.

Most years Sam would hire someone to keep up appearances around the place, but I never worked for him. I never was much of a gambler and Sam was too unpredictable in his pay. On some occasions he would pay for some chore with as much as five or six times what the job was worth, while other times he would reward a boy who had worked hard for half a day with only a thank you. Phil Shambley and his brother Leo were greater gamblers than I was, and they often came away with a nice pay for a job, but sometimes came home empty handed.

Phil and his brother soon learned that it was a good idea to approach Sam for their pay if one of his daughters was visiting. When Sam was alone, pay was uncertain, but if one of the daughters was watching, Sam would ostentatiously overpay.

The daughters concluded that Sam needed a guardian to prevent him from doing something foolish with his money. They decided that the best course of action was to have him declared incompetent by a judge and one or both of them appointed as guardians. Because he lived in Hanover County but had property in both Kent and Hanover County, they could take him to court in either county. The daughters both lived in Kent County, so it was selected as the appropriate court to start with.

One nice May day, Martha Ridenour came to visit and asked Sam if he would like to take a ride. Sam was very pleased to take a ride, so they set off for Mt. Pleasant where Martha had arranged to have them appear before a judge. As they came into town across the viaduct on South Main Street by the railroad station, Sam said, "I gotta go. Let's stop at the Texaco station by Zink's Fruit Market. They gotta rest room."

Martha didn't really need any gasoline, but she pulled up to the pump and Sam got out and disappeared around the corner of the station. Martha asked the man to put in a dollar's worth of gas and waited for Sam to return. When the gas was in the tank and she had paid the man, Sam hadn't come back, so Martha pointed toward the corner of the building asked the man, "Go around to the rest room and see if my father is OK. He went around there when we came in."

"There ain't no rest room around there, lady," the man replied. "The men's room is inside by the grease rack."

"I better go see where he went!" Martha was alarmed and got out of the car and hurried around the corner of the station. There was no rest room, just as the man had said, but there was an alley that ran parallel with Main Street. There was no one in sight.

"Hey," protested the Texaco man. "Your car is blocking my pumps and I got customers waiting. Move your car first."

"I gotta go find my father first!" Martha replied.

They got into a discussion of which was more important, the waiting customers or Martha's finding where Sam had disappeared to. Since their priorities were quite different, the argument became somewhat heated. Neither could hear the other very well because of the sound of a Greyhound bus that was just then pulling out of the station that was next to the alley where it joined Gambier Street. The bus was making conversation somewhat difficult and loud, and the argument had attracted a lot of attention by this time.

A Mt.Pleasant policeman stopped to see what the commotion was about.

The result of the affair was a reproach for Martha and an apology to the Texaco man. It was very embarrassing to Martha and she missed her appointment with the judge who was going to decide on guardianship for Sam. She spent some time looking around for him and finally gave up and went home.

In the meantime, Sam had gone directly to the bus station and bought a ticket to Centerburg. He was on the bus that made so much noise during Martha's discussion with the Texaco man. When he got to Centerburg, he walked home, enjoying the pleasant day.

When Martha found out what he had done, she was pretty upset. Sam explained that he knew she must have had some shopping to do and he had been enough bother for the day, so he had just gone on home by himself. He couldn't seem to understand why she was upset.

Some time later, the daughters got Sam to a judge who was more sympathetic to them than he was to Sam. Sam was declared incompetent and in need of a guardian. He was moved to a nursing home shortly after that, John Hudson went back to live in his own place again, and Sam's grandson Sid Crandall took over the management of Sam's property. Sam didn't live much longer and his descendants got his property.

BELL

When the Sap Flows

Nearly all the farmers in central Ohio made maple syrup in the spring. At least those with a woods lot did. Sugar maple trees are common in that part of the country and syrup was a staple on farm tables there. It also was a cash crop at a time of year when there weren't many other sources of income. It takes a lot of sugar water to make a gallon of syrup, about 50 gallons. Gathering that much water and collecting enough wood to boil it down is a lot of work. When the sap is running, the work goes on 24 hours a day too. Many farmers boiled syrup all night long and gathered sugar water during the day. A farmer's life is not an easy one.

Corn Binder

Ernest Shambley lived next door to Sam Harris for years. Ernest's ancestors had probably come to North America from France because the name was most likely an Americanization, There is a small village in southern France named Champlemy and another small village in the north of France named Champlin. Or it may have come from some other French name. In any case, Ernest's family had been in America so long that any trace of French culture had been thoroughly subdued. Ernest was as American as all the rest of his neighbors, in spite of the French sounding name.

Ernest, like many farmers, had a corn binder. In corn harvest, a farmer had several choices of how to do it in those days. He could cut the corn by hand and stack the sheaves in shocks, which many did. Later the shocks would be pulled down and the corn husked by hand or the sheaves would be fed into a corn shredder which husked the ears and shredded the fodder much like the threshing machines that were used for wheat and other grains. In any case the corn would be left in shocks until the corn grains had dried out some.

Hired men often cut corn by hand for a fee. The farmer had a dilemma at that time; if he paid them so much per shock, he would get a lot of small, hastily stacked shocks which would often blow over in the first wind of autumn. If he paid the men by the hour, he would get shocks that would stand up in a hurricane but it would take twice as long to cut a field of corn.

An alternative that was often used was to cut the corn with a binder similar to the grain binders used for wheat, oats, and small grains. This machine was pulled by a team of horses and, like the small grain binders, took its power from a drive wheel, called the 'bull wheel'. It cut one row of corn and tied the stalks in sheaves and dumped them out on the ground to be picked up by hand and stacked in shocks like the hand-cut corn.

Farmers would often use one method one year and another the next, so when Ernest Shambley asked Sam Harris one year if he could use the barn next to Sam's gravel pit to store a corn binder in, Sam didn't think much about it. The barn was sitting empty anyway and Ernest didn't have enough room to store the binder in out of the weather at home. So after the corn was harvested that year, Ernest took the binder over to Sam's barn and put it away. That would have been about the first of November.

The following year Ernest didn't use the binder, so it sat in the barn collecting dust for another season.

The following spring, a year and a half after the binder had been put in the barn, Leo Shambley, Phil's older brother, was helping Ben Phillips plant corn. As they were filling the hoppers at the end of one round, they saw the junk dealer drive past them going toward Centerburg towing a corn binder behind his old Chevy truck.

"Ain't that your dad's corn binder," Ben asked Leo.

"Sure looked like it," Leo said, "but it can't be. Dad's binder is stored in Sam's barn."

"Might be a good idea to call your Dad and ask him to take a look in the barn," Ben suggested.

Leo walked over to the house and called his Dad and told him what they had seen, so Ernest hurried over to the gravel pit to see what he could see. There were ample tracks around the doors to indicate that there had been some activity and, sure enough, when Ernest looked in the barn, the binder was gone.

Ernest immediately hurried back home to get his car and drove over to Sam's place to find him. However, shortly after the junk dealer had driven away, Sam had remembered urgent business over in Mt. Gilead, and had driven away himself. Ernest could find no one at home so he drove over to where Ben and Leo were still planting corn.

Ben told him what they had seen and Ernest hurriedly drove over to Centerburg to the junk yard, where he found the dealer and his corn binder. It cost Ernest $10 to get his binder back and he towed it home behind his car. Then he went looking for Sam.

It was several days later when Ernest next saw Sam. Ernest had been unable to find him at home whenever he went up there, but one day Sam was walking down the road past Ernest's to get to his tenant farm. Ernest went out to accost Sam and get his money back.

As soon as Sam saw Ernest approaching, he lay down in the middle of the road and commenced shouting, "Help! Help!" as loud as he could.

Ernest was somewhat taken aback by this tactic and stood back a few feet.

"Oh stop yelling." Ernest protested. "I ain't gonna hit you. I oughta give you a thrashin' but I ain't. Stop yellin'."

"You ain't mad?" Sam stopped yelling and sat up.

"A course I'm mad, but I ain't gonna hit you. What made you sell my binder?"

"Didn't think you wanted it no more," Sam had gotten to his feet by now. "It had been settin' there since ever so long an' when the junk dealer came lookin' fer old iron, I sold it to him."

"Well it cost me ten dollars to get it back and I want my money"

"I never got no ten bucks. That man cheated you. He only give me five."

"You sold my good binder for only five bucks! It was worth a whole lot more than that anyway. 'Sides, I want my money back."

"Sure," Sam reached into his pocket and brought out his billfold. He pulled a ten dollar bill out of it and handed it to Ernest. "I figured that five bucks was more than I had in it and you didn't want it no more."

That was the end of the affair. Ernest had his binder, he wasn't out any money and Sam wasn't out a whole lot, the barn was empty again (Ernest had decided to store the binder at home.), and the junk man had made an easy five dollars. All in all, a most satisfactory day for all concerned.

Probably the least trusted member of the community was the junk dealer, perhaps with good reason, perhaps not.

No matter how good the deal is,
the customer is always suspicious.
Unknown

Stoney Creek people could never afford to hire a moving company, so it was always hard work for everyone concerned. They used whatever vehicle was available, car, team and wagon, truck, trailer, wheelbarrow, whatever they had. Perhaps that is why the people pretty much stayed where they were whenever they could.

There are three reasons why lawyers are replacing rats as laboratory research animals. One is that they're plentiful, another is that lab assistants don't get attached to them, and the third is that there are some things that rats just won't do.

Unknown

Fast Moving

Sam Harris had several tenant farms, including one on the Sussex County side of the County Line Road. It was just to the west of Ernest Shambley's place and had a small two story house with a porch that ran across the front of the house, a good barn and several good outbuildings. It was normally occupied by one or another of Sam's tenants.

About the time I entered high school a family named Samson lived on that farm. They had four children, two of them in the lower grades of school and two not yet in school. The Samsons were not the brightest of people, actually a little on the dim side, but Mr. Samson was a hard worker and did the farm work well the first summer they were there. They had moved in about plowing time in the spring and the crops had done well that year.

In late October, Sam was sitting in Samson's kitchen one evening discussing the work they would do the next day. They planned to haul some shocked corn into the barn and husk it out on the barn floor. It was rainy and dreary and the work would better be done indoors. Sam planned to come down and help first thing in the morning.

Early the next morning Sam walked down the road to the tenant farm. He noticed that there was no smoke coming from the chimney and that seemed a little odd. What seemed even odder was that when he got to the house it was deserted. All the furniture was gone, the people were gone, the stove was as cold as though it had been out for hours, and there was no sign that anyone had lived there for months. The chickens had been fed some time before, and there were no other animals, so that was not a problem. There was no note or any indication of the Samsons ever having been there. Since Sam and Mr. Samson had not settled up completely for the summer's crops, most of which were still in the bins or corn crib, it was a real mystery why or where they had gone.

Sam arranged for Phil Shambley to feed and water the chickens for the winter and then Sam made inquiries around to find the Samsons. He had no luck and the following spring he was talking to several other possible tenants about coming in to run the farm before plowing season set in. At the time, tenants were not so easy to find; times had gotten better and there were not so many poor farmers around as there had been earlier in the 30's. He needn't have worried as it turned out.

One morning in March, when Phil went down to feed the chickens he found the Samsons eating breakfast. The chickens had been fed and watered and everything appeared normal.

Samson's ran the farm that year as they had done before. What arrangements were made with the children who were in school, I have no idea, but the kids rode the same school bus that Phil and I rode. When they were there the kids went to the Centerburg school, what they did through the months of November, December, January, February, and part of March, I never did learn.

The following October the same thing happened. The Samsons were there one evening, the next morning they had disappeared without a trace. Sam was not quite so surprised that year and didn't spend much time looking for them. Neither did he try to get someone else to run the farm the next spring. Sure enough, the next spring they appeared as usual, and also as usual, behaved as though this was perfectly normal behavior for anyone.

About the third or fourth spring they had been Sam's tenants, my dad was working for Curtiss Wright in Columbus and rode in a car pool that left from over near Dan Rogers's farm. (Dan was Sam's cousin and had a large farm on the Sugar Creek Road west of where Samsons lived.) I was driving my Dad over to catch his ride one morning when we met a car pulling a trailer along the County Line Road over near the Sugar Creek Road.

Dad said, "Wasn't that the Samsons?"

I replied, "I don't know. All I noticed was a car going the other way with a trailer bouncing all over the road behind it."

"Well, I think it was the Samsons moving back in," Dad said.

As I returned toward home, I came over a rise in the road just before reaching the Samson home. The car we had met was pulled up in the lawn and parked with the trailer sitting beside the porch. Mr. Samson was in the trailer, the older boy was in the lawn between the back of the trailer and the porch, and someone was just inside the front door because I could see a pair of hands come out every few seconds. As I slowly drove past, Mr. Samson grabbed a chair and threw it out of the trailer onto the lawn. The older boy grabbed it on the first bounce and threw it at the front door, a pair of hands reached out of the door and grabbed the chair and pulled it in out of sight. By the time that chair was on its way in the door, Mr. Samson had grabbed another piece of furniture and thrown it to his son who repeated his action with the chair, and so on. No wonder they could move in or out overnight. Also no wonder their furniture looked like three days of bad weather.

By the time Sam would get there around breakfast time, the Samsons would be all settled and eating breakfast. Another year was about to start.

We never learned where they went in the winter. They often left before all the crops were sold in the fall, but they apparently knew that Sam would settle up fairly when they came back. I don't know what ever became of them; I left home for college that next fall and never heard any more about them. By the time Sam had been replaced by his grandson Sid Crandall, I suppose the Samsons had moved on to other fields.

The Hunting Season is On!

Rabbit Hunt

Sam Harris was one of the few farmers around Stoney Creek who would permit hunting on his farm. Most farmers have a very low regard for hunters, particularly city hunters. Too many gates are left open, fences broken down from climbing over them, windows shot out, and livestock killed or wounded, for farmers to consider hunters much better than vandals. But Sam never seemed to care. He always grinned and waved his hand for hunters to go ahead.

When Sam had been allowing hunters the run of his place for many years, he began to wonder what possible attraction there was in hunting. He'd heard men say that the swamp in his pasture across the road from Ernest Shambley's was good shelter for rabbits and pheasants, but he'd never checked it out personally. After a few drinks one November day, he decided to find out first hand how much fun hunting could be.

Because he didn't own a gun, Sam walked down the road to Ernest's place to see if he could borrow one. It was a cold day so Sam wore a cap with ear muffs, an old wool scarf around his neck, a heavy sheepskin coat over two sweaters and a flannel shirt, two pairs of pants tucked into 4-buckle overshoes. He had two pairs of wool socks inside his shoes and, of course, long winter underwear next to his hide. With thick wool mittens on his hands Sam had difficulty getting the pint bottle of Pagetown's Best (PB) in his coat pocket, but he wouldn't leave home without it, so he managed.

Although he looked like an animated pile of old clothes as he walked along, with a few slugs of PB in him to keep from freezing, he could hardly feel the cold November wind. He could hardly walk either, but that was not because of the PB; a little alcohol had never bothered him much. He was accustomed to it.

Sam knocked on Ernest's door and was welcomed into a warm kitchen. He pulled off his hat and mittens and sat down.

"What brings you out on such a cold day?" Ernest asked.

"Cold?" Sam acted surprised. "Hell, I ain't cold. I'm like to melt. How come you keep your house so damn hot?"

"Take off yer coat an' set a spell." Ernest invited.

"Nah, I can't stay. I jist wanta borrer yer ole shotgun to go huntin' with."

"Huntin?" Ernest exclaimed. "I never knowed you to go huntin'."

"I ain't. But hunters been smashin' m' fences and leavin' m' gates open fer forty years. They've shot out m' barn winders and even kilt a pig fer me onct. How that pig got mistook fer a rabbit, I ain't sure. Anyway, they say that ole swamp 'crost the road by the gravel pit is good cover fer rabbits. Now I thought if huntin' is so much fun, maybe I'd best not miss it fer no longer."

"OK, sure. Yer welcome to the use o' m' gun. I'll even furnish the shells. Whatcha want, bird shot er rabbit shot?"

"They's a difference?" Sam was surprised. "Hell, gimme both kinds. Maybe I'll get both."

"You ever use a shotgun?"

Sam knew Ernest's weakness for explaining things in more detail than the listener really wanted, so he hurriedly said, "Sure I do! Ain't nuthin' to shootin'."

This was a bald-faced lie. Sam didn't know which end of the gun to put the shells in, but he'd rather figure it out for himself.

"OK, if yer sure" Ernest got his shotgun out of the corner behind the stove and handed it to Sam. He then shook a handful of shells out of a box from the clock shelf and said, "I only got bird shot, but I guess it'll do fer rabbit if he ain't too far away."

"I won't let him git far", Sam promised, putting the shells in the coat pocket with the bottle.

Sam pulled his hat and mittens back on, picked up the shotgun and started for the door.

"Hey, you can't shoot with mittens on," Ernest protested.

"Whatcha want me to do, freeze m' fingers off?"

"Well, you sure can't pull the trigger that way," Ernest pointed out. "Here, take my gloves."

"Well, OK." Sam pulled off the mittens, put on the gloves and headed for the door.

Sam walked down the road to the old barn by his gravel pit to get out of sight of Ernest and out of the wind before inspecting the shotgun.

After a few minutes of fiddling with levers, the shotgun suddenly broke open at the breech.

"Oops, now I done it. I broke it," Sam moaned, but a few more minutes of fooling with it showed him that this was the way to load it. He pulled two shells out of his pocket and loaded the gun. He also took a couple more pulls on the bottle that was in the pocket with the spare shells.

Sam examined the gun enough to discover how to cock it by pulling the hammers back until they clicked, and he stepped out into the wind and walked over to the edge of the swamp behind the barn.

The water lying in pools around the edge of the swamp was frozen hard and Sam walked carefully out onto the ice. He worked his way along the underbrush and clumps of grass growing up through the ice watching for any sign of movement that would betray the presence of a rabbit or pheasant.

Suddenly a rabbit leaped out of a clump of grass almost at Sam's feet. It hopped away as fast as it could, but it had made only about three jumps when Sam pulled the trigger. Sam's reactions were pretty good and he remembered that Ernest had said not to let the rabbit get very far away if he wanted to get it with bird shot. To be sure of the shot, he pulled both triggers at the same time. (Why carry around two barrels if you are going to use only one?)

The roar of the gun nearly deafened him. The recoil of both barrels at once nearly tore his shoulder off. The ice underfoot caused his feet to slip out forward and he landed flat on his back with a thump that knocked the wind out of him in spite of all the clothes he had on and the ice gave him a nasty whack on the back of his head.

Sam lay quietly for a moment recovering his breath and hoping the throbbing in his head would cease and that his ears would stop ringing. He found that his interest in hunting had been reduced a great deal, in fact it had quite disappeared.

He sat up painfully and reached into his coat pocket for the bottle of PB and found only some shards of glass and wet shotgun shells. He threw the now useless bottle neck and cap into the brush, got up, picked up the shotgun, rubbed his shoulder with his left hand, and went looking for the rabbit.

"Might's well get that much out of it anyway," he muttered to himself.

He found the rabbit a few feet away. Both barrels had hit it and it was now shredded. He picked it up by one hind leg and held it at eye level. The head nearly touched the ground and was held by only a shred of skin.

"Damn," Sam mused, "It sure don't look like much to me. Can't see why anybody'd wanta eat somethin' like that."

Sam walked slowly back to Ernest's to return the gun and the unused, and probably unusable, shells. His right shoulder was beginning to throb and his ears were still ringing, but his head had pretty much stopped hurting. Sam was anxious to get home to a fresh supply of PB, his old reliable painkiller.

He knocked at the door and when Ernest answered the knock, Sam said, "Here Ernest. You like rabbit so you take this'n. I ain't got much stomach fer game." He handed the shotgun, shells, and gloves along with the shredded rabbit to Ernest and went on to say, "The shells got kinda wet so I come in. Guess I'll hafta git you some more."

"Aw, that's OK," Ernest looked dubiously at the rabbit as he took it and the gun from Sam. "You musta been right on top of him."

"Well, you said not to let him git much of a lead. I don't guess I'll be needin' the gun agin. Huntin' don't pleasure me much." Sam turned toward home, rubbing his shoulder.

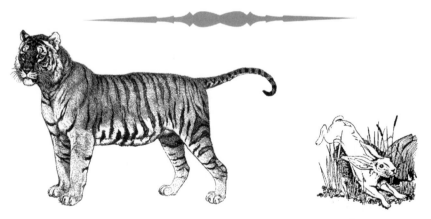

If you are looking for rabbits in a country where there are tigers, you must always keep a lookout for tigers, but when you are looking for tigers, you can ignore the rabbits.

This is a rule often given to engineers when troubleshooting problems

Sam Harris's Model A Ford, as it looked when he bought it new. It was a 1929 model, standard coupe, model 45A, without a rumble seat. It looked pretty good when it was new.

I had occasion to drive one like it from Greensboro, NC, to Dearborn, MI, in 1978 at the celebration of fifty years of Model A's. A friend of mine asked me to go along with him in his restored A because he didn't want to drive it alone. After driving for about two hours, I understood why he didn't want to drive it alone. It would cruise steadily at about fifty-five or sixty mph and could keep up with traffic on interstate highways well enough; that wasn't the problem.

The problem was that the steering wheel vibrated so much with the engine that the driver's hands became numb in about two hours. Henry didn't believe in mounting engines with rubber shock absorbing engine mounts; the A engine was bolted firmly to the frame of the car. The frame and everything else vibrated exactly as the engine did.

Most people didn't drive A's very far at a time. Those who did learned to stop every two hours or so to rest and get the feeling back into their hands.

Fender Bender

Sam Harris was a sociable man. On Saturday evenings he could often be found in one or another of the beer joints in Mt. Pleasant , passing the time with friends. He usually managed to stay sober enough to drive home without mishap.

Late one summer Saturday night he had more than his usual number of drinks and drove his Model A slowly, in second gear, down Main Street on his way home. He brushed against every car parked on one side of a couple of blocks down the street. He said later that he thought there were a lot of friendly people out in the street behind him, waving and shouting greetings at him as he drove along. He waved back and continued on his way.

The next morning, the Kent County Sheriff knocked on Sam's door but got no response. Sam's car wasn't in the drive or the shed, so the sheriff asked Sam's nearest neighbor, Paul Miller, if they had seen him.

He hadn't called "Breakfast!" as usual that morning and the Millers hadn't seen him that day.

On Monday, the sheriff called again several times, but Sam was nowhere to be seen.

On Tuesday and Wednesday, same thing.

On Thursday, Sam arrived home in what appeared to be a nice shiny new Model A Ford. The old scratched and battered Ford had been repaired, cleaned up, and repainted. It looked great. Not a scratch or dent on it. While it had once been light green with black fenders and cream colored wheels, now it was a light cream color with black fenders and red wheels.

Sam told Paul Miller that he had been in Columbus at a body shop getting the car fixed up. Sam had grown tired of the way the car looked and decided that it could stand some improvement.

On his way back to Stoney Creek, Sam had stopped at the sheriff's office in Mt. Pleasant and had agreed to pay damages to all of the car owners whose vehicles had been scraped. The sheriff had no grounds to charge Sam with any traffic violation or driving while under the influence because the sheriff did not see anything happen, and when Sam stopped to see the sheriff, Sam was sober.

It wasn't too long before the pretty cream colored Ford had a few scratches on the fenders and body. Sam wasn't always too careful about appearances.

Taking Your Chances:

There are always risks associated with any activity but most of us don't really appreciate the relative risks between activities. We fear the wrong things. The following figures are approximate relative risks between some common events. They are rounded and are average numbers. They are for comparison purposes and not to be taken literally in each case. They come from National Safety Council data. They are the average number of deaths annually in the United States from various causes.

Automobile Accidents	42,000
Airline Accidents	200

(**Worldwide** the number of fatalities in airline accidents in 1999 was 512, less than half the 1,046 in 1998, and the lowest number since 1946.
The number of passenger-miles has increased astronomically since 1946.)

Poison (includes food poisoning)	6,500

(To increase your safety in flying, avoid the meals served by the airline. Statistically the meals are far more likely to kill you than the airplane.)

Murders	22,000
Falls	13,000
Choking on Food	2,900
Falling Objects	800
Medical Treatment Accidents	2,500
Bathtub Accidents	300

It sure would make me nervous living on the 29th floor.

Illegal Coon

Those who didn't know my Uncle Ben Phillips thought he was rather sober and even a little on the slow side. He had a subtle sense of humor and few people outside the family or very close friends ever saw him laugh aloud. He loved what has been called a mental hot foot, but often his jokes had a serious lesson behind them.

Ben made a fair living from his farm at a time when many folks were hard pressed. He worked hard, was good with livestock, and was a good business man. His farm was mainly on one side of the Croton/Five Corners road but he managed a woods lot across the road from his house. The woods lot ran back to Sherman Cooley's place along Whitcomb's lane which crossed Sugar Creek by a small bridge.

When I was a boy, I used to play along that creek, which ran down across my dad's pasture field on the other side of Whitcomb's lane from my Uncle Ben's woods. Minnows, tadpoles, crayfish, and dragon flies were abundant, and I often saw tracks of raccoons along the creek. I wasn't the only one aware of coons either; Sherman Cooley was well aware of all game animals in that part of Ohio.

Sherman had a fair farm of his own at the end of Whitcomb's lane, about a third of a mile off the Croton/Five Corners Road. Sherman trapped and hunted to supplement his income as well as for pleasure. He was not always too strict with himself either about legal seasons or the various game laws.

One sunny fall day, a short time before legal trapping season, Sherman walked down Whitcomb's lane to his mail box on the main road. As he crossed the bridge over Sugar Creek, he paused and looked around. No one was in sight, so he stepped down off the road into a thicket along the creek on Ben's wood lot. The fence around the woods went into the thicket and then down across the creek close to the bridge. Sherman had placed a trap close to the fence where a coon was likely to come fishing for crayfish along the bank. The fact that the start of trapping season was a couple of weeks in the future made Sherman a little nervous about anyone seeing him. The fact that neither Ben nor my Dad, who owned the land on the other side of the road, permitted anyone to trap on the land merely added to Sherman's nervousness.

Lady Luck smiled on Sherman that day and he had caught a young healthy coon. It hadn't been there long and was still full of fight and apparently hadn't been hurt much. The coon hadn't yet started to chew its leg free. Sherman now had a dilemma.

He couldn't very well kill the coon and carry it home along Whitcomb's lane. He and Joe Whitcomb were not on very good terms at that time because Joe had put a padlock on his granary after he had suspected that his corn was disappearing rather fast. Sherman took it as a personal insult that Joe would suspect him of stealing corn so he wasn't speaking to Joe. This made him reluctant to be seen carrying a coon up the lane past Whitcomb's before trapping season had started; Joe just might call the game warden.

Sherman continued on down to the mail box while he pondered the problem. He got his mail and decided that his best bet was to go on home, get his car, and drive down to get the coon. Then he could drive past Whitcomb's without anyone knowing that he had a dead coon in the car.

Sherman didn't notice that as he picked up his mail, Ben was starting out from his barn with a tractor pulling a trailer loaded with some wire and fence repair tools and supplies headed toward Whitcomb's lane. Ben saw Sherman getting his mail and starting toward home, but didn't wave or speak because he was too far away and Sherman didn't look toward him. Ben was planning to do a little fence repair along the woods lot.

Ben pulled into a gate near the bridge and shut off the tractor. Sherman had disappeared over the rise in the lane without looking back and seeing Ben, so he was unaware that Ben was now pretty close to the coon in the trap. Ben picked up a hammer and staples and started working his way along the fence toward the creek. As he approached the creek he saw the coon in the trap. Lady Luck had turned her back on Sherman and now smiled on the coon.

Ben stared thoughtfully at the coon for about a minute considering the possibilities. The trap could possibly belong to one or another of the Stoney Creek boys, but this was a bit far afield for them. It wasn't likely to belong to Enos Myers; Enos always asked permission before trapping on anyone's property and besides, with game still plentiful, Enos wouldn't likely be hungry. About that time, Ben heard Sherman's car approaching along Whitcomb's lane and knew immediately what the situation was. He knew Sherman wouldn't walk down for mail if he was going to be driving down the lane right afterward.

Ben stepped up into the lane, and without waiting for Sherman to stop or slow down, waved at him to stop as though he expected Sherman to drive right on past.

"Hey, Sherman, come over here. I wanta show ya something." Ben called as Sherman stopped the car. Sherman looked uncomfortable. All chance for profit seemed to have disappeared but maybe Ben didn't know whose trap it was, so he responded, "Whatcha got, Ben?"

"Look," Ben said, parting the bushes, "Someone's caught 'em a coon"

"Well, I'll be damned," Sherman replied, "He's a big un ain't he?"

"Sure is," agreed Ben. "Wonder who caught 'im? Don't see any name tag on the trap."

"Damifino," said Sherman. "Whatcha gonna do with 'im?"

"Don't look like he's hurt much, Sherman. Why don't we jist let 'im go?"

"Man, you can't do that. That hide is worth at least five dollars." Sherman was shocked.

"Worth more'n that to the coon," said Ben. With that he waved his hat in front of the coon to distract its attention while he stepped firmly on the spring of the trap. The jaws opened and the coon took off like a shot down through the woods, hardly limping in its hurry. Sherman watched it go in dismay.

Ben pulled up the trap and looked it over for identification. Ohio law at that time forbade anyone setting a trap without an identification tag on it, but this one was bare. Ben looked it over and said, "There ain't no identification on it. Guess I'll just throw it in the trailer and take it home with me."

Sherman's day was spoiled. He climbed back into his car and drove on out to the main road and turned toward Centerburg. He couldn't very well go on home immediately or Ben would suspect what he had brought the car for. He had to stay out of sight for a while before he could go back past Ben who would be working the fence for a few hours.

Ben whistled softly as he worked his way on down the fence. He mused to himself, "I'll probably lose some corn to that coon but he sure brightened my day. I'll probably lose a bag or two of corn to Sherman too when coon huntin' season starts, but its worth it. He won't be speakin' to me for a few months either, most likely. I guess I can stand that."

September Morn—the first day of school.

Winter Barnyard

The chickens are usually shut in overnight in the winter in the chickenhouse on the right. Foxes, weasels, and skunks are common in central Ohio, and in the winter especially, they like to raid chickenhouses. Through the day, the chickens are pretty safe and they are allowed to run outside if they wish.

The granary/corncrib is the building to the left and that is where the farmer heads first in the morning. The cows and horses need to be fed and watered. Usually the watering is done by letting the cattle outside after the milking is finished. The horses and cattle are usually allowed to come and go outside as they choose. On cold winter days the ice in the water trough must be kept broken to allow them access to water.

When I was a boy, the main source of water for the animals was the nearby Sugar Creek which ran through our pasture. It seldom froze over completely but often would freeze in the wide still areas enough that I could sometimes skate on it. But the narrower rapid sections seldom froze and the animals could get a drink.

Winter was a pretty time of year, but it wasn't a whole lot of fun for farmers. Chore time lasted the better part of the daylight hours.

Les Robins

Les Robins was custodian at Centerburg School when I was in the lower grades. He lived in Stoney Creek in the house that was up on the hill near the cemetery, back from the road about 150 feet or so. It was just across the street from Harley Quinn who lived on the corner of the road that heads southwest out of Stoney Creek toward Olive Green. Les's house had a long stone walk that came down to three steps at the mailbox by his driveway.

Les and his wife Anna had two daughters, Mary who was a couple of classes ahead of me, and Martha who was a couple of years older than that. Les and Anna didn't always see eye to eye on things and when they had a disagreement, everyone in Stoney Creek knew about it.

I remember Les at the school, standing in the hallway downstairs at recess and lunchtime. When it was good weather he would shout "Outside" to send the smaller kids outdoors to play instead of running up and down the hallways. Also, he always rang the bell outside to call the children in at starting time, recess end, and after lunchtime was over. He kept the bell rope tied about seven feet off the ground so that mischievous small children couldn't reach it, but when it was time to ring the bell, if any small children were waiting, Les would let them pull the rope and ring the bell for him.

Les was pretty understanding. Before I was old enough to start school, we lived across the street from the school so that my sisters could attend high school. They didn't have bus service for high school kids until sometime in the 1930's so they had to get there the best way they could. My folks moved to town during that time. Anyway, my sisters never have been on time for anything and they would wait until the bell rang before racing out of the house and across the street to the school in the morning and at lunch time. The rule was that they weren't late if they were in their seats before the bell stopped ringing. Les would keep the bell ringing until he figured that they had time to reach their room.

I remember Les telling stories about World War I. He was a locomotive engineer during the war and spent some time in France and Germany. He would be asked to speak to the school assembly on Armistice Day, and if I remember correctly, could still get into his uniform. I remember his stories as being very exciting, but I can't remember any details anymore.

After Marty and I were married and living on the farm with my mother, she used to urge me to go visit Les. He had retired and was living in Stoney Creek and knew all sorts of interesting stories about the community, but to my everlasting regret, I never did go to visit with him. I should have gone with a tape recorder. Ah well, if we had to live the time over, would we do anything any differently? I doubt it. I never seemed to have the time.

About the time I finished the lower grades of school, Les found a better job in Columbus, something more in his specialty of stationary engineer. That means a job running a boiler or something similar in a stationary installation. The job has a great deal of responsibility for seeing that it doesn't blow up and destroy property not to mention human life and limb, and requires a license in most states. The job required him to live in Columbus during the week and he came home only on weekends. Les didn't have a car so he would take the Greyhound bus from Columbus to Centerburg and walk home from there. He might get off the bus at the intersection of the Croton/Five Corners road with Route 3 south of Stoney Creek about five or six miles and walk home from there. The distance was about the same.

To get back to his disagreements with Anna, they never were reticent about letting their feelings be known. Whenever they had an argument, it always went about the same way. Their voices were both loud, and when things got too hot for Les in the house he would walk down to the steps by the mailbox and sit down. He would shout his arguments back toward the house from there. Everyone in Stoney Creek could hear him quite well, and I'm sure that Anna could too. She would shout her replies back toward him from the front door.

When both had reached the point of desperation, Anna would go upstairs, throw Les's suitcase out the upstairs window, and follow that with his clothes. Then the argument would continue for a while until one or both got tired of it. Then Les would walk up to the house, pick up his clothes and pack them in the suitcase, and then carry it back in the house. The rest of Stoney Creek would go back to their regular chores at that time and everything would get quiet until the next time.

Christmas Cheer

Years ago, that is in 1944 or 1945, Centerburg and the rest of Ohio had a lot of snow. Snowplows kept the main highways reasonably clear, but streets in town had snow piled up along the sides so that parking along the curb was virtually impossible. There was a large ridge of snow down the center of Main Street so that traffic could go only along a narrow lane on either side of the center of the street. It was possible to get across the streets only at intersections, and the snow had been there long enough to be packed hard. There was no danger of cars hitting any traffic in the other lane; the snow was an effective traffic barrier.

The snow had started in early December and the snow that came down was still on the ground by spring. More snow had been added in subsequent weeks and by the middle of December there was a nice accumulation. This was the weather situation when Ike Shelton came home from Chicago to spend Christmas with his brother Bill in Stoney Creek.

Ike had a business in Chicago and Bill had a farm near Stoney Creek. Both men were in their thirties and neither had married. They shared a weakness for strong spirits and also shared the family characteristic of wanting to fight someone whenever under the influence of those spirits. People in Stoney Creek and Centerburg knew when it was wise to keep a little distance from any of several Shelton boys.

In order to celebrate Christmas in the Shelton tradition it was necessary to make a trip to Mt. Pleasant, about thirteen miles away, a few days before Christmas. Centerburg had no liquor store and over the holidays the two beer joints would be closed. Ike didn't have a car in Centerburg so he and Bill went to Mt. Pleasant in the rolling goat's nest that Bill called a car.

The car was not very old, only about ten years or so, but it had had a hard life. There were dents and scrapes on the fenders and body, The front bumper was badly twisted and the driver's door was held shut with wire wrapped around the door and door post because the latch was broken. The windows of both the front and rear doors on the left side had to be left down enough for the wire to wrap around, and of course neither door on the left side could be used. That was all right though, Bill could slide across the seat whenever he needed to get in or out. The heater didn't work, but then it never had been any great shakes anyway. Very few car heaters were much good in those days.

After making their purchases in Mt. Pleasant, Bill and Ike sampled some of the wares. This was thought advisable for several reasons. They wanted to be sure that the stuff was any good before driving all the way to Centerburg and it was damnably cold in the car so it was thought that a sip or two of the cup that cheers would help ward off frostbite.

It took roughly a half hour to drive to Centerburg and by the time Ike and Bill reached the edge of town they were both feeling the effects of the liquor a little. There was no one else in the car to fight with so they began to argue between themselves. By the time they reached the traffic light at Hartford Avenue, the only traffic light in town at the time, they had begun to exchange blows. Driving the car distracted Bill enough that he was getting the worst of the fight, so he reached across Ike, opened the right door and pushed Ike out. He then followed his brother and they continued the fight on the sidewalk.

The traffic light was at the highest point of Main Street which sloped gradually downward toward the edge of town, about a half mile away in either direction. The car's engine was idling with no one's foot on the throttle and third gear was engaged because Bill hadn't had time to take it out of gear. The track between the ridges of snow kept the car from straying off the main path so the car chugged along slowly toward Columbus until it got to the cleared highway at the edge of town where it eased over to the shoulder of the road, ran into a snowbank and stalled. It didn't hit anything but snow and didn't do any damage.

Bill and Ike didn't continue the fight very long on the sidewalk; it was too cold for comfort. They soon adjourned to George Bowers's pool room on the corner. George had a barber shop in the front and several pool tables in the back room and it was usually filled with men either waiting for a haircut, a table, their turn with the cue, or just watching the activity. Bill soon tired of fighting and sat down on a bench along the wall.

Ike was jumped by three of the men in the place and wrestled to the floor, so Bill got up from the bench, grabbed a man with each hand and pulled them off Ike. Ike could handle one man, but three was just too much. Bill sat his two down on the bench and went over to help Ike. Somehow, one of my classmates got in the way of the scuffle and Bill threw him through the plate glass window at the front of the barber shop.

Fortunately, the young man wasn't cut or hurt much, although he did say later that it didn't feel very good, but the barber shop and pool room began to get pretty cold, so Bill and Ike moved on down the street to Dick Tate's beer joint. George Bowers had called the State Police by that time, and when the patrolman arrived he found Bill and Ike having a beer. He arrested both of them and took them to Mt. Pleasant to the pokey to sober up.George Bowers went across the street to Hutcherson's Hardware and got the last piece of plate glass that Hutcherson had that was big enough to replace the broken window. As he was removing the broken pieces from the frame, he leaned the new pane against the wall. Justin Case the insurance man, curious about the fight, came along to ask George about it and inadvertently leaned against the new pane and broke it.

George had to get a piece of plywood to replace the window until he could get a new plate glass pane from Columbus. This arrived a couple of days later.

Bill and Ike appeared before the magistrate the next day, sober and contrite. They paid the fine and damages in cash and went to retrieve Bill's car. The battery was run down but that was a minor problem with that car, considering all its other defects. Presumably, Bill and Ike had a merry Christmas.

This is a 1935 Dodge like the car that Bill Shelton drove except that Bill's car was a not as neat as this one. Bill didn't take very good care of his car, but if he had, it would have looked like the one above.

Ben Phillips saw this sheep in his flock when he returned from Centerburg one spring day. When Ben had left for town his man Bill Hess had been shearing sheep at Ben's lower sheep barn and most of the rest of the sheep in the flock were freshly shorn.

"What happened?" Ben asked Bill when he reached home, "Lunch time sneak up on you?"

"Huh?" Bill replied, "Oh, you mean about that sheep? Naw, the shears broke when I was about half done and I couldn't find another pair."

"Well, I'll go borrow some tomorrow," Ben said. "In the meantime, let's get that sheep inside the barn. No need to let the neighbors think the dinner bell rang when you was half done."

Uncle Ben is holding his team on the left and my Uncle Nolan is between the teams. My cousin is on the wagon holding the reins to my Dad's team and my Dad is leaning on the fork. The boy with the dog is the writer at about age 10. This is a typical load of hay in the middle 1930's; not many farmers had balers at that time.

This farmer is hauling wheat to the threshing machine. Wheat shocks in the foreground show how it was stacked to dry out between cutting and threshing. Oats were shocked the same way . I always preferred to pitch oat sheaves onto the wagon for threshing because they are so much lighter than wheat sheaves.

Thrashin' Time

Ben Phillips had a threshing machine and big Case tractor to run it. In the 1930's the wheat that every farmer raised was cut with a binder, stacked in shocks by hand for the grain to dry out, and along in late July or early August the threshing crew came around to "thrash wheat".

The women came along too as a rule, because "thrashin' dinner" was traditionally a gala occasion. Every woman prepared a specialty and the men were always hungry after a hard morning's work. The men always sat at "first table" and there was much banter as they stowed away the food. Early gardens were "in" and there'd be plenty of green onions, radishes, new potatoes, early tomatoes, green beans, peas, and maybe even early sweet corn. Always there were biscuits, store baked bread, lots of home-made butter, as well as baked beans, several kinds of meat such as roast beef, meatloaf, fried chicken, ham, along with gravy and several kinds of cheese. For dessert there would be pie, cake, and puddings. Also there were salads and deviled eggs for those who wanted them, and the fare was all hearty country food to satisfy hard-working men as well as growing boys. It probably hastened the formation of artery clogging plaque and early heart attacks, but it was good eating.

After the crew had eaten, the women would clear and reset the table for their meal. It was time to visit and enjoy each others' company. Almost everyone enjoyed threshing time, even though it was hot tiring work.

Some of the jobs I detested and was not very good at, such as manhandling the bags of wheat from the machine to the granary and into the bin. It was always noisy and dusty around the machine and the grain. The bags were always about sixty pounds each and I never was notably strong in the arms so it was a struggle for me. The job I liked best was pitching the sheaves up to load the wagons in the field. The sheaves weighed about fifteen or so pounds and one had to pitch them up about as high as one could reach with the sheaf on the end of a pitchfork to get them on the top of a load. That was not really very hard but by the end of the day, you knew you had been working. It was out in the fresh air away from the noise, and between loads there was usually a shade tree nearby with a jug of water under it. You could talk to the wagon driver while you were loading and could actually hear what was said.

Most of the job assignments were pretty well fixed in our crew. Grandfather Ed filled the bags at the chute by the machine. Uncle Ben stayed on or very near the seat of the tractor all the time the machine was running so that in case of any emergency he could stop it very quickly. Bill Hess was the only person permitted to handle things on the machine such as moving the straw discharge spout, putting wax on the belt when it was moving, or clearing any jams in the machine that might occur. (Ben didn't want anyone but Bill to ever get inside the machine so that, if he could see Bill outside the machine, he knew that it was safe to run it.) Usually the owner of the farm where the work was would drive the truck or team and wagon hauling the bags of grain from the machine to the granary to put it in the bins. Other farmers would drive their teams and wagons to the field to haul in the sheaves of grain. Usually the boys would be put to work hauling bags of grain or pitching sheaves up to load the wagons.

The others used to chuckle at Sherman Cooley because he was not expert at loading a wagon and the slope of the load at the front and back was such that the men used to say it would shed water. He also sometimes lost a load part way to the machine from the field because he stacked it so loosely on the wagon. I always liked to pitch up sheaves to him because he never put the load up high and I never had to stretch to reach a sheave up to the top of the load as I did with some of the men. Paul Miller could really load it high and level; the last few sheaves for his loads required a toss of the sheave to reach. He had a good big wagon too, and I can't remember him ever losing a load. He was interesting to talk with though which made up for the extra work loading for him.

If the machine clogged, as it did often in the morning when the straw might be a little damp, Bill would need to open the door of the machine by the straw blower and clear out the jam. It was necessary for him to stand on the wheel and reach inside, usually up to his waist, to reach the worst of the jammed straw. When he was done, he would step back off the wheel and wave to Ben who never left the tractor seat when anyone was inside the machine. When he saw Bill wave, Ben would race the engine a time or two to signal that he was ready to start up again, and then slowly let in the clutch and increase the speed of the belt to drive the machine.

Ernest Shambley always knew the best way to do anything and was quite ready to share the knowledge with anyone. He had quite a lot of difficulty standing around waiting while Bill cleared jams, because he knew how to do it better and faster. One day he got to the door of the machine before Bill did and was unlatching it as Bill arrived.

"Better let me do that," Bill said. "Ben don't want nobody in there but me."

"Now jist let me do it," Ernest insisted, "I kin git it done a whole lot quicker than you kin."

"Ben don't want nobody but me in that machine," insisted Bill. "Ah, he won't know the difference an' I kin git it done in no time." Ernest had the door open and was pulling damp straw out of the machine by the handful by this time. Bill stepped back and looked down toward the tractor at Ben and shrugged his shoulders. Ben had been watching but said nothing.

As soon as Ernest had leaned way into the machine with only his rear quarters showing, Ben raced the engine of the tractor a couple of times. At this signal, which Ernest knew as well as anyone, Ernest frantically backed out away from the deadly blower. He lost his straw hat and he bumped his head on the top of the access door and then he lost his footing on the wheel he was standing on. He backpedalled frantically to keep from falling down backwards as he got away from the machine. All of the men watching laughed loudly, and this seemed to irritate Ernest.

Ernest turned red in the face and then reached back into the machine to recover his straw hat. Then he glared at Bill and started marching down toward the tractor. He thought that Ben had been playing a joke on him, but Ben looked as serious as a judge. Ernest came as near to swearing as he ever did.

"Condemn you, Ben Phillips! You mighta killed a man!" Ernest shouted as he approached.

"Was you in there, Ernest?" Ben replied seriously. "I saw Bill outside and thought it was safe to start up again."

"You darn tootin' I was in there. I was clearin' the straw out so's we could run agin."

"I'm surprised at you Ernest. You knew that was Bill's job. Maybe you better let him do it. I'd hate for anyone to git hurt around that machine." Ben replied.

Ernest was pretty sure that Ben knew what he was doing, but he wasn't completely certain. The other neighbors knew very well what Ben was up to and remembered the lesson. Threshing machines were dangerous and more than one farmer had lost limbs and lives to them. Leo Blackwood had lost an arm one year in a corn shredder by violating a safety rule about reaching into moving equipment. Ben never lost a man or any part of one, and he ran dangerous equipment for years. One of the reasons for this was his constant alertness to safety and his hard rules about who was to get into equipment and who was not. He never did specify any firm rules about it, but he had a way of embarassing anyone who didn't follow his safety practices.

Ernest never tried to get into the threshing machine after that and neither did any of the other men around it.

Ben used to let me drive the tractor when I was not yet big enough to drive horses. He had a Case which had a hand-lever clutch; you pulled it back to engage it and this could be done easily and gently. To disengage it, you simple gave it a push forward and it disengaged by itself. It would lock in the engaged (rear) position but even a small boy had no trouble disengaging it. Steering was not powered, but if the tractor was moving, it was not difficult to steer and the speed was controlled by a hand throttle. You could select the gear you wanted at leisure because nothing was engaged until you pulled the clutch lever and it would start moving in any gear. The tractor was huge, but even as a small boy I was permitted to drive it. My Uncle Ben was very good to me and I worked with him a lot when I was growing up.

There were a lot of jobs I didn't like on the farm, but threshing was one I really enjoyed. That was the season I liked the best.

Stoney Creek in the springtime would be lined with wildflowers, at least in the portions where livestock couldn't graze. Ohio has, or had when I was a boy, lots of wildflowers, and a favorite place for them was along the banks of creeks. Some portions of Stoney Creek didn't have many stones; it actually was marshy in places. That is where the wildflowers were most abundant.

Duck, Here Comes the Goose — or Something

Boys living on a farm usually learn at a young age what to be afraid of. When I was pretty small, my Uncle Ben had a young man working for him who had a lot to learn.

One evening, as they were letting the cows out of the barn after milking, Walter Feasel looked at an old gander which was walking close by.

"How much does one of them weigh, Ben?" he asked.

"Don't know, never weighed one" Ben answered.

Walter reached down to pick up the gander and Ben warned him.

"Don't know as that's a very good idea, Walter."

"Aw, I ain't gonna hurt it," said Walter and picked up the gander.

"I wasn't worried about the gander," said Ben.

The gander reached around and grabbed Walter's nose with its bill which, like all gander's bills, was very rough and very strong. Then as Walter loosed his grip, the gander flailed Walter with its wings. Ganders have a knot at the joint of the wing which is about the size and hardness of a man's fist and they use these knots in fighting other ganders. This gander connected with Walter's jaw with both wings.

Walter staggered back against the barn, a lump rising on each side of his jaw, and his thoroughly scraped nose beginning to swell. The gander stood in front of him and hissed, threatening to repeat the treatment.

As soon as Walter recovered a little, he quickly retreated into the barn. He never tried to weigh a gander or a goose again. Ganders don't hold with being treated that way.

Walter was a bit thick, but he learned a lot working for Uncle Ben. For example, he was afraid of the dark when he came to work for Ben, but he learned to overcome that fear, at least partially.

Walter was about eighteen and came from over near Olive Green. He was beginning to take notice of girls and when Nora Whitcomb hired a young girl to help with the housework, Walter began to spend several evenings a week at Whitcombs. Summer evenings were long, but it does get dark eventually. Walter was nervous about that walk home beside the dark wood along Whitcomb's lane, but the pleasure of feminine company in the evenings helped overcome his fear.

There is always a lot of work to do on the farm in the summer, and the days begin pretty early. Ben was amused at Walter's overcoming his fear of the dark, but he was less than amused at how tired Walter sometimes was in the mornings when there was work to be done. Walter sometimes got home pretty late at night.

One evening as it was getting along toward dark, my parents and I were sitting on the porch cooling off in the late evening breeze. Uncle Ben stopped at our house carrying a bucket and sat down on the edge of the porch.

"What are you up to?" Dad asked.

"Thought maybe you might help me a little while", Ben replied, "I got some whitewashin' to do."

"At this time of day?" Dad asked, "What on earth are you gonna whitewash?"

"Rocks. C'mon and bring a brush."

The last glacier scattered all the rocks it had gouged out of what became Lake Erie in the moraine of central Ohio. All farmers around there had dragged the rocks off the surface for years and piled them in the corners of the fields. Dad was no exception and there was a big pile of rocks in the corner of our pasture where Whitcomb's lane joined the Croton/Five Corners road. There was another big pile beside Sugar Creek where it flowed under Whitcomb's lane out of Ben's woods.

Dad and Uncle Ben whitewashed both piles of rocks just as it was getting dark and then sat down in the edge of the woods by Sugar Creek and lit cigarettes to wait for Walter to come home.

There was just enough moonlight to see fairly well, but the shadows were deep and dark as Walter started homeward. He came nervously along the woods by the lane, whistling softly now and again. As he neared the bridge over Sugar Creek, he noticed something large and white in the dim moonlight, something beside the lane across the creek, something scary that he had not seen when he went back to Whitcomb's before dark to see his girl.

Walter stood still and scuffed one foot in the gravel of the lane for a few minutes. He then climbed the fence into Dad's pasture field and gave the white thing a wide berth. This forced him to jump the creek a ways downstream from the bridge. He almost made it. He also stumbled into Dad's herd of cows that were sleeping near the creek and startled both himself and them. He worked his way over to the Croton/Five Corners road and began walking up toward Ben's house and safety, his wet shoes squelching a little.

As Walter was working his way through the pasture, Dad and Uncle Ben walked quietly up to a spot near the Croton/Five Corners road where they could see Walter as he approached the corner.

As Walter got near the corner, he noticed that the large white object had moved to the corner by the road and was waiting for him there. This was an even more frightening thought; the monster or whatever it was had been stalking him.

This time, Walter didn't hesitate. He climbed the fence into Ben's field next to the road and gave the white thing in the corner another wide berth. He had to climb another fence into Ben's pasture field and then cross Sugar Creek a second time to get to Ben's house. This time he just waded across; his feet were already as wet as they could get.

As he crossed the porch in the dark to get to the front door, he encountered something soft and large which felt mansize and menacing. It seemed that after Walter had left that evening, Ben had hung his sweat-damp shirt and overalls from a coat hanger to dry out. He had put it where the breeze on the porch could help the clothes to dry and it just happened to be between the porch steps and the front door of the house.

The next morning, Walter announced at breakfast that he believed his dad needed him to help on the farm at home near Olive Green. He left shortly after breakfast.

About that time, Ben hired Bill Hess to work for him. Bill was married already and wasn't afraid of the dark.

May those who
   are not kind,
   and gentle,
   and pure,
And follow God's
   teaching,
May they always
   hope for good luck.

An old Gaelic blessing

May those who love us,
   love us
And those that don't love
   us,
May God turn
their hearts;
And if He doesn't
turn
   their hearts,
May He turn their
ankles
So we'll know
them by their limp-
ing.

An old Gaelic blessing

Fearless watchdog and man's ever faithful companion. Appearances count. Fangs and a fierce expression are the two essentials for a good watchdog, and this dog had both. Actually, this dog was a bundle of phobias and she went to hide at any unusual noise.

Shaggy Dog Story

For a number of years my sister had a yellow dog that kept getting under foot. My brother-in-law Ed used to grumble that the dog was always in the way.

One day, as he was starting to go downstairs, the dog got in his way and both dog and man went down the stairs together. The dog was yelping and my brother-in-law was swearing as they landed with a crash at the foot of the stairs.

My sister came to the head of the stairs and shouted, "Did you hurt the dog? Did you hurt the dog?"

Ed replied, "Not yet! But I will!" and he did.

That dog was the source of a spot of trouble for me on one occasion. My sister was pregnant with her third son at the time and asked me if I would drive her two other sons back from our parent's home when it came time for the baby to be delivered. Ed could drive them there and I could go get them when it was time for them to come home. That was fine with me because I often drove back home for the weekend anyway.

I had my first new car at the time, having been working in Cleveland, about 120 miles from Stoney Creek, for several years. The depression and World War II were over and times were pretty good.

When I arrived at home to pick up the boys, I was dismayed to see the dog too. That dog was known to get carsick after a few miles and even if she didn't, she shed yellow hair all over and I didn't really like the idea of having my new car all redecorated inside.

My mother said, "Don't worry. Tomorrow go into Centerburg to the vet's and get some sleeping pills. She will sleep all the way."

That sounded good to me so I went to Doc Haberman and asked him for some phenobarbital pills for the dog.

"How heavy a dog?"

"I don't know how heavy. Maybe forty pounds or so. I don't know. Why?"

"How many pills you need depends on the dog's weight. Well, I'll give you six. That should do it. Give her four, wait about a quarter hour and if she isn't asleep, give her two more. Once she is asleep, she'll sleep for about 4 hours."

That sounded good to me. The trip should take about three hours.

The next day I got the boys ready to go home, gave the dog four pills and watched. In about ten minutes, the dog's front legs crossed and she fell on her chin. She got up and staggered around the room for another ren minutes or so but wouldn't lie down to sleep. She fell down a lot, but wouldn't stay down. So I held her down in a chair and she went to sleep.

I loaded the boys and the luggage in the car and put the dog on a blanket on the floor behind the driver's seat. The dog promptly woke up and started to leave the car. So I gave the dog the last two pills and held her in the car for a few minutes and she went back to sleep again.

We started out. When we reached Mt. Pleasant, about twenty minutes into the trip, I stopped at a traffic light and looked over my shoulder to see how the dog was doing. She was awake and trying to get on the back seat.

I grabbed her by the collar and put her back on the floor. The light changed and we continued on our way. Every time we stopped for a traffic light or anything else, the dog tried to climb on the back seat. As long as the car was moving, she stayed on the floor, but she didn't sleep. She whined loudly and continuously all the time the car was moving. This went on for about three hours.

When we arrived at my sister's home, the dog went staggering into the kitchen where my sister was sitting at the table. The dog saw my sister and rushed over to her, staggering and falling down on the way.

"What's the matter with her?" my sister wanted to know.

"She's just drunk." I answered.

The dog slept all day the next day but I had to be back at work. At least she didn't get sick in the car, but there was a lot of yellow fur to brush out of the seat and floor upholstery. I never did have much faith in sleeping pills after that.

Sensible advice: Never take a sleeping pill and a laxative at the same time.

Snow White says either Sleazy goes or she does..

In case you have forgotten, the seven dwarfs' names are:
Sordid, Sleazy, Shady, Shameful, Greedy, Tricky, and Cheap.
They are also known as:
Creepy, Scruffy, Cranky, Droopy, Rowdy, Raunchy, and Lewd.
Of course, Disney got it all wrong and called them:
Sleepy, Sneezy, Bashful, Happy, Grumpy, Dopey, and Doc.

Tales of Aunt Lois

Aunt Lois Loses Her Cat

I had an aunt who at one time lived upstairs over my sister Ruth. Aunt Lois was not packed too tightly and had a habit of losing her cat. She also was hard of hearing and often lost her hearing aids.

The cat took every opportunity to escape out the front door and when it did my nephew Ed had to find it and bring it home. Once the cat disappeared and Ed couldn't find it even after searching up and down the street and all over the lot. Lois called the fire department. (I don't know why, but the fire department used to help find lost pets.) They found the cat — in one of Lois' dresser drawers in her bedroom where she had closed the cat in and forgotten it. She probably hadn't noticed when the cat got in the drawer.

Here kitty, kitty, kitty!

A few days later the cat disappeared again and Lois got my sister Ruth to walk up and down the street calling the cat. My other sister Florence asked Ruth, "Does the cat come when it is called?" Ruth replied, "No." "Then why call it?" Florence asked. Ruth asked Lois if the cat was caught in a drawer again and Lois said, "Oh, no. The cat's not in the house this time." After four days, Lois found the cat in one of the dresser drawers. It had probably been yelling its head off, but Lois had lost her hearing aid again so she never heard it. I don't blame the cat for trying to escape out the front door whenever it could.

Driving in Convoy with Aunt Lois

Marty and I had gone to visit my sister Ruth and she had invited several family members to dinner at a restaurant in Lakewood. Aunt Lois, who lived in Rocky River at that time, was included. Lois came to Ruth's house that afternoon and when it was time to go to the restaurant for dinner, Aunt Lois asked if any of the group would like to see some of the new houses that were being built in her neighborhood. Everyone expressed politely their total lack of interest in seeing fancy houses from the outside, so Aunt Lois said, "Fine! Martha and Ed can ride with me and Robert can follow in his car with Ruth. Then after dinner I can just go on home and not have to drive so far."

I wasn't completely familiar with the route to the restaurant although I had been there once before, and I certainly did not know the route to the fancy houses Lois wanted to show us. I also particularly dislike driving in convoy with anyone, so I was less than enthusiastic about the whole thing, but I had little choice in the matter, so we started out.

At the first traffic light, Lois caught it green and I caught it red. About halfway down the block Lois noticed that I was not following so she stopped - in the middle of the street in the middle of the block - and waited for me to catch up. Several cars had to go around her, but traffic was not heavy so it didn't matter too much.

We shortly entered Interstate 90 headed away from downtown, so far so good. Lois speeded up to about seventy mph and started passing cars and trucks. She was in the left hand lane of a three lane roadway beside a truck when she began to wonder where I was. I was hanging back a bit in the center lane behind the truck. Lois slowed to the speed of the truck, about sixty-five, and stayed beside it. I could see her moving her head around searching for me in the rear-view mirror and there were enough other cars around, all doing sixty-five or so, that she was having difficulty finding me. We had only about four miles to go on I-90 so this couldn't take very long.

Finally Lois gave up finding me in the mirror, speeded up again, passed the truck, swung over in front of it and moved into the right hand lane to exit I-90 at the next ramp. I didn't pass the truck but moved into the right hand lane behind Lois and followed her up the ramp and down the street to her neighborhood.

We drove slowly, thank Heaven, up and down several streets looking at new houses until Lois found herself driving into a court with no outlet. I hung way back to see what she was going to do. Apparently, she thought that the paved driveway to one of the houses was an extension of the street so she drove up the driveway until she reached the house. She said later that she thought that street was awfully narrow. Then she started backing out of the drive, but the drive was curved a bit and she found herself backing over the lawn straight toward the mailbox at the end of the drive. Fortunately, my nephew Ed noticed and suggested to Lois that she should stop and get back on the driveway pavement.

Lois said to Martha, "I **love** to drive, but I hate having accidents." We got out of the drive and the neighborhood without further incident and got back on a main street which went past the shopping center where the restaurant was. It was several miles and there were some traffic lights on the way. One large intersection had several streets coming into it and had two traffic lights very close together. Lois caught the first one green and I caught it red. Lois then stopped in the middle of the next intersection to wait for me and while she was there the light changed. The light was directly over her car so she couldn't see it and she wondered why all the cars on the cross-street were blowing their horns at her. Finally Ed reminded her that she should keep going, so she did. I watched her car disappearing into the distance while I sat there waiting for the light to change again.

I had only a vague idea where the restaurant was located so we continued on down the street after the light changed. Ruth was searching for the restaurant close to the street while I was looking for a familiar shopping center and searching deep into the parking areas because I remembered that the restaurant was a long ways from the street. I spotted it and began looking for a parking space in the second row back. When I found one and Ruth and I got out, we saw Lois and Ed standing in an empty space in the first row looking toward the street watching for me. A car was waiting to get into the space and impatiently tooting the horn for Lois to get out of the way and Marty was over on the sidewalk trying to pretend that she didn't know those people out in the parking lot.

We got Lois away from the parking spot and later we were joined by other relatives who had not had the thrills getting to the restaurant. We did have a good meal, but Martha determined that she had had her first and last ride with Aunt Lois.

Lois drove the way she had been taught by my Uncle Fred when he was alive. Fred liked to go fast, so Lois went fast. One time she was passing a string of half a dozen cars on a two-lane road when Fred thought she was going a little too fast so he said, "Why are you going so fast?" Lois replied, "I have to go fast to get around all those cars, don't I?"

Lois didn't often criticize Fred's driving but once on the New York Throughway she thought Fred had made a mistake. The road was a glare of ice as they were approaching Buffalo. There was a toll plaza on the edge of Buffalo, a nice wide plaza with about a dozen gates. Fred was driving and didn't even slow down as he went barreling through one of the gates.

Lois turned and looked back and said, "Weren't you supposed to stop and pay toll back there?"

Fred replied, "I couldn't have stopped, Lois. I was doing seventy miles an hour and if I had tried to stop I'd have been all over the road."

One day Lois' nephew Ron drove over to see her and noticed that there were large black streaks on the left side of her car, the wing mirror was hanging loose and the trim strip on the side of the car was missing. The black streaks were in a swirling pattern as though a giant buffing wheel had massaged the side of the car and left streaks.

Ron asked Lois what caused the damage to her car and she said, "Oh, I hit the curb when I was parking the other day and dented the back fender a little. Ron hadn't noticed the minor damage to the right side of the car.

"No, I meant the left side of the car. What happened?" Ron asked.

"Oh! I don't **know**!" Lois replied. "I was just going along Interstate 90 the other day and suddenly I heard a terrible crashing and squealing noise on the side. When I got home I noticed that the mirror was broken and the car had those horrible streaks on the side. I don't know what happened."

Ron figured that he knew. Lois had been driving at her usual speed in one lane of I-90 and a truck had passed her on her left. As the truck got even with her car, Lois had moved over to the left enough to brush the wheels of the truck and the truck tires had left big black streaks on the finish as well as ripping off the trim strip and mirror. This must have happened at seventy or eighty miles per hour. The trucker probably didn't know what had happened either; he might not have even felt it.

Lois lived a charmed life. She was well into her eighties when she died of natural causes. She had had numerous property damage accidents, but survived without personal injury. What a woman!

Catch the Parakeet

When our children were small and our house was too, Aunt Lois decided that what our children needed was a parakeet. The fact that we had four cats and a dog had no effect on her decision that what every household needed was a parakeet, so she gave us a parakeet complete with a cage as well as a stand which held the cage precariously about four feet or so off the floor. We put it in the living room behind the rocking chair.

One of the cats, Sam, liked to have a bowl of milk in the morning and then take a nap in that rocking chair. He was not a particularly observant cat and didn't notice the bird in the cage. As soon as he closed his eyes however, the bird chirped.

Sam's eyes popped open and he listened carefully. One could imagine his thoughts:

"That sounded like a bird. I'm in the house and there are no birds in the house. It sure sounded like a bird though. I must have dreamed it."

Just then the bird chirped again and this time Sam turned and looked at the cage.

"I be damn! It is a bird! They are serving hors d'oeuvres today! How about that!"

He then climbed up on the back of the rocking chair for a closer look, but Marty had a broom in her hand and gave him a swat to remind him that this bird was not for eating. Birds outdoors were fair game, but birds indoors were to look at but not touch. Sam had a good memory and from then on he ignored the bird in the house.

One day I fell victim to some bug that upset my digestion and I stayed home from work. I found that if I lay completely immobile and didn't even move my eyes, I no longer felt nauseated or had the need to rush to the bathroom. So I lay quietly in bed in my room. I could hear the normal quiet rustling from the other rooms as Marty went about the usual household tasks but other than that, all was peaceful.

Suddenly there was a crash in the living room and then the sounds of running feet and shouts of dismay from Marty. It seemed that one of the lesser disciplined cats, Claude, had decided to get a close look at the bird and had climbed onto the back of the rocking chair. From there he had leaped to the cage but he had not realized that the back of a rocking chair is not a stable platform for leaping and he fell slightly short of his goal. He had, however, managed to catch the lower part of the cage with his front feet and carry the cage over with him as he fell to the floor. Hence the crash.

On the way to the floor, the cage had hit the potted plants that Marty had on a shelf by the window, and several of them had crashed to the floor as well. Naturally they broke and scattered plants and potting soil all over.

The cage door had popped open and the bird was now free in the house and Marty was trying to catch it before one or another of the cats did. Hence the sound of running feet.

My curiosity overcame my sense of nausea and I went to the living room to see what was happening. Sam, who had been asleep in the rocking chair when this started was clinging to the door knob trying to get outdoors. He obviously did not want to be involved. Marty was chasing the bird with a dish towel in one hand and swinging a broom at the cats with the other hand. Claude was trying to help catch the bird and running back and forth on the floor as the bird flew about the room. Pepper, our Manx cat and mighty hunter, who had not gotten involved until the bird got loose, was leaping from the back of one chair to another trying to help catch the bird.

I found that it was all too confusing so I just watched.

Marty managed to get Pepper captured and put out the door without losing the bird outside as well. She also let Sam outside and he disappeared for a few hours. Pepper jumped onto the window sill on the outside where she could watch the activity in the living room with her nose pressed against the glass. Claude kept on running here and there avoiding the swipes with the broom.

Finally Marty managed to catch the bird using the dish towel as a net, and the bird promptly bit down on Marty's thumb in gratitude for her saving its life. She righted the cage, shook the bird off her thumb, and slammed the cage door. I decided that the best thing for me to do was to return to my sick bed without making any comment.

The next time Aunt Lois visited, she brought us another bird because she thought the first one would be lonely. So we ended up with two parakeets. When we moved to North Carolina we insisted that the birds would be better off with Aunt Lois, and we left them with her.

Xenophobia

In Paris they simply stared when I spoke to them in French; I never did succeed in making those idiots understand their own language.

Mark Twain

You can tell German wine from vinegar by the label.

Mark Twain

If a lump of soot falls into the soup and you cannot conveniently get it out, stir it well in, and it will give the soup a French taste.

Jonathan Swift

Southern Exposure

A "D" in spelling? How could that be? This from a fourth grader who had never had anything but "A's" on her grade card before? There must be something wrong.

We had just moved to North Carolina from central Ohio and this was the first grading period for our children in their new schools. Molly had been advanced enough that she had skipped a whole grade in her previous school and she still had excellent grades in everything except spelling. A quick test of her spelling ability at home showed that she had no trouble spelling words that were more advanced than the fourth grade she was in at school. So something was wrong.

An interview with the teacher showed us in about ten seconds what the problem was. The teacher was from South Carolina and had an even richer southern accent than the people in North Carolina. Whenever this teacher called out words for spelling, Molly had been spelling them the way she heard them.

We suggested that in the future, the teacher use each word on the list in a sentence when she called it for the children to spell. That solved the problem. Molly got a good spelling grade on the next grading period.

The following list of words and their definitions by Jim Henderson which was published in the Norfolk *Virginian Pilot* some years ago will help explain why Molly had trouble.

The Northerner will say, "Dijeet yet?" and the Southerner will say, "Yawl etchet?" In either case, if you have eaten you should nod your head. "Abode" is a plank and "braid" is what you spread butter on.

CHURN: Progeny; little scudders. They come in lap, yard, and porch churn sizes.
FAINTS: A structure around the yard to keep the churn from running into the street.
JOGGER FEE: A book churn read in school.
LYE BERRY: Where jogger fees and other books are kept.
M: A tree; also pronoun, as in "Who's M fellers standing under that M tree?"

Churn

Helm

HELM: A song people sing in church.
HEP: Assistance; aid.
HARD HEP: Someone paid to render assistance.
GREET: A tee-ninecy piece of sand. Plural, finely ground hominy, as in "Please pass the greets."

Raffle

RAFFLE: A firearm. Also, a verb construction affecting Ralph, as in "Raffle be here directly."

CHEER: An item of furniture. Also an adverb of locations as in "Put it rat cheer."

RAID: A color. So are WHAT and GRAIN.

ROTTEN: Communication through symbols: "Who are you rotten that letter to?"

TOP: To pick out the words on a top-rotter.

Cheer

BUD: Noun, a flying animal. Verb, interred.

WOBBLE: To sing like a bud.

PANE: Putting out money for goods or services.

PAIL: What the doctor tells you to take when you're sick.

WRETCHED: A man's name. Call him Dick for short.

SHED: Verb, divided. "John and Wretched shed the pie."

FARM: Adverb form, as: "How farm I from town?"

KAYO: An animal that gives milk and is cut up for steaks if it doesn't.

Bud

DAINTY: An interrogatory, as in "John did that, dainty?"

TEAK: Half of the sound a clock makes.

TALK: The other half of the sound a clock makes: "Teak, talk, teak, talk."

SPECKLE: Verb form: "Speckle go into town this evening."

Kayo

Along about the same time as Molly was having trouble understanding her teacher, I was having a bit of difficulty myself in conferences and business meetings with colleagues. For example, at one early morning meeting with some other engineers, one of the men arrived a little late. He apologized by saying, "Sorry I'm late. I had to carry my car down to the Buick garage for servicing."

I could just imagine him carrying his car on his back down to the garage, but it turned out that he simply meant that he had taken his car to the garage for routine maintenance. "Carry" in the south means "take" or "escort" as in "I carried my girl to the movies last evenin'", or "I had to carry my mother back to her home after she was stayin' with me for a week." No one had to be literally carried.

This is just one of the expressions that are common in the south which at first sound odd to northerner's ears. "You all" is an expression that northerners seem to think is the same as a singular "you" whereas when a southerner uses it, it actually refers to more than one person being addressed. Another expression that I particularly liked and began to use myself is the customary farewell. Instead of saying "goodbye," one says, "Come see us." What a gracious way of saying farewell. You all come see us.

Eine Kleine Nachtmusik

Picture and caption printed with permission from WCVE, Richmond, VA

I decided to quit my job at the bank

Drawing by Charles Dana Gibson, ca. 1900

Waiting for the Trolley

This picture is actually a composite from several drawings of Charles Dana Gibson which were published about a hundred years ago. Gibson published many books of his work and illustrated a number of books for other authors.

When I was a boy in the 1930's, my parents had a copy of The Gibson Book in two volumes, a collection of eleven of his previous books. The Gibson Book was published in 1907 and the copy that I remember was a bit worn, some of the pages were loose, and mice had chewed at the edges of the pages. I have no idea what became of the books.

Recently, I found and bought a set of the two volumes. This set is in remarkable condition, almost like new. Except for that it is just like the set I remember. This picture is from that book.

Book Three
Retrospect

Backward, turn backward, oh time in your flight.
Just thought of a comeback I needed last night.

Tom Wyant

Sometimes it doesn't pay to look back. Consider Lot's wife. She looked back and turned into a pillar of salt. Of course, sometimes turning into something is not all that bad. I knew a driver once who drove down the street and turned into a driveway.

(Something has always puzzled me: why do we drive on a parkway and park in a driveway?)

Retrospect

The great Satchel Paige is supposed to have said, "Never look back. Somethin' might be gainin' on you."

That may be good advice for the faster creatures of this world but for a small car on the interstate highways, it is not a particularly good idea; large trucks do not like small cars to get in their way and large trucks always, **always** have the right of way. (Have you ever seen a truck stopped by a highway patrolman?) Drivers of cars should be grateful that the truckers let the cars on the interstates at all and therefore should stay out of their way. Don't ever try to dispute the right of way with a truck; you are not arguing from a position of strength.

Even eagles, like the one above, find it advisable to look back from time to time. This one thinks he may have missed something back there and wonders if he should go back and see about it.

Another retrospect

Through the Looking Glass

"It's long," said the Knight, "but it's very, **very** beautiful. Everybody that hears me sing it — either it brings **tears** into their eyes, or else ——"

"Or else what?" said Alice, for the Knight had made a sudden pause.

"Or else it doesn't, you know. The name of the song is called *Haddock's Eyes*."

"Oh, that's the name of the song, is it?" Alice said, trying to feel interested.

"No, you don't understand," the Knight said, looking a little vexed. "That's what the name of the song is **called**. The name really is *The Aged Aged Man*."

"Then I ought to have said 'That's what the song is called'?" Alice corrected herself.

"No, you oughtn't: that's quite another thing! The **song** is called *Ways and Means*: but that's only what it's called, you know!"

"Well, what is the song, then?" said Alice, who was by this time completely bewildered.

"I was coming to that," the Knight said. "The song really is *A-sitting On a Gate*: and the tune's my own invention."

> Lewis Carroll in
> *Through the Looking Glass*

The following news item from the *Associated Press* dated July 29, 1998, was printed in our local newspaper, *The Richmond Times-Dispatch:*

Rolls-Royce auto brand sold to BMW, not VW

London —*The grandest name in British motoring, Rolls-Royce, was shaken up yesterday in a deal that will see separate German automakers producing Rolls-Royce and Bentley models.*

BMW will make Rolls-Royces after buying the rights to the brand, while Volkswagen AG will keep the Rolls-Royce factory it just bought and continue producing Bentley luxury cars.

VW paid $790 million for Rolls-Royce Motor Cars Ltd. early this month but didn't get the rights to the Rolls-Royce brand name and logo. They were held by the British jet engine maker Rolls-Royce PLC, which said yesterday it would sell the Rolls-Royce auto brand to BMW for $66 million.

If Lewis Carroll were writing today, this is probably what the passage would sound like:

"It's long," said the Knight, "but it's very, **very** beautiful. Everybody that sees me drive it — either it brings **tears** into their eyes, or else ——"

"Or else what?" said Alice, for the Knight had made a sudden pause.

"Or else it doesn't, you know. The name of this model is called *Limousine*."

"Oh, that's the name of the car, is it?" Alice said, trying to feel interested.

"No, you don't understand," the Knight said, looking a little vexed. "That's what the name of the car is **called**. The name really is *Rolls-Royce*."

"Then I ought to have said 'That's what the car is called'?" Alice corrected herself.

"No, you oughtn't: that's quite another thing! The **car** is called *a Bimmer*: but that's only what it's called, you know!"

"Well, what is the car, then?" said Alice, who was by this time completely bewildered.

"I was coming to that," the Knight said. "The car really is a *BMW*: and it's made in Germany."

"But I thought that Rolls-Royce was made in Crewe" protested Alice.

"Oh, no!" said the knight, "That's the Bentley, but that's only what its name is called, you see. It really is also a German car called a VW and it is made in Crewe."

"Now I'm confused," said Alice.

"Oh, but you don't have a degree in business. If you did, you would understand completely." said the knight. "Would you like to buy one?"

"No, thank you," said Alice.

Wagner's music is better than it sounds.
Bill Nye (1850-1896)

Sympathetic plain friend to inconsolable young widow: The last time I saw your dear husband he stopped and spoke to me with such a sunny greeting that I was the happier for it all day long.

Young widow (still oblivious to everything except her loss): Yes, that was just like dear David. There was no woman so humble, or homely, or unattractive, or dull, but that he could find something pleasant to say to her and would take the time to say it.

This cartoon was done by Charles Dana Gibson in 1895. The young widow certainly has a way with words, doesn't she?

A Study in Courage

In *The Lord of the Rings*, J.R.R. Tolkien tells the story of Frodo, who has volunteered to carry the Ring on a dangerous mission into enemy territory. Several companions, including Gimli, have agreed to accompany him. When Frodo stands up in the council and volunteers, Elrond, the leader of the council says:

"It is a heavy burden. So heavy that none could lay it on another. I do not lay it on you, but if you take it freely, I will say that your choice is right."

Then Elrond turns to the companions and says, "The Ring-bearer is setting out on the Quest of Mount Doom: on him alone is any charge laid — neither to cast away the Ring nor to deliver it to any servant of the Enemy, nor indeed to let any handle it, save members of the Company and the Council, and then only in gravest need. The others go with him as free companions to help him on his way. You may tarry, or come back, or turn aside to other paths as chance allows. The further you go, the less easy it will be to withdraw; yet no oath or bond is laid upon you to go further than you will. For you do not yet know the strength of your hearts and you cannot foresee what each may meet on the road."

"Faithless is he who says farewell when the road darkens," said Gimli.

"Maybe," said Elrond, "but let him not vow to walk in the dark who has not seen the nightfall."

"Yet sworn vow may strengthen the quaking heart," said Gimli.

"Or break it," said Elrond. "Look not too far ahead. But go now with good hearts."

Stephen Ambrose in his book *D Day* tells of one soldier who was found part way up the cliff behind the beach in Normandy completely unnerved, huddled in a hole and crying hysterically. One of the others in his outfit commented later that this man had been the most "gung ho" soldier in the outfit during training. He apparently had not realized how dark the road would be. Some others showed incredible courage. Who knows how heroic a person will be until the situation arises?

1929 Chevrolet

My aunt and uncle who lived on the next farm to us owned a 1929 Chevrolet sedan like the one in the picture. It had a six cylinder engine instead of the 4 cylinders that the Ford had and was a bit more luxurious. Chevrolet had brought it out to compete with the Model A Ford, but it had one basic flaw that didn't show up for several years. The Chevrolet had a wooden frame covered with metal whereas the Ford had a steel frame. The wooden frame tended to rot out and after a few years the door hinges and latch felt pretty loose.

I had a cousin who was three years older than I and of course he learned to drive before I did. One day shortly after he had learned to drive he was going to town on an errand for his mother and he felt particularly proud to be entrusted with the family car. Unfortunately, as I saw him coming down the road past our house, I waved enthusiastically and he misinterpreted the wave to mean that I wanted him to stop. He applied the brakes with vigor and the right front door flew open because the frame was too loose around the latch. The door hit our mailbox which went flying across our lawn and the window in the door shattered into many shards. No safety glass in side windows in those days.

My cousin was very embarassed and shaken by the experience and he decided to turn around and drive home instead of continuing to the store. I don't remember that he received any punishment for the accident; it really wasn't his fault and I think his parents realized that.

A winter scene such as this is, or at least was in the 1930's, quite common. Quail, or Bobwhites as they were called, were present on every farm and earned their keep. They did eat a bit of grain but their diet was mostly insects, insects that would destroy a lot more grain than the quail would eat. Most farmers liked having

the quail around, but some would shoot them as game, illegal in Ohio, but legal in some states. Nowadays, in some states, quail are grown domestically for their meat, just like small chickens.

A Parting Shot—The Death Penalty

"I believe that people would be alive today if there were a death penalty."

This statement received an enormous amount of ridicule from the press back in the 1980's. The press is noted for putting words in prominent peoples' mouths, but if Nancy actually said it, she was absolutely right when you consider the number of murder victims who have been killed by a paroled murderer, or by some murderer who had been turned loose because he had served a brief sentence or because of some minor technicality in his trial.

Mercy to the guilty is cruelty to the innocent.

Adam Smith

Thomas Sowell in his *The Vision of the Anointed* asks the question: how many innocent murder victims are we willing to sacrifice to save one innocent defendant who has been mistakenly convicted of murder? The media can and does show the poor convicted man on death row but they cannot show and do not even attempt to mention the poor innocent victim of a murderer who is pleading for his life. Is it worth sacrificing ten innocent victims, or a hundred, or more, just to prevent the possibility of executing one innocent convicted defendant who happened to look suspicious enough to persuade a jury of his guilt. The convicts on death row are not there because of some whim of a policeman or judge. They are there because a jury believed that they were guilty and did not grant their victim the endless appeals for mercy.

Quips and Quotes

Sickness comes in on horseback
and departs on foot.

Dutch proverb

My grandfather started walking five miles a day when he was sixty. Now he's eighty-five and we don't know where the hell he is.

Ellen de Generis

I'm not crazy, but I think everyone else is.

Peter O'Toole

Another victory like that and we are finished.

Pyrrhus

The trouble with him is that when he is not drunk he is sober.

William Butler Yeats

If you want an audience, start a fight.

Old Gaelic proverb

Never sell more of yourself than you can buy back with skill and performance.

Contractor's motto

Many states permit the hunting of quail, and bird dogs are trained to point out the birds to the hunter. Quail will often run rather than fly away from dogs or hunters as the quail in this picture are doing. This makes them very difficult to shoot because shooting at them on the ground is considered ill-mannered. Pheasants

will often do the same thing, and birds that survive their first hunting season are more likely to die from some other cause than a hunter's gun because these birds are not stupid. They quickly learn that the ones that fly get shot at while the ones that run do not. Both quail and pheasants are incredibly fast either way.

Old English Monetary System

two farthings = one ha'penny
two ha'pennies = one penny
two pennies = one tuppence
three pennies = one thrupenny bit
two thruppence or three tuppences or six pennies = one sixpence
two sixpences = one shilling or bob
two shillings or bob = one florin
one florin and one sixpence = one half crown
four half crowns = ten bob note
two ten bob notes = one pound or 240 pennies
one pound and one shilling = one guinea

This system was used up until the British decimalized the monetary system about 1970. Many people resisted the decimalization for a long time because the new system was too complicated.

One p = One penny
Two pennies (two pence) = Tuppence
Three pence = Thruppence
Five pence = Five p
Ten pence = Ten p
Twenty pence = Twenty p
Fifty pence = Fifty p
One pound coin = One hundred pennies =One pound

See how much more complicated that is. Many Americans are reluctant to visit the United Kingdom because they don't understand the monetary system.

USA Monetary System

one penny = one cent
one nickel = five cents or pennies
two nickels or ten cents = one dime
two dimes and one nickel or twentyfive cents = one quarter or two bits
two quarters or five dimes or fifty cents= one half dollar or four bits
two half dollars or four quarters or ten dimes = one dollar or one buck
five dollars = one fin
ten dollars = one sawbuck
one hundred dollars = one century note or one C note
one thousand dollars = one big one or one thou or one grand

A teacher is better than two books.
Unknown

When the candles are out, all women are fair.
Plutarch

This heated discussion, probably about politics, in a cobbler's shop could have taken place in any one of hundreds of small stores across the country only a couple of generations ago. Cobbler's shops have largely disappeared because many of the shoes we wear cannot be repaired in the old traditional ways that cobblers have used for centuries. Judging by the fact that most of the men in this picture are

wearing chin whiskers, a style that disappeared about a century ago, the setting for this picture is most likely any small country community of the early twentieth century or late nineteeth century.

Pictures such as this were used to illustrate magazine stories and articles until photography replaced drawings about sixty years ago.

This country road is between Zelah and Perranzabuloh in the southwest corner of Cornwall, England. It is wide enough for one vehicle with passing places here and there. If one meets a vehicle, one looks for a passing place to pull into and then blinks the headlights for the other to come on and pass. As they pass, the driver moving waves his thanks. These unclassified roads are quite common all over the UK.

Those hedge rows beside the road are not quite what they seem. The invading troops in Normandy found hedgerows just like them in France and they are virtually impossible for even tanks to get through. When the farmers built them they piled rocks in rows and packed dirt in between them. The walls are about five feet thick at the bottom, about five feet tall, and about two or three feet thick at the top. Of course berry bushes, vines, and trees promptly took root and formed an almost impenetrable hedge around and above the wall. These hedge rows are pretty typical in Cornwall, but they are not typical of the stone walls one finds elsewhere in the UK. Each area has its own style of wall or hedge. They certainly make pretty roads to drive on.

One reason that Marty and I like the UK so much is that the villages and countryside are so much like those we remember from childhood. The towns and villages have much the same atmosphere that our country villages had fifty or sixty years ago. Many of the villages have shops and stores that are like the ones we remember and the people, in general, are as open and friendly as the people we grew up with. Call it nostalgia if you will, but it is a very pleasant place to be.

Drawings by Lamplight

During the middle 1930's and through all of the 1940's, my parents drew and sold cartoons to various farm magazines in the Midwestern states. Only after the late 30's were the drawings done by electric light; before that my father would do most of the drawing by lamplight in the evenings. He drew in pencil because he

"IT'S BED-TIME" — BY RAY C. BELL- CENTERBURG, OHIO

preferred it as a medium, doing most of the action drawings and animals, leaving the background and detail work to my mother who would also go over his work the following day with ink. My mother also painted in oil, but my father preferred to work with pencil and didn't use color at all.

"LAST CALL FOR BREAKFAST" BY RAY C. BELL— CENTERBURG, OHIO.

"THE FAMILY REUNION   BY RAY C. BELL — CENTERBURG, OHIO — STAR ROUTE

Family reunions in the 1930's were a bit different from those in the 1990's but the people haven't changed much. They still have the same characteristics and foibles as their ancestors. Note the enthusiasm of the one man for battle in the middle right side of the picture. Also note the attitude of the family leaving in the lower right side. Judging by the automobiles, this drawing was made in the early 1930's.

SANTA CLAUS HAS COME AND GONE.
BY RAY C. BELL — CENTERBURG-OHIO.

The illustration of the young man being irritated at receiving four books on good manners for Christmas is based on a true story. One of my aunts married a young man many years ago who had some manners that the family found undesirable. At the first Christmas he was in the family, he received four books on good manners. I have been told that this was unplanned and that it didn't improve his manners in the least, but I don't really know first hand; he and my aunt were divorced long before I was born and she had married again. The second husband was a good man with good manners.

* 'CMON WITH THAT SAP, THE PAN'S ABURNIN' — BY RAY C. BELL — CENTERBURG — OHIO.

This is a very early Bell cartoon. Probably drawn about 1932.

GOOD NIGHT, PAW, DON'T WAKE THE CHILDREN

PAW'S WANT AD BRINGS THE MAN OF THE HOUR

TURKEY, AS USUAL

Family reunion.

The Wiener Roast

By Ray C. Bell, Centerburg, Ohio

This is the only Bell cartoon in my collection that I know how old it is. This one was drawn in the autumn of 1947, about two years before the last cartoon of this type was drawn by the Bell's.

"THE SPRING-WORK GETS UNDER WAY". — BY RAY C. BELL — CENTERBURG - OHIO

There was always plenty to do on an Ohio farm in the spring.

"THE FAMILY REUNION" BY RAY C. BELL — CENTERBURG, OHIO

It is obvious that the family reunion was a favorite topic for the Bell cartoons.

"OUR ANNUAL REUNION" BY RAY C. BELL — CENTERBURG, OHIO.

Hallowe'eners will git you if you don't watch out.

By Ray C. Bell - Centerburg, Ohio

Do you have any of those new invisible hearing aids?

Accident on I-95

Bill Harris arrived late one morning at his office in Richmond, Virginia. He explained that he had an automobile accident near the downtown interchange on Interstate 95 that had totally wrecked his car but he hadn't been hurt.

Asked how it had happened, Bill explained, "Well, I'm driving in the usual morning rush traffic, see. An' I was doing about sixty or sixty five when I hit a pig."

"You hit a pig on I-95 near downtown Richmond?" his listeners exclaimed.

"Yeah, an' it wasn't just any old pig either. It was a frozen pig that had fallen off a meat truck that was ahead of me. Man, you ain't lived till you've hit a frozen pig at sixty miles an hour. It went right under the car an' tore up the whole underside of my car. Everything was all bent to hell. I was all over the highway for a minute or so. Didn' hit anyone though, but cars was sure going crazy tryin' to keep out of trouble. Truck never stopped."

"What happened to the pig?" we asked.

"Oh, it wasn't worth much when the car got done with it. The wrecker truck hauled what was left of it away. Make dog food with it maybe."

It must have made an interesting insurance claim when Bill turned it in. He had a new car a few days later. Even an unfrozen pig can do a lot of damage to the underside of a car, but a frozen one is hard to beat.

A Fond Look Back

This part of the book has been a fond look back at earlier years and amusing incidents of years gone by as well as cartoons and quotations collected over the years. I think most of us, as we get older, like to look back at what was and what might have been. We seem to be able to remember more clearly what happened fifty or more years ago than we can remember what we came into the kitchen to get a few minutes ago.

No one knows whether other animals reminisce; we do know that they often look back. Just look at some of the animal and bird photos used to illustrate this book.

Part of this book is devoted to happenings of some sixty or more years ago. Not everything was better then; very few things were in fact. But remember the good things, the funny things that happened and forget the slights and sorrows. You can't change them now anyway.

Baby Alligator

During the 1930's a favorite souvenir of Florida was a "live baby alligator". Perhaps some of the early ones really were alligators, but the supply soon ran out and alligators were hard to find and even harder to catch so the entrepreneurs who dealt in these souvenirs switched to baby caimans, South American crocodiles. It was a lot safer because these could be obtained from South American natives who risked **their** lives and limbs to capture live baby caimans from their rivers and swamps. Adult caimans are more aggressive and nastier than alligators and they, like alligators, tend to keep trespassers away from their nests. Caimans look enough like alligators, especially as babies, so that tourists could easily believe that they were buying real live Florida native baby alligators.

Sometime about the middle 1930's my sister Ruth went to Florida by bus for a short vacation and during her visit she bought a small "alligator" to give to her then current boyfriend in Cleveland. What possessed her to do so escapes me, but she wanted a real live souvenir of her vacation and wanted to surprise her boyfriend with a nice gift. The alligator was about eighteen inches long and was quite active, noisy, and aggressive. By bending its tail a little, Ruth got it in a shoe box to haul it back to Cleveland

The rules of the Greyhound bus company forbade hauling live animals on the bus. It was permissible to put small animals in cages in the luggage compartment, but not in the passenger compartment. However, Ruth didn't want to subject the poor little alligator to the discomfort of riding with the luggage so she carried the shoe box with the alligator inside onto the bus to come home. She boarded the bus in the late evening for an all night ride. It would be several days before she reached Centerburg to spend a few days with us at Stoney Creek before going on to Cleveland.

After the bus lights were dimmed so that people could sleep, a woman in a seat a few rows forward from Ruth started screaming that there was an alligator under her seat. Her screams woke the whole busload of people and the driver stopped the bus. He came back with a flashlight and looked carefully around under the seats nearby but found nothing that wasn't supposed to be there. The driver assured the lady that it was her imagination; there were no alligators anywhere close and certainly not on the bus. He then went back to the front and drove on. Everyone settled back to rest.

When things had quieted down again, Ruth carefully opened the shoe box to see how her alligator was faring. Alas, to her dismay the shoe box was empty! She could not imagine what had happened because she had put it on the floor under her seat and knew that the alligator was in it at that time. She did conclude that she knew where the alligator the lady had complained about had come from, but Ruth thought that perhaps she had better not say anything until the alligator was found and could be returned to the box.

About an hour later the lady screamed again, waking everyone on the bus and causing the driver to stop the bus again. Again she complained that the alligator was under her seat so the driver made another search. All of the other people on the bus (except one) were complaining that the lady had an overactive imagination and was dreaming again because no alligator was found.

This happened three or four more times during the night and the passengers were getting very little rest. By morning some of them were ready to throw the lady off the bus. However, when the morning came and people could see better, they found the alligator — under the lady's seat as she had maintained. Ruth admitted that it was hers and she was asked to leave the bus and get a more secure cage for her alligator and take it on the next bus — with the luggage.

When she arrived at our home, we put the alligator in one of the bedrooms in the unused part of the house. We put a pan of water and some raw ground beef on the floor for it to eat. Whenever anyone would open the door to see how it was doing, it would run directly at the person, hissing loudly and snapping its jaws. It was not hard to catch and one could hold its jaws closed easily, but it never quit trying to do grievous bodily harm to anyone it saw. It would obviously make a most desirable pet for any animal lover.

Ruth stayed with us for the few remaining days of her vacation and then went on to Cleveland with the alligator. She took it over to her boyfriend's house when she arrived. He was at work so Ruth showed it to his mother. They put it in the bathtub until he could get home and decide what to do with it.

When the boyfriend came home from work that evening, his mother was in the kitchen preparing dinner. He went on upstairs to his room to change clothes and on the way stopped in the bathroom. His mother heard him shout and slam the bathroom door just before he came clattering down the stair and into the kitchen.

As soon as he saw his mother he shouted, "There's an alligator in the bath tub!"

"Yes, I know." she replied.

I never heard what became of the alligator after that. Ruth and her boyfriend broke up about that time and she started dating someone else.

Old Bess

I've often heard my Dad tell of the troubles that his brother, my Uncle Jay, had when he was courting Hattie Mitchell. At that time Jay lived with my dad and mom in the house where the two brothers had grown up. Dad and mom had been married only a couple of years and had twin baby daughters. This was sometime before World War I and the two young men were operating the home farm.

The house was large and at that time my parents' bedroom was at the northeast corner of the house on the ground floor. The location of the room is important later in this tale; the northeast corner of the house was the front of the house nearest the driveway.

Jay was a fun loving man with a slow gentle manner with people and animals. He was sparing of his words and his serious expression hid a cheerful disposition and quick wit. He was as full of mischief as a monkey, but most people outside the family were fooled by his serious demeanor into thinking him a bit slow and somber sometimes. He rarely laughed out loud except in the presence of the family.

The Mitchells lived about three miles north of Stoney Creek and Jay began to ride his horse up to see Hattie pretty regularly one summer. Jay and my dad had grown up on the farm and their dad, Ed Bell, had always kept good horses and prided himself on having the fastest steppers in the neighborhood. Jay and dad were accustomed to handling spirited animals and at the time Jay was courting, the favorite of all the men in the family was a black mare named Bess.

Bess was fast and good natured, reasonably gentle with people, but she was inclined to be a bit headstrong and she definitely had a mind of her own. As long as Bess wanted to do what the driver wanted, she was the best horse in the stable. If she wanted to do something else, a compromise was usually reached by the driver capitulating. But she was handsome and fast so Jay preferred Bess over any of the other horses for riding or driving .

One snowy night in December after Jay had been courting Hattie for several months, Jay hitched Bess to the sleigh and drove up to the Mitchell home for a Christmas party. He put Bess in their barn while he went to the party. He stayed rather late and Bess was a bit restless when he harnessed her and hitched her to the sleigh to come home. Jay drove around to the front of the house and then went up to the front porch to kiss his girl goodnight.

The goodnight kiss lasted longer than Bess wanted to stand waiting on a cold night so after a few minutes she started walking toward home. Jay came hurrying out to catch the sleigh but Bess had started to trot. Jay ran faster trying to catch the sleigh but Bess went even faster and Jay began falling behind. Soon Bess was galloping toward home and a warm barn. Jay resigned himself to a three mile hike.

About a mile from home farm the main road makes a slight jog at a cross road and Bess was going pretty fast at that point. She made the turn nicely but the sleigh swung far enough to the side to hit the ditch and tip over. From there the rest of the way home, pieces of the sleigh kept falling off until by the time Bess reached our driveway, only the shafts of the sleigh were left.

When Bess turned into the driveway, she was going fast enough that she ran across the lawn and barely missed crashing into the house. The shafts of the sleigh which were still dragging behind her did hit the house. There was a mighty crash, right on the corner of the bedroom where my parents were asleep. This woke them suddenly and Dad thought maybe he should go see what that was all about.

Dad found Bess standing at the barn door waiting to be let into her stall. She wasn't breathing very hard even after a three mile run and the weather was cold enough that she wasn't overheated. Dad let her into the stall and removed what was left of her harness. He rubbed her down and put a blanket over her and went on back to the house. He figured Jay would be home after while.

After that Jay tied Bess to a fence post when he went to say goodnight to his girl. Even this wasn't quite good enough, as he discovered one night the following summer. Jay had ridden Bess that evening and when he was ready to go home he went to the Mitchell barn and saddled Bess for the ride home. When he rode around to the front and got down to say goodnight, he tied Bess to the fencepost.

As he was again taking too long to suit Bess, she grabbed the line with her teeth and pulled it loose. Then she started for home without a rider. Jay again tried to catch her but wasn't quick enough so he again had a three mile hike in the dark. This time Bess did no damage to the equipment and Jay unsaddled her and put her in the barn when he finally got home.

Black Bess

Jay was more careful about how he tied Bess after that but on one occasion my parents were reminded about Bess and her habits. They had driven Bess with a buggy into Centerburg to pick up a package that had arrived at the freight office of the railroad station. Dad left my mother in the buggy while he went into the station to get the package. As he was waiting for the agent to get the package, Bess started walking toward home.

My mother knew very little about how to handle horses. She took the reins and pulled, shouting "Whoa" as loudly as she could, but Bess paid no attention. Dad came running out of the station carrying a package and chasing after the buggy but Bess merely went a little faster. Dad resigned himself to a long walk.

As Bess neared the edge of Centerburg with the buggy and a shouting woman pulling on the reins, she approached the house where my grandfather often stopped to visit when he went to town. Bess slowed as she neared that drive and when she reached the driveway, turned quietly into the drive and went up by the house and stopped. When Dad arrived, he stowed the package in the back of the buggy, got in, took the reins, and drove Bess home.

My mother and my Aunt Nellie took Bess and the sleigh one winter day and started to drive to a neighbor's house for a visit. The weather was foul and the road was icy and they should never have attempted to go out in such conditions, but they were very young and inexperienced in handling horses. Sure enough, part way to the neighbor's house Bess fell down.

She apparently wasn't hurt but the two women were frightened and thought that Bess would get up and run away, so they both got out of the sleigh and stood by the side of the road. Bess turned her head and looked at them as though expecting them to help her get up. When they didn't, Bess gave them a disgusted look and struggled to her feet. She turned the sleigh toward home and waited for the women to get in. Then she carefully made her way home.

On another occasion, my mother and my Aunt Nellie had driven Bess and a buggy to another friend's home and were making their way home again after dark. The road was difficult to see and a light fog made it even worse. At one point on the way home there was a sharp turn in the road with a steep bank into a creek at the turn. As they reached that turn, the women couldn't see well enough to know where the road went.

Bess started to make the turn as she should but my mother tugged on the reins to make her go straight. Bess insisted on the turn. My mother insisted on going straight because she couldn't see where the road turned and believed that Bess was trying to put the buggy in the ditch. Bess won the struggle and turned. As she made the turn, the women could see beside the buggy that if they had won the struggle they would be in the creek.

By the time I was old enough to remember, Bess had been retired for a number of years and spent her days in the pasture and her nights in her stall. By this time she had gone blind but she could find her way around the barnyard and pasture without trouble. Our work horses were nearly twice her size but Bess was the senior horse and the others deferred to whatever Bess wanted to do. They sometimes would kick at anything walking behind them in the stable, but they never kicked at Bess. Dad said that was because Bess would kick the stuffing out of them if they had and they knew it. She was gentle with people but would stand for no nonsense from other horses.

The old saddle hung on rack in the barn near Bess's stall and the sleigh was in the buggy shed. I used to wonder why Dad kept such useless things around. I think I know why now.

Castles and the Errors

Recent documents have been located in the Tower of London which show that even in 1300 kings had difficulty with bureaucrats and contractors. Edward I (1239-1307) was so irritated at the delays, cost over-runs, and expensive errors in the building of fortifications, especially at Caerphilly Castle, that he dictated a special decree:

I, Edward, Ruler of England, etc., etc., defender of the True Faith, and all those good things, do hereby issue this decree so that future royal servants may cover their rears and protect themselves from disaster.

Having defeated the Welsh Llewellyn ap Gruffyd and killed him but having yet failed to subdue his people completely, it became my wish some time ago to have builded a castle surrounding the tower in the Welsh village known as Caerphilly. Therefore, to this purpose I did hire many skilled artisans and scribes and designers of fortifications and makers of machinery for building fortifications and say forcibly unto them: build me a castle worthy and strong and be damnably quick about it.

Great was the number of permanent designers, supervisors of designers, engineers, and scribes to the number of seven thousand two hundred and seventeen plus a few hundred temps and contract designers. Large portions of the castles known as Chepstow, Skenfrith, and Ludlow were allotted to these designers and craftsmen and no expense was spared to ensure their comfort.

Many times did the moon wax and wane and many times did the managers and chiefs among the designers report to me on the wonderful results I could expect from the castle when it was completed. And yet none could show me finished

drawings or even concept sketches of what the designers envisioned. So I hied me to the offices at Chepstow to observe first hand what marvels these artisans and designers had wrought.

Behold, I found not artisans and designers working diligently as I had decreed. Instead I found layabouts, drinkers of tea and munchers of crumpets, and tellers of tales which are known as bull dung. So I expressed my royal displeasure which did disturb them a great deal.

"See here, O mighty ruler," said the Chief Engineer, as their head designer was called," Some things cannot be rushed. Our men strive mightily even unto the wee hours of the night under very primitive conditions, but without adequate accommodations. Results will take some time." He poured himself another cup of tea as he spoke these words.

"But thou hast the greater parts of the three palaces known as Chepstow, Skenfrith, and Ludlow." I protested. "What more canst thou ask?"

"Perhaps the scribes could be provided with quills of the peacock instead of the goose, and with the ink known as India." said the Chief Engineer. "And the draughtsmen would like silver and brass candle holders to light their work tables."

"Thou shalt have these things and more," I replied," Anything thou desirest, get it. But build for me a castle and make haste about it." And I returned to my throne and resumed my royal duties in the realm.

Again, many days passed and yet no castle was builded. Once again I journeyed to Chepstow to observe and determine what progress, if any, had been made. "What goes on?" I inquired.

"O mighty ruler," the Chief Engineer wailed,"Have mercy upon us. We have received many drawings and designs from Skenfrith and yet more from Ludlow, both for the castle and for the machines to build the castle. But forsooth, no artisan here can understand the drawings. For the designers at Skenfrith call a stone one thing and the designers at Ludlow call it something else. The draughtsmen at Skenfrith use a strange numeric system called metric while the draughtsmen at Ludlow use an old fashioned system they call English, but it is an archaic version which our people here have long since abandoned. The conversions require much effort and lead to all sorts of mistakes."

So I, King of all Britain and major parts of France, did issue a decree that from henceforth and now on all locations would use the same system. I, being generous and not wishing to seem arbitrary, did unwisely not specify which system should be used.

Many weeks later it came to my attention that no location had in fact changed their system. Each insisted that their system alone was the right system and all other systems were false. I thereupon did issue an arbitrary decree that from henceforth the system to use was the English system in use at Chepstow, thereby irritating all designers and draftsmen at Ludlow and Skenfrith and satisfying no one but some few designers at Chepstow.

I commented to my court that it did amaze me that men with such swiftness of mind should have so little judgment, likening it to the sense of asses.

And once again, many days did pass and no castle was started, no ground was broken, and the Welsh did gain in arrogance and did show themselves to be in need of chastisement. But because I was still without the castle it was impossible to impress upon them the need to be good citizens of the realm. So I once again visited Chepstow to learn what the problem was this time.

"O King, every day from dawn to dark, we struggle with the designs, attempting to build machines with which to erect the castle walls. But every day, the designers of machines tell us that the designs we have are obsolete and that they have revised the designs to a new and better design. Then our artisans tear down the machines they have built and start on the design changes."

Then I, Edward, did issue another decree stating that from henceforth and now on no design changes should be made, that the designs should be considered to be cast in bronze and frozen in ice. And the construction of the castle should be started immediately with the designs we had in hand. And so it was done.

But many days did pass and the walls did rise slower than the oak tree grows from an acorn to its full height. So I did hie me once again to Caerphilly to see what the delay was this time. And it was reported to me that the foreman of construction was running short of stone masons.

"Well, hire some more," I suggested.

"I have hired more. I have even gone to Ireland and France and even unto Italy and imported foreign masons of admittedly inferior quality because skilled masons will not stay. Even the unskilled masons leave as soon as they learn that the design of the granite facing stones is such that the mason must work between them and the rough masonry behind them. When the facing stones are in place the mason cannot get out and must therefore spend eternity between the stones. It is difficult to recruit masons for that kind of work and there is necessarily a continuing and increasing shortage of help."

I then did rescind my decree against a change in design and call for a redesign which cost many pounds of gold and more months of delay. And again, many days did pass and the castle was still not builded. So once again, I trod the now familiar path to Chepstow and Caerphilly to hear what excuses would be used this time.

"O king, for many months we have been waiting for the stones to be delivered from Blaenau-Ffestiniog to use in the the inner walls."

"Is it so hard to get stone from Blaenau-Ffestiniog — how do you spell that anyway? If it is, then why not get the stone from somewhere else? All of these hills here are full of stone."

"The designers have specified that the height of the inner walls must match the height of the outer walls within two inches or less so that the cross beams will line up. The stones for the outer walls are three feet and four inches high but the stones for the inner walls, which are of slate from Blaenau-Ffestiniog have a much smoother surface and they are only three feet high and when the stackup reaches the proper height, they don't line up within two inches but are off by two and one half inches."

"Well, cut a half inch off the top row of stones"

"Oh, we can't do that or the whole design would look wrong. The surface of the inner stones has an artistic design which is done by artisans from Betys-Y-Coed which cannot be easily altered and cutting one half inch from it would ruin the symmetry of the stone."

"Well, then add an extra half inch of mortar at the top tier of stones on the outer wall"

"O king, we tried that and the designers of the machines insisted that this violated the building code for Welsh castles, Volume III, Section LIV, dated 1203, so we had to abandon that idea too. So we are waiting for the stone masons from Betws-Y-Coed to alter the surface design so that the stones can be the right height to begin with. If they cannot do that, the outer wall of the castle will need to be redesigned and done over."

I thereupon vented my royal spleen and did take royal action. I can now avouch that the designers of castles do not have the ability to walk on water nor even to swim, for if they did they would surely have escaped from the moat of the castle into which I had them thrown. I then issued this decree from which no designer or artisan is to deviate.

This decree is to be posted at all places where designers congregate to drink tea and munch crumpets and is to be memorized by them and recited in public once each week as a condition of employment.

The Edwardian Code

When a part is named, it shalt have that name from henceforth unto eternity. Thou shalt not call that part by any other name nor shall any other part be called by that name.

When a part is numbered, it and it alone shall have that number from this day henceforth forever.

When a number system for dimensions shall be decided upon, that system shalt be used for all parts of the system whether designed at that location or at some remote location.

Thou shalt specify and design with standard sizes and parts wherever possible. Do not waste time with oddball sizes or designs just to be pretty.

Thou shalt not fail to attend to the most important things first. Waste no time on unessentials.

Thou shalt design something so it can be built without using four hands or exceptionally long arms. The workmen of today who will be building thy design are men, not chimpanzees.

Thou shalt not continue to design a part to perfection when the time for its need is come unless of dire necessity. If the time for its need is gone past, it has not met its need. Timeliness is as important as perfection.

Thou shalt always remember that everything thou design is a balance of time, quality, cost, and function. If thou ignore these rules then thine employment will be brief and miserable. If thou attend to all four, then thou wilt not be required to demonstrate thine ability to walk on water, nor even to swim.

A man was flying in a hot air balloon and realized he was lost. He saw a man in a field below him so he lowered the balloon and shouted, "Can you tell me where I am?"

The man below said, "Yes. You're in a hot air balloon hovering 50 feet above this field."

"You must work in information technology," said the balloonist. "I do," said the man, "but how did you know?"

"Well," said the balloonist, "everything you have told me is technically correct but it's of no earthly use to anyone."

The man below said, "You must work in business." "I do," said the balloonist, "but how did you know?"

"Well," said the man, "you don't know where you are or where you are going, but you expect me to help. You're in the same position you were before we met, but now it's **my** fault."

Stoney Creek in Winter

Winters in Ohio can be bitter, with dreary cloudy skies, sleet, freezing rain, wet snow, cold wind, and mud. They can also be incredibly beautiful with clean white snow covering all the drab fields and woodlots with a clean clear sky above. The winters in the 1930's that I remember were longer and colder than the winters of the 1990's, but I lived in Ohio during the 30's and I live in a Middle-Atlantic state these days. If I lived in Ohio I probably would conclude that the winters now are as cold and as long now as they ever were.

Nostalgia has a funny way of allowing memories of good times come flooding back while blocking from our minds all of the bad memories. Making a living was hard on farms in the 1930's and it is hard today. The activities and needs are a bit different, but making a living is a full-time job for most farmers. There aren't many vacations and a forty hour week is for city folks. Of course for the better educated and for the self-employed, the forty hour week is a dream even in the city. But times were **so** much better when we were young, right? Maybe just being young had something to do with that.

Winter on a farm in the 1930's meant having to get up at dawn or before, dress quickly to prevent freezing, hurry to the outdoor "facilities," and go to the barn to feed and milk the cows before breakfast. The other animals could wait until a little later in the morning to be fed and watered, but the truck to pick up the milk cans came at an early hour and the milk had to be in the cans before that.

Mother had to be up early too. The fire in the cookstove had to be started so that breakfast could be on the table in time for the children to eat before catching the schoolbus. The heating stove had to have the ashes shaken down, wood added, and the draft opened so that the room would be reasonably warm soon. Water had to be pumped by hand from the well pump. Luckier folks had that pump on the back porch or even in the kitchen, but it had to be primed before you could get any water. If the water were not let down the pump would freeze overnight and then one really had the problem of thawing it out before water could be pumped.

Breakfast was usually cooked breakfast, cold cereal was an uncommon treat. At our house there was usually oatmeal porridge, bacon or ham and eggs, with coffee for the adults and milk for the young, with home-made bread toasted over the open fire in the cookstove. (The stove lid would be removed and the bread held with a fork over the coals or flame until it looked about right.) Often we had fried mush because that was a favorite of both Dad and me. Dad liked to put maple syrup on his but I liked it with just butter. Both the syrup and the butter were home-made.

Some of the people reading this may not have had the privilege of knowing what fried mush is like. They may however know what the Italians call polenta, ground corn meal boiled with water and salt to a very thick porridge-like consistency. For fried mush, this polenta is allowed to cool and congeal, sliced into about 1/4 inch thick slices which are fried until crisp and tasty. Really good eating for breakfast.

After the school bus has come and gone, the farmer must get back to the barn to feed the horses, pigs, and chickens. He then must turn out the animals to get water from the creek or from the water trough. In cold weather the ice must be broken in the trough but only in really cold weather was the creek frozen. When the animals were outside, the farmer had to clean the stalls and pens and put out clean straw for bedding. For the baby animals, water had to be carried; they couldn't stand deep snow and cold wind. But even the babies soon grew big enough to fend for themselves unless it was really bad weather.

If the farmer also had sheep, they were attended to after the other chores were completed. Dad had to walk about a half mile to the lower sheep barn, carrying a forty or fifty pound bag of grain for the sheep. He would put about half of it in the feed trough in the barn lot for about half of the sheep. These had access to the barn lot and water through the night and they could eat while he threw down hay from the mow and filled the mangers for all of the sheep. The half who were closed in the barn overnight started on the hay.

When the half of the flock in the barn lot had finished with the grain in the trough and had come into their side of the barn to eat the hay, Dad would shut their door confining them to the barn for the day. Then he would refill the feed trough and let the other half of the flock out to eat and drink. They were then allowed access to the barn or barn lot as they wished through the day. In the late afternoon, this routine would be repeated.

After the sheep had been cared for, the farmer's work was pretty much done for the morning. He probably would have about two hours of unstructured time before the noon meal, always called dinner on the farm. In that time he could repair harness for the horses, husk corn, grind feed, split wood, run errands, or do any of the always present odd jobs that accumulate in any household.

Afternoons were a repeat of morning chores but in slightly different sequence. Usually the farmer would try to get done before dark because lanterns, the only source of light in the barn after dark, were not only inadequate but dangerous. It gets dark early in Ohio in the winter, so afternoon chores were started about two o'clock in mid-winter. Milking the cows was usually the last chore at night, just before supper.

In the evenings, light was provided in the house by oil lamps. No one I knew used candles for light, lamps were the normal light. It is not difficult to read by lamplight, but fine work such as sewing was almost never done by lamplight. My Dad often sat at his drawing board with a pencil in one hand and a cigaret in the other and drew cartoons for my mother to go over with ink the next day. Cartoons were a major source of income for my parents when I was growing up. The cartoons signed Bell that appear in this book and others are some of their work. Much of the drawing was done by lamplight.

This is not the farm where I grew up but it is typical of what Ohio farms looked like in the 1930's

Outhouse

In the dark days of the great depression of the 1930's the people of Stoney Creek had no running water in their houses. They never had running water in their houses so no one thought much about it. It did make for a lack of some conveniences, such as what is sometimes euphemistically called indoor plumbing.

Every house had an adjunct out back known by various names but typically called the outhouse. Some were fancier than others but all served the same function and all typically smelled pretty bad, especially in the summer. They were pretty cold in the winter too, because no one I knew provided heat in them. But we survived.

At Halloween, a favorite vandalism of the teenage boys was to tip over the outhouses of neighbors. This was easy to do by three or four big boys and it wasn't a great big job to set it up again. It did take a couple of men to push it back upright though, and it got rather inconvenient if one needed the outhouse before the men could get together and set it back in place.

As a make-work project during the days of the Roosevelt administration, the government would send a crew around to homes and build a new outhouse for just the cost of the material. They had a standard design which was much nicer than most of the older houses and included a sanitary holding tank made of concrete to keep the waste from soaking into the ground. Periodically these tanks had to be emptied and the waste disposed of in a safe place, but that was a small inconvenience compared to the risk of the waste contaminating the well. Nearly every house had a well, and most people placed the well a safe distance away but sometimes this was difficult to do.

Before Howard Clay had enough money to buy a better house, he lived in a small old house which didn't have running water so naturally he had the same kind of outhouse that his neighbors had. Then when he had a chance to do so, he had the government crew come in and build a nice new modern outhouse with a concrete holding tank. It was strictly first class, just like everything that Howard wanted, and was painted a nice white with green trim. Howard was very proud of it.

As Halloween approached, Howard became apprehensive about his new outhouse and worried that it might be damaged if vandals tipped it over. So for several nights before Halloween Howard stayed up until about midnight watching over his new outhouse. To be precise, he was watching the inside of it; Howard figured that it would be better to hide from any vandals and that he could hear them if he was close.

That wasn't all that smart. Howard fell asleep about 10 o'clock on Halloween, just about the time that several teenage boys came by and pushed it over. They pushed it from behind so that it fell on the door and although Howard was awakened, he was trapped inside and could only shout imprecations at the boys, who of course had long since run away.

The outhouse wasn't seriously damaged, just a few scratches, and Howard was soon released. His wife had heard the crash as the outhouse fell over and had gone for help. Some of the neighbors helped put it back in position and get the door open. Howard was pretty mad, but he was a quick learner and vowed, "I'll never do that again."

The following year, Howard kept watch again but this time he stayed on the back porch. He had alerted Warren Semple, Stoney Creek's special constable, that he was watching for vandals and that Warren should pay special attention to Howard's house. The citizens of Stoney Creek took up a collection every year to pay Warren to watch for vandalism and prevent the boys from doing serious damage to any property. Warren was not too swift in his thinking, but he took this responsibility seriously and watched carefully for any activity by teenagers.

Along about ten o'clock Howard was alerted by a little rustling in the gravel of the alley behind his house and began watching very carefully. About that time he heard shouts from out in front of his house.

"Hey Howard," Warren was shouting, "I caught 'em Howard. These boys was going onto your property but I got 'em. Come out here and tell me what to do with 'em."

Howard didn't want to go out front but Warren was insistent and kept shouting, so Howard went to see what all the commotion was about. As he got out there and found that Warren had two boys by their arms, they heard a crash from the back as the outhouse tipped over.

Warren let the two boys go and they disappeared into the darkness before Howard could protest that these were simply decoys to draw attention away from the outhouse and allow their friends to tip it over. Warren helped Howard set it back in place again.

The following year Howard was really determined that this vandalism would not happen again. The outhouse had not been seriously damaged, but it had become a matter of principle with Howard.

The evening of Halloween, Howard and his friend Bill Payne got a case of beer and put it on the back porch of Howard's house. They set two comfortable chairs beside the case of beer and prepared to stand watch. Just after it got good and dark they went out to the outhouse and carefully moved it forward about six feet, just enough to uncover the holding tank of waste. Then they went back to the porch and started in on the beer. They didn't light any lantern or lamp so it was pretty dark, with only a half moon to light the back yard.

After a couple of hours they heard a crunch of gravel in the alley and became alert. They couldn't see anything, but they heard a boy's voice saying, "C'mon you guys. He ain't anywhere around. C'mon, let's go." They recognized the voice as Billy Crump, a tenth-grader at Centerburg High School and old enough that he shouldn't have been out playing vandal. Then they heard footsteps hurrying on the gravel and then a splash and sounds of dismay.

The boys with Billy were far enough behind him that they stopped short of disaster but Billy was standing in the tank and very upset. He didn't smell very good either and that sort of put an end to the evening's activities for Billy. The other boys lost a great deal of interest in any further activities too and all went home. Billy found that his friends kept a little distance away and were careful to walk up wind from him.

One of his friends pretty well expressed what the others were thinking when he said, "You're a nice guy, Billy, but please stay down wind."

The following year the REA, Rural Electrification Act, brought electricity to Stoney Creek and most of the houses installed bathrooms. The days of tipping over outhouses had passed.

A man who lived in an area that was subject to flooding was sitting on his porch one rainy day when a police car came by with a PA system warning people to move to higher ground because the levee was being breached by the flooded river. As it came by, the policeman called to the man to come and get in the car and move to higher ground before the flood came this far.

"Oh, no thank you," the man replied, "The Lord will take care of me."

Later, the flood came and forced the man to climb up on his roof. As he was sitting there, a rescue boat came by with several people on board who had been in the same situation. The boat pulled up to the edge of the roof and the pilot of the boat said, "Here, come get in the boat and we'll take you to higher ground"

"Thanks," said the man, "But the Lord will provide for me. Go help someone who needs it. The Lord will save me."

"Okay," said the pilot of the boat, "But I'll send a helicopter to get you then."

A little while later the helicopter came by and the rescue team sent a man down with a basket to rescue the man.

"Thanks," the man said, "but you don't need to go to such a bother. The Lord will save me."

So the helicopter left him sitting on the roof and the water rose still further. Eventually the man drowned and went up before the Lord in Heaven.

"Where were you when I cried out to you?" the man protested. "I cried and prayed to you but you never saved me!"

"Don't give me that nonsense," said the Lord, "Three times I tried to save you. I sent a police car, I sent a boat, I sent a helicopter, and you told them all to go away. So I say to you, you can go away too."

Cows and Cats

When I was a boy every farm had cows and cats. They seem to go together like berries and cream or pancakes and maple syrup.

Farm cats seem to have it made. They adapt well to their environment and the Stoney Creek farm environment was nearly ideal for cats. They had a hay mow full of sweet smelling hay to burrow in for warmth on cold winter nights. There was usually an adequate but not overly ample supply of game such as mice and other small mammals around to provide a protein supplement to their regular ration of milk morning and evening. There was always company because almost no farm had just one cat; there were always several. And all farms had cows. What more could a cat want?

Cows on the Stoney Creek farms were generally placid creatures, unaccustomed to hurry. They walked leisurely most of the time, grazed contentedly in the pasture, loafed in the shade on hot days, and gave as little milk as they could get away with.

Every boy who grew up around Stoney Creek learned to milk cows. It was considered to be a strengthening exercise for the hands. There was no need to go to a sporting goods store to buy mechanical hand grip exercisers; we just milked half a dozen cows twice a day. Our hands and forearm muscles became plenty strong. After a few years the knuckles of our hands became oversize too, but our grips became firm and hard.

The cats always sit around the cows' feet at milking time. By squirting a thin stream of milk at them, a boy could teach a cat to sit up and drink milk as it squirted into its mouth. This encouraged the cats to sit even closer and sometimes try to get into the bucket as it was being filled. Such impatience was discouraged, but when the milking was done some of the milk would be poured into a pan for the cats to enjoy.

I finished milking my cows one summer evening before my dad was done with his. I hung my bucket on a nail and leaned against the stable wall, chatting with Dad while he finished up his last cow. The cats were sitting around as usual waiting for Dad to finish and pour out their evening ration.

The cow was switching her tail at the flies that always bothered the cows during the summer. Occasionally she would lift a hind foot to kick at a fly on her belly, all the time peacefully munching on the scoopful of grain in her feed box. All perfectly normal behavior.

Then the peace was shattered explosively. One of the cats took advantage of Dad's inattention to the bucket as he was talking to me and it commenced lapping milk from the bucket. Just then the cow lifted her hind foot to kick at a fly and inadvertently set the hoof back down on the cat's tail. The cat gave a loud screech and raked the cow's leg with both front sets of claws. The cow humped her back, gave a startled bawl blowing a mouthful of ground feed into the manger, and kicked with both hind legs.

The cat went up the ladder into the hay mow so fast that I saw only a blur out of the corner of one eye. The milk bucket came tumbling behind the cow, scattering cats in all directions and drenching them with warm milk. Dad rolled over backwards to avoid the cow's hooves; farmers had to have fast reactions at such times.

Dad was pretty mad at the cow for a minute. Then he was mad at the cat for a few minutes longer. He ended up being mad at me for laughing. By the time he had picked up the bucket and calmed the cow down, he had begun to cool off.

As we turned the cows out for the night, he chuckled a little and said, "I'll bet that cat doesn't try to steal milk out of the bucket right away soon."

After the cats had their milk in the evening they always sat around washing themselves as is their habit after meals. There'd be a cat sitting on the beam along the edge of the hay mow and another on the top of the feed storage box. A couple would follow us to the house to see if my mother would give them some extra food which she usually did. The others would come to the house later for some table scraps after supper.

One cat had an evening ritual after she drank her portion of warm milk. She would laboriously climb up the posts and beams along the south wall of the barn until she was sitting on the beam that ran under the open window at the peak of the roof. She would take her post there and wait patiently until dusk when English Sparrows came into the barn to roost for the night. They would fly to the window from outside and perch briefly to accustom their eyes to the dim light inside the barn. Then they would fly to their roosting spots under the eaves. That is, all but one. Each evening one made a dessert for the cat.

As soon as she caught a sparrow, the cat would make her way carefully back down the barn wall to the floor of the hay mow. There she would deliberately eat her sparrow and then wash up. There were always plenty of sparrows around so there was no danger of her running out. Sparrows are none too bright and the survivors never seemed to miss the losers. They never changed their habit of stopping on the window ledge as they came into the barn to roost.

The cats were all hunters but about the only birds they caught were English Sparrows. Song birds, which we attracted with feeders, are generally too cautious to be caught except on rare occasions. Sparrows were so plentiful that the few the cats caught were not missed.

Mice and rats are attracted to barns where they eat cow feed and stored grain. Cats learn very quickly where the good hunting is to be found. When cats are well fed, they hunt for sport. Some farmers starved their cats so that they would be anxious to hunt for food, but Dad always maintained that the lean and hungry cats were too weak to hunt well and could only hang around for a handout. Our cats were sleek and well fed and all were good hunters. We often found dead mice or rats on the barn floor. Cats would sometimes eat mice and we would find only a small portion, but usually we found whole dead rats.

A full grown rat is a tough customer for a cat to handle and often the cats would leave the rats for the dog to kill. As proof of Dad's theory about cats hunting for sport, he would point to a half eaten mouse or a whole dead body on the barn floor.

The cows never seemed to mind having cats around them. The incident of the cat scratching the cow's leg was exceptional because the cats rarely got stepped on. Kittens just barely able to get around under their own power would play around under the cow's feet but only rarely did a cow step on one. The cows weighed several hundred times as much as a kitten and had such big clumsy feet that it seems incredible that they didn't smash all the kittens. They apparently were careful.

Cows and cats are both curious creatures, and anything unusual attracts their attention. They will both stare and investigate if possible any object with which they are not familiar. If Dad left a wagon or sled in the pasture field for a few minutes, all of the cows would come from the far end of the pasture to see what was going on. Fence building was always done to an audience of staring cows, and most jobs around the barn were observed by one or more cats who wanted to see what was being done.

When walking to and from the barn Dad was always accompanied by one or two cats. It always irritated Dad to need to walk around them every few seconds. The cat would follow for a few steps and then run on ahead a few steps and sit down in the path. After Dad passed it, it would repeat the procedure.

Another habit cats seem to inherit from their ancestors is a reluctance to go through doors. Dad would open a door, either at the barn or the house, and wait for the inevitable cat to precede him. It always annoyed him to have the cat stop in the doorway and peer carefully in all directions before going further. One cat we had would always smell the door frame even though it had come through that door only seconds earlier and had checked everything at that time too. Another cat often would forget that it had wanted to go through the door in the first place. She would look in all directions and, seeing nothing unusual, would sit down and begin washing herself waiting for something interesting to come along.

This last habit of cats was shared by cows. The first cow to reach the stable door when Dad and I would turn them out after milking, would stop in the door with only her head outside. Then she would slowly look in all directions before going on outside. Each cow in turn would repeat this ritual and turning out required patience on the part of the farmer. Prodding and urging from the rear had only slight effect and would need to be repeated for each cow in turn. Often, while gazing at the countryside and ignoring the pushes and shouts of the farmer, the cow would take advantage of the pause in an otherwise hurried existence and relieve herself on the barn floor rather than outdoors. No amount of urging could dissuade some cows of this habit.

While cows don't usually follow a person like a cat, they would stop abruptly in front of the farmer when being driven along a path. If two or more cows were being driven, the first cow would stop, the second and third and other cows would have to stop to avoid running into the cows ahead and progress would come to a halt. The farmer soon learned that trying to start them moving by whacking the rear cow was like trying to push a rope. The line of cows would simply collapse on itself until the lead cow decided to continue on her way.

Cats and cows are a lot alike despite their vastly different proportions as anyone familiar with both will agree. Both are interesting to watch but cats make better house pets.

Appropriate Names for Occupations and Products

Lois Steem	School Guidance Counselor
Rosetta Stone	Language Professor
L. G. Brah	Mathematics Teacher
Abbey Ration	Psychologist
Frajel and Riketti	Construction Engineers
Seymour O'Fencis	Head of Security
Linus Bizzy	Communications Consultant
Justin Case	Insurance Salesman
Bud Weiser and Michael Loeb	In charge of refreshments
Vehemint	he chewing gum for angry people
Detrimint	the chewing gum that damages your teeth

Book Four
Reflection

    The beauty of such a vista depends on one's viewpoint. The comment of the first white settlers in our American west when they first beheld this scene was, "Oh Lord! More mountains to cross! Will they never end?"

    This is the fourth in a series of books. None are limited to one subject. They all include whatever I thought was interesting at the time and what I thought my friends and relatives might also find interesting or amusing.

    I hope you enjoy reading the material as much as I have enjoyed putting it together.

Robert E. Bell

Reflections

Reflections can be beautiful and most of us could benefit from more reflection. Of course, most of the time when we think we are reflecting, all we are doing is wishing for something we don't have. But then what else is there to wish for? This part of the book spends some time on reflection, but most of it is just a mixture of thoughts, quips, quotations, and memoirs.

Upon reflection, certain truths become evident or at least obvious. For example:

Apathy is a universal problem but no one seems to care.

If the customer wants vanilla, for heaven's sake, give him vanilla.

For a speech to be immortal, it does not need to be eternal.

Anyone who uses foul language is an ignorant oaf.

There is no substitute for a genuine lack of preparation.

I took this picture at Stourhead Gardens in the Cotswolds section of England a few years ago. When I was looking through the prints of the pictures after they were developed, I saw this picture and wondered what was wrong with it. I knew it wasn't right, but it was only after I turned it upside down that I realized what was wrong. That's why I printed this text upside down so you would see the picture as I first saw it.

G-BJOB stands for "great big job" which is just what this one was. It is a 1960 Jodel which Tom Beck and Martyn Smith bought when it was in pieces stored in a barn. They had a big job restoring it.

Tom Beck and Martha Bell are looking at a small homebuilt plane that Tom and Martyn built before G-BJOB. It can carry the pilot and that is it. Tom and Martyn are both Captains with a British airline and spend a lot of time in airplanes at work. In their spare time they go flying.

When you starve with a tiger, the tiger starves last.

Unknown

The first Christian gets the hungriest lion

Ernie Doczy

"I see nobody on the road," said Alice.

"I only wish I had such eyes," the king remarked in a fretful tone. "To be able to see Nobody! And at that distance too! Why it's as much as I can do to see real people by this light!"

Lewis Carroll
Through the Looking Glass

It's not whether you win or lose, it's how you place the blame.

Robert Vesco

Nothing dries sooner than tears.

Latin proverb

The comforter's head never aches.

Italian proverb

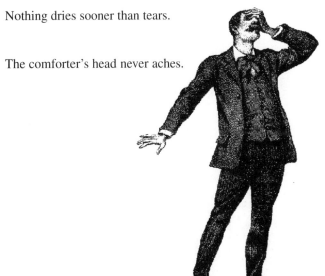

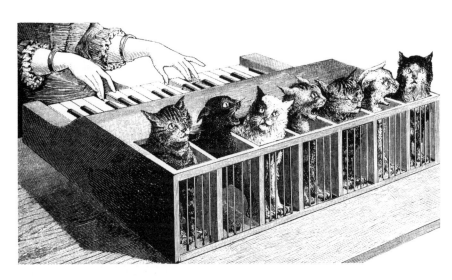

Of all noises, I think music is the least disagreeable.

Samuel Johnson

A friend in need is a pain in the butt.

Anonymous

The above drawing is by Charles Dana Gibson. It was originally published in 1904.

Little Willies and Gentle Janes

Little Willie, full of gore,
Nailed his sister to the door.
Said Willie's mother, with humor quaint,
"Careful, Willie, you'll spoil the paint."

Little Willie in bows and sashes,
Fell in the fire and was burned to ashes.
Later on the room grew chilly,
But no one cared to stir up Willie.

Little Willie fell down the elevator.
There they found him six months later.
Willie's mother said, "Gee, Whiz!
What a spoiled child Willie is!"

Little Willie was a chemist.
Little Willie is no more.
What he thought was H_2O
Was H_2SO_4.

Little Willie, feeling bright,
Found a stick of dynamite.
Curiosity seldom pays.
It rained Willie seven days.

There was a young fellow named Sidney
Who drank till he ruined a kidney.
He sat there and drank
Till it shriveled and shrank,
But he had a good time at it, didn' he?

Cannibals, exceeding rude
Once cooked Gentle Jane for food.
Though a nature mild she had,
Gentle Jane got boiling mad.

Gentle Jane at midnight's hour
Dreamed she heard a thunder shower.
Waking from her pleasant sleep,
Jane was struck all of a heap.

A Cure for the Flue

In 1942 when I was in high school my Mother had major surgery and was restricted from any activity for several weeks. During her convalescence my two older sisters took turns spending a week at a time keeping house at the farm for my father and me.

At the time we had two stoves in the kitchen of the farm house, one for cooking and a space heater for keeping the house warm. (Cookstoves are notoriously poor heaters for the house except in the summertime.) We burned wood when it was available but most of the time we burned soft coal which produces enormous amounts of soot and strong odors as well as heat.

The two stoves each had stovepipes which joined as they entered the chimney and both had to be removed from time to time to clean out the accumulation of soot. The chimney also tended to clog with soot and had to be cleaned at least once a year.

One day as I arrived home from school on the bus, I had just started toward the house when I noticed an enormous black cloud emerge from the chimney and shoot a long way straight up. As I watched the cloud spread out and tiny black flakes began to drift slowly downward from it. I stepped up on the porch to be away from the fallout and watched for a moment before I opened the kitchen door.

As I opened the door, I could hardly see more than a foot or so inside the room; it was full of what appeared to be a black fog, not smoke but tiny particles of soot suspended in the air. A small black boy, my nephew, appeared out of the fog. He had been white when I left for school that morning, but he was black now. Then a much larger black figure, my sister, appeared out of the fog.

"What happened?" I asked

"The stovepipe blew up. It wouldn't burn all day. I kept trying to keep the fire going but it wouldn't burn and it wouldn't burn. So I put some kerosene on it to make it burn but all that did was make more smoke. Then when I closed the stove door, the pipe blew up. It just blew up!"

If there had been some flame in the stove when my sister threw on the kerosene, it would have flashed into flame immediately. Because there were only embers, the kerosene merely evaporated and filled the stovepipe and chimney with fumes until the mixture was in the right proportions to explode, and explode it did. All the accumulated soot in the stovepipe and chimney were removed in one huge blast and it was fortunate for everyone concerned that the house did not catch fire. The chimney was open enough and the pipe was loosely connected enough that the expanding gases had somewhere to go and only made a mess.

And make a mess they did. Behind the kitchen was the spare bedroom where my sister and nephew had been sleeping. The stopper from the chimney in that room, which was used to close off the chimney opening when there was no stove connected, had blown completely across the room and that room too was filled with the black cloud of soot particles. Directly above the kitchen was my bedroom and the chimney went up through the clothes closet in the room with a stopper over the stovepipe opening there. It also had blown out and there was a thick round black spot on the back of the coat that was hanging in front of the chimney. The door to the clothes closet had been closed so the soot cloud was confined to the closet and the air in the bedroom was clear.

We spent several days cleaning the rooms that had been affected and the stoves both burned beautifully the rest of the winter. There was no more trouble with the chimney not drawing properly. It really was a cure for the flue, but not one I would recommend.

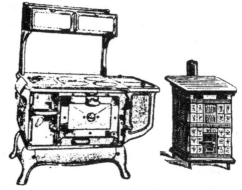

Stoves like these graced the kitchen in my boyhood home.

The farmhouse at Stoney Creek. Picture taken about 1920.

Squirrels in the Walls

When I was small we lived in a farm house in central Ohio. The house had been built about 1840 and about 1890 an addition was put on which nearly doubled its size. Both parts of the house had been built with materials from the farm. The old part had a full basement with walls made from large stones gathered from the fields and held together with mortar. The beams were rough hewn from big hardwood logs and bark was still on parts of the beams. The wood used throughout the house was hardwood cut from trees on the farm. (It really was hard too; it was almost impossible to drive a nail into it after a few years of seasoning.) The construction was good, but over the years the spaces inside the walls had become accessible to small creatures like mice.

Mortar between the stones in the basement had eroded in places so that it was impossible to prevent mice and even rats from getting into the basement. My parents set traps for vermin constantly to keep the population under control, and they plugged obvious openings whenever they could be found. Once a mouse was inside the basement, it could find access to the space between the wall studs and could go anywhere in the house inside the walls. The attic was as available as the basement to small creatures and we never stored anything in the attic without protecting it from vermin in some way.

Vegetables and fruits stored in the basement were placed in bins suspended on wires from the ceiling so that mice and rats couldn't get into our winter food supply. Seed corn for the next season was also hung from the ceiling in the attic for the same reason. Walnuts and hickory nuts were spread on the floor in the attic so they would stay dry but these were not protected from mice and rats because their shells were too hard for the small critters to chew into.

But one year we discovered that somehow red squirrels had gotten into the

walls. Mice and rats are fairly quiet in the walls; we could occasionally hear one gnawing on the wood, but this could be stopped by simply banging on the wall with one's fist or a shoe and all would be quiet again for a while. But squirrels are a different kind of rodent. Squirrels sound as though they are wearing hobnailed boots and they don't stay still for more than a second or two at a time. They also ignore any other noises so pounding on the wall is useless.

The squirrels also found the winter supply of nuts in the attic and thought that they had died and gone to heaven. They would run across the room and leap onto the supply spread on the floor and slide with a rolling thunder until they hit the opposite wall with a crash. Then they would grab a nut, take it to the top of one of the partitions and eat it. The squirrel would then drop the empty shell which would fall, bouncing from one inside of the wall to the other as it went all the way to the basement. Then the squirrel, apparently believing that there may have been another morsel of nut meat in that shell, would race down the inside of the wall to the basement, retrieve the nut, and scramble noisily all the way to the top to inspect the shell again. Then, concluding that it was right in the first place, the squirrel would drop the shell again which would clatter all the way to the bottom of the wall. The squirrel would then go get another nut from the supply and repeat the performance. This noise in the walls kept up for hours and really did nothing to encourage sleep. The squirrels apparently slept in the daytime or else they never slept. Their presence was quite a nuisance to my parents, and they tried various things to stop it.

They even resorted to putting the best hunter-cat we had, Nimrod, in the attic to see if he would at least discourage the squirrels. We found him the next morning at the foot of the attic stairs wanting his breakfast but he had apparently done nothing about the squirrels. He was reluctant to go into the attic the following night and after a few more nights, my parents decided that was a waste of time.

One summer day my father was behind the house when he noticed a squirrel running along a downspout which angled across the back of the house to carry water from one side of the house to a cistern on the other side. The downspout ran at about a 30° angle and crossed just under one of the windows upstairs. Dad noticed that the squirrel suddenly disappeared as it passed under the window.

Looking carefully as he could from the ground, my dad couldn't see any thing unusual about the side of the house under the window by that downspout. With closer inspection by leaning way out of the window itself and using a hand mirror to look under the sill, Dad could see an opening into the wall just large enough for a squirrel to enter. At last, after months of looking, he had found where the squirrels had gotten into the house. He then put a piece of metal over the hole to stop the access. Squirrels already inside the house would be forced to find water somewhere and would eventually die of thirst; at least in theory. Squirrels outside the house would be forced to find another source of food other than our winter nut supply. It was warm weather when Dad found the hole so there probably were no squirrels inside the house, unless the one he had seen stayed inside. At any rate, we didn't hear any more squirrel activity in the house after that.

The Walking Song

The road goes ever on and on
Down from the door where it began.
Now far ahead the Road has gone,
And I must follow, if I can,
Pursuing it with eager feet,
Until it joins some larger way
Where many paths and errands meet,
And whither then? I cannot say.

Still round the corner there may wait
A new road or a secret gate;
And though I oft have passed them by,
A day will come at last when I
Shall take the hidden paths that run
West of the moon, east of the sun.

The Road goes ever on and on
Out from the door where it began.
Now far ahead the Road has gone,
Let others follow it who can.
Let them a journey new begin,
But I at last with weary feet
Will turn toward the lighted inn,
My evening rest and sleep to meet.

This poem does not appear in its entirety anywhere in J. R. R. Tolkien's *The Lord of the Rings*, but the several verses are printed separately in the book. The first verse is attributed to Bilbo Baggins, the protagonist of Tolkien's first book, *The Hobbit*, a children's book. The other verses are attributed to Frodo Baggins, the protagonist of Tolkien's much larger adult book, *The Lord of the Rings*.

The sentiments expressed have struck a sympathetic chord in me. I have often been disappointed that I was unable to pursue some hidden path that branched off what I perceived to be my "road". There just isn't enough time in one lifetime to do everything one wants to do or to see every place there is to see or go down every tempting path that appears.

As Robert Frost once said in one of his poems:
The woods are lovely, dark and deep,
But I have promises to keep,
And miles to go before I sleep.

Small Cars

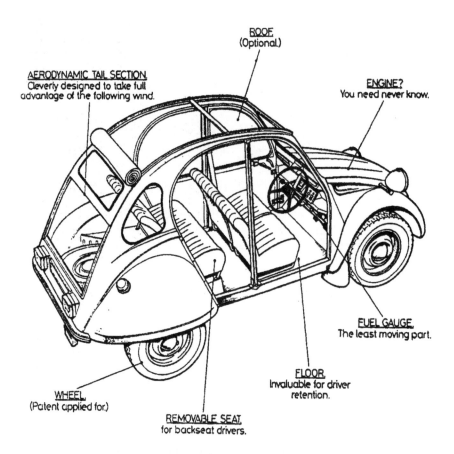

ROOF
(Optional.)

AERODYNAMIC TAIL SECTION.
Cleverly designed to take full
advantage of the following wind.

ENGINE?
You need never know.

FUEL GAUGE.
The least moving part.

WHEEL.
(Patent applied for.)

FLOOR.
Invaluable for driver
retention.

REMOVABLE SEAT.
for backseat drivers.

THE CITROËN 2CV £2,870.
All the technology you'll ever need in a car.

This picture was first published as an advertising brochure about 1980. The car is still the same but the 2001 price for a new Citroen is a lot higher than £2870. The car was still being made in 1999 and probably you can still buy a new one in Europe, right hand or left hand drive. It won't meet the USA emissions requirements so we can't import one. The basic design has not changed since 1947 when it first came on the market. The doors can be easily lifted off and set aside and the seats also can be lifted out without tools one at a time and set aside so that the interior can be used for hauling; even small livestock such as sheep, goats, or pigs can fit in.

Baby Austin

A demonstration to show how rugged a Baby Austin is

In the 1930's there was a small automobile on the market called the Baby Austin. The car first appeared in 1930 and was made in Butler, Pennsylvania by a company called American Austin Co. to distinquish it from the English company and the by then defunct American company of a similar name which had made luxury cars in Grand Rapids, Michigan until 1918. The car was small, the smallest made in the United States up to that time, and sported an emblem of a bantam rooster which caused much amusement.

It was a nice little car and sold for a very modest price, but unfortunately it came on the market at the wrong time. The depression was just starting and most people were not buying new automobiles. Also, because it was small and cute, it would be ideal as a second car, but people preferred to put their money into used larger cars which were more practical as the only car in the family. Most families didn't have a second car at that time. A car about the same size but nowhere near as cute, the Volkswagon, sold well about thirty years later when many families were buying second cars. The Baby Austin was just not considered primary transportation.

The owners of Austins had problems with pranksters. The car weighed only about 1000 pounds and therefore could be picked up by five or six strong men. A car left parked in town on Saturday night would probably be found on the sidewalk or inside some unlikely spot that would be difficult to drive out of when the owner returned. Owners would resort to trickery to prevent this happening too often.

A load of Austins on the way out of the factory. Note how much narrower they are than the truck or trailer bed.

One trick that some owners did was to grease the bumpers with a mixture of soot and axle grease so that it would not show in a darkened area. Young men of that era favored white pants when they were out on the town and it must have been disconcerting to find that after putting someone's Austin on the sidewalk and thrusting their hands casually into their pockets, the pants would be smeared with black grease. It isn't likely that this trick would work more than once; pranksters would be prepared for it the second time.

One young man who delivered papers in Richmond, Virginia, sometimes was teased when he arrived in an Austin to pick up his papers at the loading dock. One of the other paper delivery men who was particularly strong picked up one side of the back end of the car one day enough so that one back wheel was off the ground and held it so that the owner couldn't drive away. With one of the rear wheels off the ground the car couldn't move but the owner was resourceful. He put the car in reverse gear and let out the clutch. The man holding the car could see the wheel spinning in reverse and didn't dare set the car back down; it would have leaped backward onto him if he had. He would not have had time to leap out of the way, so he was forced to keep holding up about two hundred to two hundred fifty pounds of weight. After a few seconds he began to plead with the owner to stop the wheels and only after he promised the owner to leave the car alone in the future did the wheels stop.

The car was economical to run even by today's standards and would go nearly forty miles on a gallon of gasoline. It had a five gallon tank so it's range was not great but with only a thirteen horsepower engine its speed couldn't have been great and the driver's range between breaks would probably have been less than the car's range anyway. The time between fueling stops in an automobile or a small airplane is determined not so much by fuel capacity as by bladder capacity of the driver. Of course, I suppose you could buy a bigger bladder if you knew where to get one.

(See the illustration on the next page.)

Of course I know what it is, but I'd like to know where you got it.

Riding the Pig

For a brief period after I got out of the army, I helped my mother operate the farm where I grew up. I learned a great deal in that time, chiefly that I needed to find another way of making a living.

One of the things I had to do shortly after coming home was get some pigs ready for market. There were about twenty pigs in the herd, all of them about two hundred pounds or so except one who was older, wiser, and bigger than the others. She weighed about three hundred pounds and was wise to the ways to stay alive.

They were in a feed lot of about three acres behind the barn, and were allowed to roam the lot. There was water available and a shed for them to get in out of the sun and rain when they wanted. I fed them in one corner of the lot next to the main barn where there was a an eight-foot wide gate.

When I thought the pigs were ready for market, I asked my uncle how would be a good way to catch them and load them into a truck to haul them to market. (I didn't have a truck but could ask a local hauler to bring his truck around on market day and we would load them.) My uncle suggested that I put two temporary gates in place beside the eight-foot gate before I fed the pigs that morning, fastening them such that one gate could be swung around to trap the pigs in a small space in the corner of the feed lot. Then, loading through the main gate would be easy. Sure.

On market morning I fixed the gates as my uncle suggested and fed the pigs in the corner as usual. While they were eating I swung the one gate around to trap them in the corner. Just before the gap was closed, the larger pig decided that it would be a good idea for her to leave. I didn't agree with her and stepped into the gap so that she couldn't get out, at least not without running between my legs.

Suddenly I realized that my idea was not too good. I was riding backward very rapidly. A lot of scenery was retreating into the distance and I began to be concerned about the board fence ahead of the pig that was high enough for a pig to go under but not high enough for a rider on a pig to get through. So I decided to get off and look to see where we were. That was my second mistake in judgment. I should have left it up to the pig to decide where we were going.

Suddenly I felt the ground hit the back of my head and a lot of sky was sliding past my field of vision. That didn't last very long though and I found myself lying supine with a few bruises on my back and elbows. That was one of the moments when I decided to go back to university and become an engineer. Farming was too exciting for me. There had to be a more peaceful way to make a living.

The following week, my uncle helped me round up and trap the pigs and load them for market.

Coaly Mullins and His Coal.

Coaly lived about 1 1/2 miles southeast of Stoney Creek where the railroad crossed the County Line road. Long freight trains ran regularly up the track hauling coal from the coal fields in West Virginia and southern Ohio to the steel mills in Toledo and Detroit. There was a long gradual slope on the tracks for the northbound trains and they usually went through the Stoney Creek area at about three or four miles per hour, working hard.

Coaly, like some of his neighbors, depended on those coal trains for his winter fuel supply. Coaly got his nickname from his well known habit of hopping on a coal car as it went past his farm and riding it for about a mile toward Stoney Creek, throwing chunks of coal off the car onto the right of way . There was a wooded area all along that stretch of track so that if a railroad detective tried to catch Coaly, he simply hopped off the car and ran into the woods.

He would get off the train at the next crossing or thereabouts and walk home. Then he would hitch up one of his horses to a cart he had and walk back up the track putting the chunks of coal into the cart. The horse was so accustomed to this that Coaly didn't need to drive the horse; it would plod along beside the track while Coaly loaded the cart. When they reached the next crossing, Coaly would turn the cart away from the tracks and go home by way of the road; he preferred not to be caught with a cart-load of coal on the railroad property. If a train happened to come along while he was loading, the chances were good that it would be another loaded freight laboriously heading north and the horse could easily keep far enough ahead of the train to reach the road crossing without being caught. If an empty train came barreling south at the normal southbound speed of forty-five or fifty mph, Coaly would simply wave at the engineer as the train passed; he knew the train wasn't going to stop just to catch him.

It always made Coaly angry to have the Stoney Creek people come out to gather up the coal that he had so laboriously thrown off the cars, but this happened fairly often. It was easier for them to gather up the chunks of coal that Coaly had thrown off than it was to hop on the train and ride it northwest out of Stoney Creek and throw off coal themselves. Besides, the next road crossing northwest of Stoney Creek was at Peerless, about four miles away and the area that direction was not completely wooded so there was a greater chance of being caught. Coaly had to share his coal with his neighbors, but there was plenty to go around and no one needed to go cold in the winter.

Dodge the New Dodge

Dan Rogers was a lean, sort of dried up looking man with a wrinkled sun-browned face from being outdoors so much. He had a peppery temper with a short fuse on it and his animals learned to jump when he shouted at them. He worked hard like everyone else on a farm and this, combined with his small boned frame, kept his weight at about 120 pounds soaking wet.

Dan drove a Model T Ford touring car for many years. It rattled and squeaked, started hard, coughed when climbing a hill, and backfired going downhill. It had no heater and Dan's wife Lois always wrapped a hot soapstone in paper to keep her feet warm and wrapped the rest of herself in a thick blanket whenever they went anywhere in the winter. The roof leaked year-round, even when the sun was shining, Dan said, and the side curtains were not very airtight.

Dan was getting tired of the car — had been tired of it for a long time — but times were tough and money was scarce. However, Dan kept looking at used cars whenever he went into Mt. Pleasant or Centerburg and one year when he sold his wheat he decided to buy a "new" car.

The '35 Dodge he bought was almost new, and as the salesman pointed out, the roof didn't leak and it had a self-starter instead of a crank in front like Dan's old Model T. Also, it had a hot water heater which would please Lois and she wouldn't always grumble about cold feet in the winter.

It did have one important difference from the old Model T. The Dodge had a standard gearbox with a shift lever sticking up from the floor boards in the middle and a clutch pedal next to the brake. Dan was accustomed to seeing three pedals on the floor and was quite used to the idea of the gears being in neutral when the left pedal was pressed halfway down — pressing it all the way down engaged first gear. Reversing a Model T was done by pressing the left pedal halfway down with the left foot while pressing the middle pedal all the way down with the right foot. Pressing the left pedal down activated the brake and would perceptibly slow the Model T down when pressed hard enough. (Emergency stops on the T were done by pressing all three pedals simultaneously as hard as one could.) To move forward, Dan pressed the left pedal all the way down until the car started moving about 10 mph, then he released the left pedal, engaging drive gear and that was it. He was not used to twiddling a stick in the middle of the floor and shoving the left pedal in and out repeatedly.

One other difference was the idea of a foot operated throttle. Dan was accustomed to controlling the engine speed with a lever that stuck out the right side of the steering column. He had never had to keep his feet doing anything once the car was moving unless he needed to stop. All of the skills necessary to keep the T going had been mastered by Dan years before and he never gave them a thought anymore. The fact that they were almost foolproof never occurred to him. For example, one could not ruin the brake linings by driving with the hand brake set because on the T, setting the brake lever disengaged the gears so it was impossible to drive with the parking brake set.

Dan was not happy at having to learn all these new things but he listened to the salesman's explanations grimly. The roof didn't leak so he bought the Dodge anyway. Dan would have been surprised to learn that other people found the T's controls confusing and sometimes drove through the back of the garage by pushing as hard as they could on the "clutch" pedal. The T's first gear could often overpower the T's feeble rear brakes, and it was amazing how powerful the car was in first gear.

The salesman gave Dan a few instructions in driving which almost made things more confusing. Then the salesman went to take care of another prospective customer and left Dan on his own.

Dan studied the controls a few minutes and went through the motions a time or two before starting the engine. He soon grew impatient with pretending to drive and started up. He promptly caused a loud clashing of gears by trying to shift into first gear while pressing the

clutch pedal halfway down. Dan corrected this error and then stalled the car by letting the clutch out without pressing on the throttle. He stalled the car three more times and then noticed that he had failed to release the hand brake anyway. So far all he had done successfully was make a lot of noise.

Dan concentrated hard and then successfully got the car to move forward, rather slowly but moving the right direction anyway. After proceeding that way for a block or so, Dan successfully, albeit noisily, shifted into second gear and then later into third gear and chugged along peacefully toward home. By that time, Dan had regained his composure and his temper and was beginning to enjoy the way the car handled and rode. It had more power than the T and took the hills more smoothly. Dan was glad he had controlled his temper and had not told the salesman what he could do with the Dodge and demanded his money back.

Dan drove smoothly into the drive at home. He waved at Lois who came out of the house to admire the "new" car. Then Dan stalled the engine because he pushed the clutch pedal only halfway down the way he always had with the T. Dan quickly turned off the ignition hoping that Lois wouldn't notice his error. He needn't have worried; Lois was interested mainly in the fact that the car had a heater and a roof that didn't leak.

After admiring the car for a few minutes, Dan set about clearing some of the garden tools and the corn planter out of the wagon shed so he could put the Dodge inside. Dan had kept the T in the shed before, but he wanted a bit more room to minimize the risk of putting scratches on the Dodge. He hadn't worried so much about the old T.

When the shed was cleared Dan got into the Dodge to put it away. He started it without trouble, remembered to press the clutch all the way down, pressed gently on the throttle and put the gear shift lever into what he thought was first gear. Unfortunately he put it in reverse.

Dan released the clutch smoothly and pressed firmly on the throttle. To his surprise the car started moving backward toward the road. Dan didn't want to go to the road, so he turned the wheel sharply to the right, backing the car off the driveway onto the lawn. As it went through one of Lois's flower beds, she screamed. This completely unnerved Dan and he became panicky. He completely forgot everything the salesman had told him and began twisting the steering wheel to avoid obstacles as he looked over his shoulder to see where the Dodge was going. His right foot froze in position on the throttle which was about half open and his left foot tried to push out the floor boards beneath the clutch pedal.

The car swept in a long zigzag path across the lawn, smashing down a couple of small shrubs but missing all large obstacles like trees. It headed for the barn but Dan twisted the wheel in time and the car shot through the space between the chicken house and the granary, scattering squawking chickens in every direction. One came through the open window of the car and flew frantically between the front and the back seat, flapping its wings in Dan's face from time to time.

Dan fended off the hen with one hand so he could see and twisted the wheel with the other hand. He narrowly missed the wagon which was parked behind the granary as he made the turn into the main part of the barn lot. The car skidded as he swerved to miss the corner of the barn and then headed back out toward the house, almost brushing the wagon shed as it went by.

Lois had run after the car screaming at Dan to stop but she couldn't move as fast as the car. Suddenly she saw the car returning and heading directly toward her. She had to jump quickly to the side to avoid being hit and this made her angrier still; she was already pretty irritated at having her flower beds torn up.

As the car went past she shouted "Now you stop that showin' off right now, Dan Rogers! An' stay outta my flower beds!"

What with the hen squawking in his ear and flapping her wings in his face, Dan didn't hear what Lois had said. He was a bit too busy at the time to pay any attention to his wife anyway. He made another loop around and Lois again had to jump quickly to get out of the way.

This made her really angry and she stamped off toward the house muttering, "All right, show off if you want to but don't expect me to watch." She went in the house and closed the door.

Dan missed the granary again but as he swerved to miss the wagon a second time he lost his balance and his foot slipped off the throttle. The car slowed abruptly and stalled the engine.

Dan sat for a moment and then grabbed the hen that was still flopping around inside the car. He threw the hen out of the car and turned off the ignition.

"That did it!" Dan finally said. "That eternally by everlasting damn did it!"

Dan got out of the car and walked to the house, taking the key with him. Lois was watching from the back porch ready to lay into him about her flower beds. She thought better of it when she saw how he looked.

Dan handed her the key and said, "You kin jist git somebody to teach you to drive. I ain't never gonna drive another inch. You kin do all the drivin' whenever we go somewhurs agin, so you better learn quick."

He meant it too. Dan Rogers never drove a car again.

Electric Fence

My Dad had a low regard for commercial electric fences. They came on the market in the middle 1930's and were supposed to end all farmer's troubles with breachy animals who could spot a weak place in the fence from a 1000 yards away. The fence chargers used a 6 volt dry cell as power and were supposed to charge the fence with 10, 000 volts every few seconds. According to the advertisements, after a couple of days one could turn the power off; just the sight of the wire would be enough to prevent the animals from touching it. Sure.

In practice, a few animals would follow the rules but most just learned to be quick in moving through the fence; it was uncomfortable only if one lingered. Most farmers who hated to fix fence hated even worse having to admit that they had been taken in by a slick advertisement, so they told their neighbors that the fences worked and were the greatest advance in farm equipment since the McCormick reaper. Again, sure.

Dad bought one called *Weed Clipp*er which was supposed to be strong enough that even if shorted out by a weed stalk would still have enough kick to turn a charging bull. Weed stalks were a common cause of the fence not being effective, but this fence charger was no better than any other. Cattle would walk along beside it switching their tails against it and occasionally drawing an arc, but they reacted as they would to a fly. They simply switched their tails again.

No fence maker made any claims about holding sheep; the wool was too good an insulator for the sheep to feel anything. (I always thought that the sheep were too stupid to associate the fence with any discomfort even if they did get hit.) Some of the fences were reasonably effective with hogs but they were expensive. Horses would usually respect the wire, but horses are usually rather obedient creatures and stayed within the confines of the fence just because they thought they were supposed to.

The advertisements were right about one thing though. The fences were harmless to livestock. There was no way that any of them would hurt even a fly.

Then one day Dad ran across an ad for a fence controller that did sound effective. It consisted of a very simple timer kit for a Model T Ford ignition coil. The kit itself was inexpensive but the farmer had to provide the coil himself and put the kit together. The kit was a laboratory type test tube with a felt pad to put in the bottom end, a marble to roll back and forth inside the tube, a mounting bracket to hold the tube on a Ford coil, an armature with a switch on it to activate the coil, and that was it. Cheap and dirty.

Every farmer knew the power of a Model T coil. A favorite trick of the young men in the community was to thoroughly clean the tires of a T to insulate it from the ground, drop a wire from one of the spark plugs to drag on the ground, and call some poor unsuspecting person over to the car when the engine was running. As soon as the person standing on the ground touched the car, he would get an enormous shock because he would have completed the circuit. Anyone inside the car wouldn't feel a thing because they weren't grounded. There were some variations on this trick, but it was well known that the kick from a T coil might knock you down, but no permanent damage would be done, at least no physical damage from the shock. The coils put out about 15,000 volts but had no current with the voltage. Painful but harmless.

I was the first to test the new fence but not on purpose. We got ready to hook the system up to a 6 volt dry cell and I held an insulated wire close to a grounded wire to see how much of an arc it would draw. I was careful to hold the wire by the insulation only — I knew better than to touch the bare wire.

"OK, connect the battery," I said to Dad.

I knew exactly when he connected the battery. I dropped the wire instantly. I felt that jolt from my fingers to my toes. I just couldn't believe I had gotten such a shock right through the rubber insulation on that wire. I concluded that I must have touched the bare wire inadvertently so I picked the wire up again being especially careful to touch only the insulation. The little timer was clicking away as the marble rolled back and forth in the test tube and as it clicked the switch closed again, I dropped the wire instantly again. That was enough. I may be a slow learner, but I eventually do catch on.

"I thought you would be smarter than a pig," Dad laughed. "A pig would have gotten only one shock."

The next morning Dad and I strung a single barbed wire across the barn lot from the pasture gate to the wagon shed, a distance of about 75 feet. We placed the wire about eight or ten inches above the ground, low enough that a pig wouldn't walk under it and high enough that it would be unlikely to jump over. We planned to turn the pigs into the barn lot and part of the pasture, but prevent them from getting down into the orchard. Then we hooked up the new controller to the wire and placed it in the wagon shed to keep it out of the weather. We connected up the battery and carefully stepped over the wire and went to the barn to let the pigs out.

When pigs are released into a new area the first thing they do is tour the boundaries. Why they do it is a mystery known only to pigs, but I suspect they are looking for a place to get out. This isn't because they are dissatisfied but because they may want out at some future time. Pigs don't get out unless they have a reason to want to and they always know how to get back in when they need to. Pigs plan ahead.

The pigs seemed to know that Dad and I wanted them to check the new wire first, so they chose to go the other direction and check the other fences first. We knew it would take them at least half an hour to work their way around, so Dad and I sat down in the granary door to wait.

A contented grunting sounded from the other side of the wagon shed, a mud-dauber wasp buzzed around the granary door, a distant freight train whistled for a crossing, and everything was peaceful. A white rock rooster and his harem of a half dozen hens came slowly along the driveway toward the fence, pecking at the ground for morsels of grain or insects, whatever chickens peck at.

As the chickens reached the wire, they cocked their heads on first one side and then the other the way chickens do at something new in their territory. One of the hens ducked under the wire and walked on. Another hen hopped up on the wire with both feet and then hopped on over to the other side and walked on. The rooster stepped up on the wire with one foot while the other was still on the ground just as the controller clicked. The peaceful summer morning hush was shattered by the most unearthly squawk I had ever heard.

White rock chickens can't fly much better than ostriches, well, maybe a little better. But that rooster felt inspired to set a world's record for chicken flight and he found hitherto untapped reservoirs of talent. He must have flown straight up, an ability believed to be limited to humming birds, and then headed for the open barn door. That door is high enough to admit a loaded hay wagon, probably about fourteen feet or so, and was about eighty feet away. As the rooster entered the door, he barely cleared the top of the opening. He landed somewhere inside the barn and we could hear him cackling his alarm for several minutes.

After a few minutes the silence returned and peace was restored. The wasp began building a nest near the eaves of the granary, the pigs were inspecting the fence at the far end of the lot, and I began to doze. Then Dad nudged me with his foot.

A stray tom cat had been hanging around our barn and orchard for several days , harassing our resident tom cat Nimrod and making a general nuisance of himself. He was now swaggering down the driveway toward the fence. He was feeling good and carrying his tail straight up in the air. He apparently was looking for Nimrod to give him another lesson in humility and was paying no attention to the wire as he walked under it. His tail didn't quite clear and was pressed slightly downward as the cat passed under the wire.

The tail suddenly grew to enormous size as each individual hair stood on end. The cat gave a scream that must have frightened every cat within a mile radius and his legs started running before he did. I read a story by Roark Bradford one time about a man who was so frightened that he made the first hundred yards in nothing flat, improved his time  by three seconds on the next hundred yards, and then began to run. I had always thought that was an exaggeration until I saw that cat run to the nearest oak tree and not stop climbing until it ran out of tree at the top. He was still there at chore time that evening, but he was gone the next morning and we didn't see him again for months.

Eventually the pigs worked their way around the lot until they got to the new fence. Pigs are naturally cautious but curious about anything new, and they remembered a similar appearing wire a few months earlier that had a mild bite to it, so they decided to test this one to see what it was like. One pig put his nose close to the wire to smell it and a fat blue spark leaped from the wire. His tail straightened abruptly and he jumped back with a squeal. He then stood to watch what the other pigs would do. The others decided that maybe his experience was good enough for them and they walked away.

There was one pig in the litter who was either a whole lot smarter than the rest or else it was a slow learner. He was a bit smaller than the others, the runt of the litter so to speak and thus had to be a bit quicker to get his share of the food supply. This one we named, something farmers rarely do, and we called him, with a great flight of imagination, Runty.

Runty had watched the one pig get a shock and so was expecting something painful if he touched the wire.

Nevertheless, he walked up and down along the wire for a little while and then made a sudden dash under the wire. A fat spark hit his back as he brushed the wire but then he was past the wire and free. He gave a short squeal as the spark hit him but after he got out, he strolled nonchalantly toward the orchard.

I started to get up to drive him back but Dad stopped me. "If he wanted out that badly, let him go." Dad said. "He'll come back at feeding time."

At feeding time I pulled the trough out of the barn into the barn lot. Dad was stirring the ground feed into skim milk in a five gallon bucket. The pigs marched back and forth in a row about a foot away from the wire. Their squealing for their supper attracted Runty's attention and he came to get his share.

Dad carried the bucket over the wire to the trough and poured out the feed for the pigs who were pushing and shoving to get their shares. Runty now ran back and forth along the wire on the outside of the pen squealing loudly for a few seconds. Then he dashed under the wire and jumped when he got shocked, but he joined the others at the trough and pitched in heartily.

The next day, Dad and I strung a second wire a few inches below the first one. Now the wires were spaced at about five inches and nine inches above the ground, not enough room for a pig to get through. So Runty jumped over. Pigs normally are not jumpers, but when the need arises, a lean pig can jump pretty well, and Runty was a bit leaner than most of the litter.

The following day, Dad and I strung a third wire above the others a few inches, high enough to discourage Runty from jumping. This stopped him for a few hours but then we noticed that he went up close to the wagon shed where he could hear the controller clicking. He would make several false starts, apparently timing his moves to coincide with the clicks, and then he quickly squeezed under the bottom wire between clicks when there was no power in the wire. He often was quick enough to escape getting shocked, but even if he wasn't, he was through quickly enough that he would get zapped only once.

At that point we gave up and let Runty do as he wished. The others never did learn to get in and out the way he did, so the fence was pretty effective. Later we found that system to be effective against cattle and horses too. It also was effective at discouraging people like me from touching it.

The Horn Blows at Midnight

A friend had an unusual problem with her automobile. Here is the story in her own words:

The problem began in Ohio. It was a very cold winter night and I had a severe cold. I put Vicks Vaporub® on my chest and a sweat suit to keep warm and went to bed. About midnight I was awakened by the sound of an automobile horn honking continuously. I lay there wishing that whoever owned that car would go out and turn their alarm off. A young neighbor knocked on my door and told me that my horn was honking. He said that when he lived in Montana the same thing would happen to him on cold nights. It would quit if I would just get in the car, turn it on and drive around a bit.

Later, I moved to Florida and after three years had forgotten the incident. Then, as I was driving to my son's home in Arizona, I was reminded of it. I had checked into a motel for the night. It was mid winter on the high desert and nights were cold. Wearing a sweat suit with the baggy pants, I had put on a heavy pair of woolen socks to keep warm. With my teeth in a cup, I had gotten off to sleep nicely when the horn began honking. I immediately remembered what that sound was, so I grabbed my car keys and got to the car just as the man in the next room got there. I started the car and drove around for a bit.

When I returned to the motel, I realized that I had neglected to bring my room key and the door had locked automatically when I left. Toothless, in a baggy sweat suit with wool socks and no shoes, I walked up to the motel desk. Pretending that I was wearing a business suit to avoid embarrassment, I asked for an extra room key. I resolved that in the future, I would have my car keys in one hand and the room key in the other whenever I went out the door.

Good Samaritans

Luke 10:30(Revised modern version)

Jesus replied, "A man was going down from Jerusalem to Jericho, and he fell among robbers who stripped him and beat him, and departed, leaving him half dead. Now by chance a priest was going down that road; and when he saw him he passed by on the other side. So likewise a Levite, when he came to the place and saw him, passed by on the other side. After the Levite came two lawyers, good faithful members of the ACLU* and when they saw him, they said to each other, 'We must find the rascals who did this; they need help.'"

* ACLU: American Civil Liberties Union; an organization of lawyers devoted to the benefit of lawyers and [other] criminals.

Typical rural general store of 1930. This one happens to be in England.

Egg on His Face

In the evenings, especially in the winter, the men of the community would often gather at the general store in Stoney Creek and argue politics or religion or any topic of general interest. Some of the men played checkers and others watched. Charley Black ran the store and when he wasn't waiting on customers, he would repair shoes and boots. He could argue politics and repair shoes at the same time and never miss a lick at either one.

George Richards was one of the regulars at the store in the evenings. George was known to be "sorta tricky" as his neighbors put it, and men usually counted their fingers if they shook hands with him. Whenever things were lost or misplaced, people always said, "George musta been around." But George was usually welcomed around the store because he could always be counted on for a rousing political argument. He was a strong Democrat in a largely Republican community and in the days of Roosevelt's first term, partisan politics was a hot topic.

Charley Black kept eggs and other perishable goods in the back room of his store which was cooler than the main part of the store and when someone wanted anything in that line, Charley would go get it. George watched for opportunities to put small edibles in his large coat pockets in the winter and when he thought that Charley wasn't watching, George would slip a packet of candy or some other small item into his coat pocket. Most food products came "in bulk" and were not packaged the way they are today, so there weren't many foods that George could filch this way.

Whenever a customer was occupying Charley's attention up at the front of the store, or if Charley had to go outdoors and pump a couple of gallons of gasoline for someone, George might slip into the back room and snitch a few eggs. He wore a corduroy hunting cap with ear flaps in the winter, and by putting a few eggs into the hat, bending over and carefully putting the hat on his head, George could conceal some eggs for his breakfast the next day. He had to be careful not to pull the hat down too far, but that wasn't much of a problem.

Sam Harris was one of the regulars at the store too, and one evening, Sam had an idea of a joke to play on poor George. Sam usually didn't say much in the political arguments and wasn't strongly partisan for either party. But one evening he watched George slip into the back room and return before Charley came back from pumping some gasoline. George had sat down nonchalantly on a bench by the stove to listen to the conversations of the other men for awhile before he headed on home. He kept his hat on, but most of the other men did too, so that didn't attract any attention.

Sam suddenly moved over behind George and entered the discussion. In a much more vehement manner than Sam was accustomed to speak he said, "In spite of the criticism that Roosevelt has been receiving lately, I think he should be given a chance to show what he can do before we judge his plans. Every man deserves a chance. Now ain't that right, George?"

With that question, he slapped his big hand down on the top of George's hat. There was a squishy sound as the hat was pressed firmly down on George's head. A yellowish liquid ran slowly down his cheeks from under the hat.

Ben Phillips broke the silence that had followed Sam's little speech. Everyone had watched George's face getting red but no one had spoken until Ben said, "Looks like you got caught with egg on your face, George."

George didn't say a word. He just got up and walked out the front door. As the men laughed, Ben said to Charley, "Betcha don't git paid for them eggs."

" It won't be the first time George ain't paid for eggs," Charley said, "But I bet it's the last."

It was too. George may have picked up other things after that, but eggs were off his list. At least when anyone was watching.

There's no particular reason to have these cats here except that I like pictures of cats. A healthy cat is usually stalking or sleeping, which is what these two are doing.

Lose a Few

Homer Shelton was thirty-five years old and had lived all of his life in Stoney Creek. Everyone knew the Sheltons as the "Fightin' Sheltons" because whenever Homer or one of his five brothers had a snootful he'd go looking for a fight. Homer was the next to the youngest and at only five foot eight and 180 pounds, was the smallest of the brothers. In spite of his size, or perhaps in compensation for it, Homer was the most aggressive and everyone stayed out of his way when he'd been drinking.

On one afternoon, after he'd been hoisting a few beers at Harlow's on the edge of Centerburg, Homer started out toward Stoney Creek in a bad humor. As he went past Joe Baird's blacksmith shop in Centerburg, he saw Ben Phillips standing by the shop door chatting with Joe. Homer remembered that Ben had laughed at him a few days before. Homer had driven the Chadwick's Mill feed truck into the ditch out by Ben's farm when Homer was about three sheets in the wind. He was supposed to stay sober when he was driving the truck, but he sometimes slipped a little. Now he remembered that Ben had simply laughed at him.

Homer stopped his car and went over to Ben to have a few words, but Ben just laughed at him again. Homer picked up a hammer from the anvil inside the shop and started toward Ben with it. Ben, instead of running, took a couple of steps toward Homer without saying a word. Homer began to back away but Ben kept advancing without saying anything. Homer backed out of the door and began walking backward down the street as Ben kept advancing.

Homer went faster and faster, waving the hammer over his head, until he was running backward down the street with Ben a couple of steps behind him, reaching for him with his right hand. Ben couldn't quite catch Homer, but he did get a handful of Homer's shirt and ripped the pocket from it. At that point Ben stopped and turned back toward the blacksmith shop where Joe Baird was standing and watching.

Homer stopped running and stood panting for breath. Then he walked to his car hiccoughing nervously, tossed the hammer down on the ground, and drove away. Ben picked up the hammer and walked into the shop. He returned the hammer to Joe Baird, got the plowshare that Joe had welded, and went on his way.

Homer went home and gave his wife Mavis a black eye before supper. He didn't always beat up Mavis, just on those times when he'd been bested in a fight, or someone larger had called his bluff, or when he couldn't get anyone smaller in a fighting humor.

After he ate his supper alone, Mavis having retreated to the bedroom and closed the door, Homer drove back to Harlow's where he played poker until Harlow closed at midnight. When Homer got home, he found the house empty and Mavis's clothes gone. He went to bed alone.

The next day, Homer knocked on the door of Harlow's tavern.

"Whatta you want, Homer? I'm closed." Harlow said when he opened the door.

"Hows about some breakfast?" Homer asked.

"This ain't a restaurant. Go on up to Lloyd Gantt's if you want food."

"Lloyd don't like me. My wife's left me an' I'm hungry."

"Ya better learn to cook, Homer. I kin give you a beer but there ain't gonna be no food here till noon, an' ya don't need to come by then if ya don't like hamburgs." Harlow laughed shortly, "I don't make no money on eats."

"Yer sign says 'Beer **an**' Eats' both," Homer protested.

"Can't git a liquor license in Ohio 'thout servin' some food," Harlow said, "But it don't say the food's gotta be good. Now, you wanta beer or not? I got cleanin' up to do."

Homer went to work hungry, hung over, and surly to anyone who spoke to him that day. The next day was not much better, and after a few days of Homer's bad humor, his boss spoke to him.

"Yer stomach botherin' you, Homer?"

"Oh God, my stomach's like to kill me. Harlow's booze is bad enough, but his food is jist pure poison. An' I'm gittin' mighty sick of cold corn flakes fer breakfist."

"Why don't you go see if you kin patch things up with Mavis?"

"Ain't no use." Homer whined, "I tried goin' over there, but Lew won't let me in the house and Mavis won't come out. I'd a gone in anyway, but he's a old man an' I wouldn't wanta hurt him."

"Why don't you try agin? Wouldn't hurt and you've gotta do somethin'. I've had a couple of complaints about the way you've acted towards customers, an' I can't have that too long."

That evening after work, Homer drove his old Chevrolet over to the Evans house. He pulled up in front and blew the horn. He had always done this when he'd been dating Mavis, and she had always come running out to the car. Most of the neighbors figured that Homer just had bad manners, but some of them noticed that Homer was always just a little nervous around Lew; Homer often got the hiccoughs when he was nervous.

Lew Evans, Mavis's father, was a black browed Welshman who had left the mines in Wales when they were closed and come to Ohio to make a living. He was a little shorter than Homer and weighed a few pounds less, but his weight was all muscle, toned well by hard physical work all of his life. He had a deep pleasant voice with a soft refined accent, but was inclined to settle a disagreement with direct physical action if aroused.

Before Mavis and Homer were married, Lew made some attempts to prevent what he thought was a big mistake, but after the marriage no one ever heard Lew say a thing against his son-in-law.

Lew heard the horn as he was sitting at the kitchen table having a cup of tea. He leaned back in his chair so he could see out through the screen door and called to Mavis who was upstairs.

"That man of yours is outside, Mavis. Do you wish to see him or should I send him away before he runs his battery down?"

"Oh, I guess I may as well talk to 'im. I must sooner or later anyway. But I don't plan to go back with 'im."

Mavis went out to the car and stood by the driver's door as Lew watched from behind the screen door. The conversation continued for several minutes with Homer gesturing with both hands and Mavis shaking her head. Suddenly Homer reached out and grabbed Mavis's right wrist with his left hand. He pulled her close to the car and started driving away. Mavis had to step up on the running board to keep from being dragged under the rear wheel.

When Lew saw this he burst through the screen door and leaped into his own car to give chase.

Homer struggled to shift gears and steer with his right hand while holding Mavis with his left. Mavis meantime had reached into the car with her left hand and was pulling as hard as she could on the bottom of the steering wheel, trying to force the car into the ditch. The car swerved erratically as Homer tried to both steer and shift gears. The engine roared loudly because Homer had been unable to shift out of low gear. Everytime he tried to shift, he had to grab the wheel again quickly to prevent the car from going into the ditch. Mavis was struggling with the wheel and trying to break Homer's grip on her right wrist.

They had gone nearly a mile in this manner before Mavis succeeded in forcing the car into the ditch. The car scraped and bounced violently causing Homer to lose his grip on Mavis, who leaped to the roadway, falling on her hands and knees in the gravel. Homer gripped the wheel with both hands and brought the car to a stop with the right side leaning against the side of the ditch.

Lew caught up with them as Mavis was getting to her feet. He slid his car to a stop beside her and stepped out leaving the engine running.

"Are you hurt badly?" he asked, looking at her scraped hands and knees.

"No, I'm all right; just skinned up."

"Then you take this car and go find a telephone. Call the sheriff and tell him there's been an accident and ask him to send an ambulance. I'll go help the victim." Lew hitched up his pants with both hands and strode purposefully toward the car in the ditch. Homer was climbing out through the driver's window as Lew arrived.

When Homer went back to work a week later he still had a small bandage on his forehead and his eyes and lips were still a bit discolored and puffy. He chewed his food rather carefully and slowly. We didn't ask either Homer or Lew how it was that Homer got so banged up when the car wasn't damaged to speak of. We figured that Homer might be a bit sensitive about it and we just accepted the explanation that Lew had given the Deputy Sheriff when he'd arrived at the scene.

"He must have fallen." Lew had said.

Homer went back to eating corn flakes for breakfast and Harlow's greasy food for lunch and supper. He took to carrying a box of baking soda around with him, and the neighbors were all careful not to get in his way even when we knew he was sober. Homer seemed to be surly and belligerent all of the time and neighbors began to wonder when he would pick a fight with someone meaner than he was who would finish him off. Homer always seemed to be able to control his temper when he was with someone bigger than he was.

Along toward Christmas, Charley Black took on some help at his general store in Stoney Creek. Henry McAdams was a newcomer to Stoney Creek, a short fair skinned man of about thirty-five who could easily take first prize in a humility contest. He had a slight limp, from an old war wound some said, but Mac never said much about it. He was the type of man who seems to fit behind a counter and look so much like a part of the merchandise that you wouldn't recognize him anywhere else.

We noticed that Mavis began coming to the store more often than usual. She had filed for divorce and had been living at the Evans home while she looked for work. She kept the house tidy and did the washing and cooking for the family. Katy, her younger sister, was still in high school and Mrs. Evans did day work for the one wealthy family in our neighborhood. Mavis had been getting groceries a couple of times a week, but now she began to drop in for an item or two about every day.

Word must have gotten around to Homer but he professed not to care.

"Hell, she kin go where and when she wants fer all I keer. It makes me no never mind if she gits sweet on some half pint." Home declared.

One cold January day, just as it was getting dark, Homer drove up to the side of Charley Black's store and staggered a little as he got out of the car and made his way to the door. Mac was tending the store alone while Charley was at home for supper; business was usually slow at that time of day and there was only one customer in the store, Ben Phillips, who was sitting on the bench in the back by the stove.

Homer's face was red from the cold wind when he flung open the front door and almost fell into the store. He had no coat on and his flannel shirt was half unbuttoned. He grabbed an axe handle out of the hardware rack inside the door and looked around for Mac.

Mac had been adding up an order for Ben, and when he saw Homer pick up the axe handle he reached under the counter and picked up the old Luger pistol he had brought home from the Great War. Ben stepped back against the back wall of the store behind the stove.

Mac pointed the Luger at Homer and said, "Don't come no closer."

Homer stared at the large round hole in the end of the gun barrel and weaved back and forth. About 30 feet separated the men. Homer waved the axe handle around knocking over two glass jars of peppermint candies. This seemed to infuriate Homer and he smashed the axe handle down on the glass-enclosed candy case. At the same time, Mac fired one shot and a hole appeared in the floor at Homer's feet. Homer stopped waving the axe handle and stared at the hole for a few seconds, then he looked at the gun barrel again. He weaved from side to side and then staggered forward a couple of steps.

Mac fired a second shot. One of the panes of glass in the front window disappeared and the glass globe on the top of the gasoline pump outside shattered into little pieces. Mac whirled and ran toward the back door of the store.

As the top of the pump disappeared, Mavis and her sister Katy had just driven up to get two gallons of gasoline. They stared in surprise at the broken glass lying on the hood of the car. Suddenly Mac came running around the corner of the store, He swerved away as he saw the car and then, as he realized whose car it was, he swerved again and leaped for the car door. As Mavis opened it, he dived into the back seat.

"Drive away! Drive away!" both he and Mavis were shouting at Katy. She let in the clutch and they left with a spray of gravel.

As Mac turned to run, Homer raised the axe handle and started after him. As he went by the stove, Ben reached out a foot and tripped him.

Homer fell heavily face down, and the axe handle went spinning across the floor. He lay there for about half a minute without moving while Ben leaned against the wall and waited. Still without moving, Homer said, "I've lost her, ain't I?"

"I 'spect you have," Ben answered quietly.

"I've done ever'thin' I know how to do. They ain't no more use my tryin' to git her back?"

"Don't 'spect there is," Ben's voice was soft.

"That's Ben Phillips, ain't it?"

Without answering, Ben reached down and helped Homer to get up and into a chair by the stove. He then went to the front door, looked up and down the street, seeing no one. He closed the door which was still open to the cold night, and then went to the back door and closed it too.

"It's a sight and a shame the way folks go off leavin' doors open. It's gittin' cold in here." Ben muttered as he walked past Homer.

"You 'spect Charley'll let me pay for the damages in installments?"

"I wouldn't be 'sprised. 'Specially if you suggest it 'fore he does," Ben replied.

"Would you ask him fer me? He likes you better'n he does me."

"Sure, Homer. C'mon, I'll give you a ride home. You'd freeze walkin' home without a coat and you're in no shape to drive."

Mac never came back to Stoney Creek. We heard later that he got a job with a Great Lakes shipping firm in Toledo. Mavis stayed home until her divorce was final, and then she left Stoney Creek too. Some said she went to Toledo.

Doctor, Doctor, will I die?
Yes, my child, and so will I.

Old rope-skipping rhyme for children

I was getting ready for work one day while my youngest, Amy, was brushing her teeth before leaving for kindergarten. She called, "There's a wasp in the bathroom." She didn't sound alarmed but there had been a lot of hornets around our lawn that fall so I went to take care of it before Amy got stung. I looked around the bathroom but didn't see any wasp. Amy continued to brush her teeth unconcernedly. "I don't see any wasp," I said. "Right there," Amy said pointing to the wall. "That's not a wasp," I said, "That's a moth."

"That's the word!" Amy exclaimed and called loudly to her mother, "There's a moth in the bathroom."

A bit of experience with the software program PhotoShop® by Adobe® and a little experience with news media has taught me never to trust anything I see in print or on a screen. Everything can be faked, including photographs and sincerity.

REB

Just because you are paranoid doesn't mean they aren't out to get you.

Patrick Murray

Chestnuts Roasting by an Open Fire

About 50 years ago, when I was young, fancy free, and as footloose as the army would let me be, I frequently spent weekends at my Aunt Ethel's home near Annapolis, Maryland. She had a beautiful place on one of the inlets off the Chesapeake Bay and was most generous and hospitable. As a result she had many guests and often had parties.

One year Aunt Ethel hosted a Halloween party with a number of guests, among whom were my cousin Paul Baer* who was also in the army at the time, and some of his friends from his army base near Washington. Some of my friends and I were there from my army base in New Jersey and it was quite a nice congenial group.

Aunt Ethel often delegated part of the responsibilities for entertaining and refreshments to guests, and for this party, Paul and I had the refreshment detail. Included in the refreshments were roasted chestnuts which we placed on the hearth in front of the roaring fire. Unfortunately, before the evening had gotten a good start, it became obvious that those chestnuts were not going to be ready to eat until the following day sometime unless we took some other approach.

We put them on a cookie sheet and put them in the oven of the electric range in the kitchen. We set the heat on broil and went on about setting out hors d'oeuvres and pouring drinks. We didn't know how long it would take for the chestnuts to roast, but we planned to check them from time to time. It would certainly be faster than roasting them in front of the fire.

It was faster. In a few minutes, as I was pouring drinks, there was a sound like a shotgun going off in the oven. A big puff of smoke came out of the oven vent at the back of the stove and a second explosion occurred. I quickly turned off the oven burner.

Just then Aunt Ethel came hurrying into the kitchen to see what disaster had befallen her stove.

"Don't open the oven door!" I shouted.

Too late. Aunt Ethel had opened the door just as three or four more chestnuts exploded in her face.

"Close the oven door!" I shouted. Needlessly as it turned out.

Aunt Ethel had closed the door before any more chestnuts exploded. But all of the damage that was going to occur had already done so. There were shreds of chestnuts all over the kitchen and the shreds that had hit the oven burners were smoking up the kitchen air something wonderful.

Aunt Ethel was wearing a very striking pale green cashmere sweater which now was stippled thoroughly with little shreds of chestnut, pieces about the size of grains of rice. Her beautiful red hair was equally speckled with rice size shreds of chestnut and she was beginning to become irritated.

---

* Honest, that is his real name. I know I have the reputation of thinking up appropriate or interesting names for characters, but in this case, Paul's parents gave him that name before I was even born.

The chestnuts remaining in the oven were exploding now and again, but the main part of the noise had subsided a bit. Some of the guests had crowded into the kitchen to see what the noise was about and some of them had begun to laugh. With every step they were crushing shreds of chestnut into the floor which was becoming a bit sticky.

Aunt Ethel began to see the funny side of it when she learned that no permanent damage had been done to her stove in spite of the noise and smoke. Paul and I began to sweep up what we could of the chestnut shreds. The guests gave up the idea of roasted chestnuts and carried the other refreshments into the living room.

What with one thing and another, this was a party that all participants remembered. I never did have roasted chestnuts after I was old enough to remember, but I understand that they are quite tasty. I also understand now that one should punch a small hole in the shell before roasting them.

Incidentally, along that line, to prepare a hard "boiled" egg quickly, just put it in the microwave and set the timer for 90 seconds. The results will be somewhat similar to those we got with the chestnuts. The smell may be a bit different though.

I had to give your pancakes a shot with the
fire extinguisher. You want them or not?

New Tractor

As in most places, many of the humorous situations in Stoney Creek or the 1930's were laced with tragedy. Consider how the audience laughs at the clown who slips on a banana peel and breaks a leg. But even in the midst of disaster there are funny events.

Henry Sherman, known as Hank to everyone except his wife, had a modest farm about a mile and a half out of town. He worked hard and managed to show a little profit. One winter Hank decided to upgrade his farm and bought a new tractor to supplement his team of horses. The dealer delivered it one day late in March and Hank checked his fields every day to see when they would be dry enough to plow.

On the evening of April first Hank decided that the fields would be ready for him to try out his new tractor and plow the next day. He went out to the machine shed by the barn to get the tractor ready to go early the next morning. It was dark so he carried a lantern to help him see what he was doing; very few farms had electricity before the Rural Electrification Administration brought power, and Hank didn't have lights in the machine shed.

He set the lantern on the hood of the tractor and started to fill the tractor tank with gasoline.

That same evening I happened to be in town with my parents. I was in high school and had a driver's license and went anywhere the car did. My parents wanted to go to a movie but I chose to go on uptown to the pool parlor and barber shop to hang out with some of my buddies until time for the movie to let out.

There were a number of boys and men loafing and playing pool that evening when Hank came bursting into the pool room shouting "Fire! My place is on fire!"

"Sure it is," some of the men said, "April fool."

"It really is," Hank was nearly hysterical and his face was obviously burned. There were no eyebrows and what was left of his hat was pretty scorched. Hank didn't have a phone, so he had run to his car as soon as he picked himself up after the blast of gasoline explosion. He drove into town to get the fire truck to come help him save his barn; the machine shed and tractor were already gone, or would be by the time anyone got there.

All the men hurried out. Some went directly to Hank's farm to see what they could do. Two of my buddies went running down to the fire house with Ted Barry to get the fire truck. They were hoping to crank the siren on the way out of town.

Ted and the boys hurriedly opened the fire house door and Ted leaped to the driver's seat. He jammed one foot on the clutch and the other on the starter. The starter ground but the engine didn't start. Ted kept on grinding the starter and soon the smell of gasoline filled the fire house; he had flooded the engine.

He paused a few seconds, jammed the accelerator to the floor and ground the starter some more. Still nothing. Finally the starter ground more slowly and eventually quit altogether. Ted asked one of the boys to operate the accelerator while he got out and cranked the engine by hand.

Ted cranked and cranked until he was nearly exhausted. Just about then, one of the boys realized that in the excitement, Ted had failed to turn on the ignition. When that was turned on the engine started easily.

They went racing out of town with the siren sounding. When they got to the scene of the fire, the machine shed was still blazing but was obviously beyond saving. The men were throwing buckets of water on the nearby barn to keep it from burning and some of the men had already gotten the animals out of the barn. The sides of the barn were hot enough that the water was steaming as it hit the wood.

Ted got the hose from the fire truck hooked up to the pond north of the barn. [The ponds near the barn which some farms had served a dual purpose. They provided water for the animals and they provided what little fire protection the farms had.] Ted soon had a spray of water going on to the barn and what was left of the shed.

Soon after that I had to leave to go meet my parents when the movie let out so I never saw the end of the fire. The shed and tractor were a total loss but the barn and animals were safe. I assume that Hank had some insurance to help cover his losses because he remained farming there.

Poor Ted Barry took a remarkable amount of kidding about his ability to drive the fire truck, or at least about his ability to start the fire truck. Poor Hank learned that a lantern near open gasoline is a hazard. He was fortunate to be alive after being so close to the explosion, suffering only a few burns and some bruises where he was thrown out of the shed door by the blast. He never did that again.

The REA came through a year or so later and most farmers installed electric lights in their barns and out buildings.

An Immutable Law of Nature

If an appliance is going to fail, it always happens on Saturday afternoon

REB

No one can have a higher opinion of him than I have, and I think he's a dirty little beast.

W. S. Gilbert

I had a supervisor once for a brief period and this was my opinion of him and his ethics.

REB

A Service of your Local Government

Hank Sherman had another problem after he had recovered from the fire and had rebuilt his machine shed. The shed and chicken house nearby were being undermined, literally. Several groundhogs had moved in and had excavated their burrows under the buildings. The result was that the foundations were undermined and the buildings were sagging.

Hank discovered that it was not a simple matter to get rid of groundhogs. He tried gas by putting a hose from the exhaust of his new tractor, a replacement for the one that had blown up, into the burrows and running the engine for a while. He hoped that the carbon monoxide would kill the groundhogs and that no one would move in when they were gone. After several hours, Hank concluded that was enough to kill anyone. He was wrong.

He considered buying a cyanide bomb that the feed store sold to get rid of groundhogs but Hank was a little afraid that he might do grievous bodily harm to himself if he tried to use that. Cyanide is pretty potent poison and Hank was a little aftaid of it.

He next tried shooting the groundhogs. He found that a groundhog is very shy and doesn't like to show itself to humans, particularly armed and dangerous humans. Hank got tired of waiting for one, any one, to show himself. He waited for a long time, in vain. He tried this on several occasions but still no luck.

Someone suggested poison so he tried to think of something that groundhogs might eat that he could poison. Unfortunately the favorite food of the groundhogs was clover and there was a large field of clover just behind the shed and chicken house. It didn't seem practical to try to poison the whole field, so Hank gave that up.

Then he thought of a trap. He didn't dare set a regular animal trap because of the several cats and dogs around the place so he tried to find a trap he could use. He found a Hav-a-Hart® live trap in a catalog and decided to give that a try. This trap consisted of a wire cage large enough to hold a small dog with a trigger on which bait could be placed to tempt the victim into the trap. When the trigger was tripped, a door would drop down at the end of the cage and latch securely. The animal could see out readily and the wires were far enough apart that a really small animal could escape easily. It obviously would not do for mice or rats, but would be very good for groundhogs. That is, if one could tempt the groundhog into the trap and persuade it to trip the trigger.

Hank set the trap one evening behind the machine shed and crossed his fingers. He had debated on what to use for bait and finally settled on peanut butter, hoping that a groundhog might have a taste for something exotic after the plain fare of clover. Hank was always an optimist.

The next morning Hank checked the trap and found one of his terriers had a taste for peanut butter and had spent the better part of the night trapped in the cage. That evening Hank tried a different bait, celery, in hopes that the dog wouldn't be interested but the groundhog might.

The following morning Hank found one of his cats in the cage. The cat had been simply curious and had not eaten any of the celery but had inadvertently tripped the trigger and trapped itself anyway. Hank decided that celery wasn't all that great an idea either so that evening he baited his trap with a melon rind, figuring that neither the cat nor the dog would be interested in melon rind but that the groundhog might be drawn to the different smell.

As usual, first thing in the morning, Hank checked the trap to see what exciting things had happened overnight. This morning he was surprised and dismayed to find that the melon rind had tempted a skunk. Now Hank had a real dilemma; how to get the skunk out of the cage without getting himself sprayed. The skunk did not appear to be very happy about spending a few hours in the trap and the wires were plenty far apart for the skunk to take offensive action on anyone who approached. Hank's reactions had been pretty quick and he had ducked back around the corner of the shed before he had gotten hit when he first discovered the skunk.

Hank pondered the problem as he peered at the skunk from a safe distance. Several ideas occurred to him and he abandoned them all. None of the plans would result in the trap being fit to use again nor would they guarantee his not getting sprayed. Hank finally did what any red-blooded American rural citizen would do; he called his Township Trustee.

In most states the lowest ranking elected office in rural areas is the Township Trustee. He has various civic duties such as seeing that the roads are cleared in snowy weather, keeping the grass mowed in the cemetery, and providing services that government entitles the citizens to such as removing skunks from live traps. Hank had never thought that this was a service he was entitled to but he couldn't think of anything else.

Harry Logan, the Trustee, arrived shortly after Hank called. He assured Hank that he could get the skunk out of the trap without damage to the trap, his pride, or his clothes. Harry would not guarantee no damage to the skunk, however, and he did suggest that Hank might provide a tarpaulin or blanket that he no longer needed for anything else.

Hank provided an old horse-blanket. He no longer had horses so he figured that the blanket could be sacrificed. Harry held the blanket stretched out widely in front of himself and moved carefully around the corner of the machine shed. He moved slowly, keeping the trap completely out of sight and himself completely out of sight of the skunk. When he got close enough, he draped the blanket over the trap, completely covering the trap with the skunk inside. Then he carefully wrapped the blanket around the trap making sure that all sides, ends, and bottom were completely covered. He then tied binder twine around the blanket to secure it, picked up the trap, skunk and all, and put the package in the back of his pickup truck.

"I'll bring the trap back to you tomorrow," Harry said as he drove away.

"Don't bother," Hank said, "I don't think I'll be usin' it any more."

Hank never asked what Harry did to the skunk; he didn't want to know. The groundhogs continued to live in peace. Hank simply shored up the sagging buildings and reinforced the foundations. Wildlife won again.

Savages

On the outskirts of Stoney Creek there was a small group of houses occupied by some of the really poor folks. Everyone in Stoney Creek was hard pressed for funds during the dark days of the depression in the 1930's, but the Savage family was really poor, even by Stoney Creek standards.

They also had the reputation, deserved or not I leave up to you, of being a bit thick. The modern term for that condition is "specially challenged" or some other similar euphemism for slow witted. In any case, the children did below average work in school.

When I was in first grade, one of the Savage boys was in my class. He had completed first grade at least once before but that didn't give him a great deal of advantage over others in the class. "Charles" was the name the teacher called him; everyone else called him "Dynamite" or "Dynie" for short. Dynie was good natured and friendly and everyone liked him, but he was not only a bit short in intelligence, he was also short in stature. He was about 2/3 the size of the average child his age.

Early in the first grade, Miss Brown our teacher, had everyone line up across the front of the room and, in turn, count to ten. The first one to do that was on his own, the second had an advantage, and the last one in line had a real advantage of having heard all the others recite. But that didn't seem to help Dynie much. He was dead last.

Miss Brown called on him to count. He hesitated so Miss Brown prompted him.

Teacher: "One"

Dynie: "One"   A long pause.

Teacher: "Two"

Dynie: "Two"   Another long pause.

Teacher: "Three"

Dynie: "Onetwothreefourfivesixseveneightnineten"   So fast that even Miss Brown was stunned. It sounded like one word.

Dynie repeated each of the lower grades several times. He stayed in school until he was grown. Even at full growth, Dynie was somewhat under five feet and probably weighed about 75 pounds. After he got tired of going to school he wandered the streets and roads of the countryside, visiting with anyone he saw. He was cheerful and pleasant, but his conversation was not what one would call sparkling. I suppose that the way the community cared for him was as good as any.

The community cared for all of the Savage family essentially the same way. That is, they left them alone, provided enough support that they could have enough to eat, clothes to wear, and had a roof that didn't leak. The men worked at odd jobs as they were available and the women cared for the households.

One of the Savage women, the matriarch of the tribe, came walking into town one cold windy day to buy some groceries. She was red faced and her nose was dripping from the bitter cold wind she had faced directly into on the mile or so walk to the store.

"That wind is pretty strong today, ain't it?" the storekeeper asked.

"Yes," she replied, "An' I sure hope it changes direction before I go home."

Dynie had an older brother Andrew who was nearly average in size and intelligent enough that he was eligible for the draft in the early part of WWII. Andrew came home for a brief furlough after his basic training and on one of his evenings home decided to go to Mt. Pleasant for a little celebration with a friend.

Andrew was driving his friend's car, a 1933 or 34 Ford V-8, one of the favorites of young people because it was faster than many other cars of that time. It also had a feature that no other car had until the Naderite nutfudges forced all cars to have it. The ignition key was on the steering column and when the ignition was off, the steering wheel was locked.

On the way to Mt. Pleasant, the friend played a joke on Andrew; he reached over and turned the ignition off. The car slowed slightly but not soon enough. They left the highway on a curve and flew down a slope into a pasture field where the car flipped a few times before it stopped. The friend survived the accident; Andrew did not.

Because Andrew was in the army, he had a $10,000 life insurance policy which was effective no matter how the policy holder died. The Savage family suddenly found that they had more relatives than they had ever heard of, all needy. They also had a number of advisers on how to spend the money.

Fortunately, a wise and kindly county judge also lived in our town and he was well aware of the situation. He had the beneficiaries declared incompetent and arranged for the insurance money to be doled out to the family in modest monthly payments rather than a lump sum. In this way Andrew's insurance provided a monthly support payment for the family for the rest of their lives so that they could live in the manner to which they were accustomed without worry. Andrew thus became the primary support for the family, a role he perhaps would not have chosen had he any say about it.

Dynie also had a younger brother, Franklin. He was not named for President Roosevelt as many people thought; he was born before Roosevelt was elected. Franklin was about average size and had about the same intelligence level as the rest of the family.

A neighbor of the Savages was a highway patrolman who had known the family for a number of years. He was only a few years older than Franklin, and at the time of the following incident had been a patrolman for four or five years.

One night Franklin had been drinking a bit more than he should have and became somewhat unruly in the pool room uptown. The proprietor of the pool room called the State Highway Patrol; Stoney Creek did not have a full time constable. The patrolman on duty happened to be the neighbor of the Savages and he had no difficulty in persuading Franklin to get into the patrol car for a ride to Mt. Pleasant for a night in the jail to sober up.

As they approached Mt. Pleasant, Franklin had some second thoughts about a night in jail and became reluctant about going on into town. He began to argue with the patrolman who had allowed him to sit in the front seat beside him rather than put him in the back. It didn't really matter anyway because there was no grill between the seats; the patrol car was not normally used for transporting prisoners unless there were two or more patrolmen present. In this case, because the patrolman knew Franklin, it seemed unimportant.

In the course of the argument, Franklin reached over and pulled the patrolman's hat down over his eyes. Ohio State Highway Patrolmen wore the "Smoky the Bear" type hats at that time. All in all, this was not a very smart thing to do because they were proceeding along the highway at normal speed, but Franklin must have thought it was a good idea at the time.

The newspaper account of the incident reported that "the patrolman subdued the prisoner" and they proceeded on to the jail. I don't know any more about it, but I suspect that Franklin was somewhat contrite about the whole thing. He was not normally a belligerent person, but he couldn't hold his liquor.

I have sometimes wondered how the patrolman subdued the prisoner, but he never said. I'll bet it was exciting for a few seconds though.

More Xenophobia

San Francisco is like granola. Take away the fruits and the nuts and all you have left are the flakes.

Unknown

In Marseilles they make half the toilet soap we consume in America, but the Marseillaise have only a vague theoretical idea of its use, which they have obtained from books of travel.

Mark Twain

In visiting the various tourist spots in England, it is easy to spot the German tourists. The men wear their jackets over their shoulders like capes, and they obviously abstain from the use of underarm deodorants.

REB

I hate to spead rumors, but what else can one do with them?

TV commercial in Britain

First shade: There's one good thing about Hell.
Second shade: What is that?
First shade: We can smoke.

The Devil in Texas

The Devil I'm told in hell was chained
And a thousand years he there remained.
And he never complained nor did he moan,
But he determined to start a hell of his own.

So he asked the Lord if He had on hand
Anything left when He made the land.
The Lord said, "Yes, I've plenty on hand
                And I've left it down on the Rio Grande."

The Devil went down to look at the place,
    And what he saw brought a smile to his face.
    "It's already about as good as can be.
    With a few little touches, it'll suit to a tee."

He scattered tarantulas over the roads,
Put thorns on the cactus and horns on the toads,
He sprinkled the sands with millions of ants,
So the man who sits down must wear soles on his pants.

He lengthened the horns of the Texas steer,
And added an inch to the jack rabbit's ear.
He put mouths full of teeth in all of the lakes,
And under the rocks he put rattlesnakes.

He hung thorns and brambles on all of the trees,
    He mixed up the dust with jiggers and fleas,
    The rattlesnake bites you, the scorpion stings,
The mosquito delights you by buzzing his wings.

The heat in the summer's a hundred and ten,
Too hot for the Devil and too hot for men.
And all who remain in that climate soon bear
Cuts, bites, and stings, from their feet to their hair.

He quickened the buck of the bronco steed,
        And poisoned the feet of the centipede;
                The wild boar roams in the black chapparral;
                It's a hell of a place that we've got for a hell.

Anonymous

A Few News Items

Inmates Botch Jailbreaks and other news

In Cambridge, MA, A prisoner really messed up a poorly planned jailbreak when torn-up sheets he had lowered toward the ground in the hope of hoisting a gun from the street below were far too short to reach.

The prisoner, whose cell was on the 18th floor of the Middlesex County Courthouse, reportedly tried to drop the line to his girlfriend and a friend who were to attach a .22 caliber handgun.

Unfortunately the line got stuck a few floors from the prisoner's jail cell window. Police already knew about the plan nearly a week before and were watching anyway.

In a separate incident, three convicted killers attempted to escape from a Dallas, TX, jail by braiding sheets together and lowering the "rope" from an upper floor. As they were descending, a disgruntled prisoner who had not been included in the escape plan, used a razor blade and cut the sheets. The three escapees fell several floors and one suffered a broken bone and was hospitalized. The others were treated for abrasions and bruises and returned to their cells.

In Florida, a jury cleared Kmart of negligence in the case of a thirteen-year-old boy who was killed when a twelve hundred-pound soda machine fell on him.

The boy was rocking the machine outside a store in 1995 when it tipped over and fell on him. The boy's parents sued Kmart for putting the machine on a sloped floor without being securely anchored.

Witnesses testified that in several months before his death, the boy had broken two windshields, burned a friend with a lighter, and threatened to hit his mother.

[He had apparently been trying to destroy the soda machine and was successful beyond his wildest dreams. Editor.]

Police reported that several grocery store employees had caught a shoplifter Monday and held him. Suddenly a woman entered the store, hit one of the captors and sprayed others with pepper spray.

But the captors were stubborn and wouldn't free the suspect, so the woman left the store, got her car and rammed it into the store's foyer several times. She threatened to run everyone over if they didn't let the man go.

The captors released him, and the woman then ran over the man. From underneath the car, the man scrambled out and grabbed onto the hood ornament as the car was backing out of the store. He then managed to get into the car before it pulled away. Police say he had tried to steal a bottle of liquor and a box of detergent. There were no arrests.

[Obviously the woman was really eager to get what he was trying to steal, but I wonder which of the two items she wanted more. Perhaps she had some clothes that were really dirty. Sounds as though they had been watching the movie *Raising Arizona*.]

In still another incident according to police it was the incessant chatter of the victim, that caused the man who was stealing her truck to give up and leave. A woman intercepted the man before he could drive away, and despite his having a gun, held him and began talking nonstop. She reported later that, "He sounded irritated. He said, 'I can't believe how this is going. This is like something out of the movies.'" She finally gave him a T-shirt to wipe his fingerprints off the truck and he fled.

Defense Mechanism

One evening a few days before Christmas, the door bell rang. When I answered I found one of our neighbors standing there in tears. I thought the worst; her husband is known to have a heart problem. It turned out that she was not unhappy, she was furious.

"We are going away over Christmas and the young man who was going to stay with our dog just called to say that he has changed his mind. Now we have no one to stay with the dog. Could you go over a couple of times a day and see that he has food and water and can go out into the back lawn each day?"

The chores were not onerous. The dog slept in the laundry room which was warm and during the day he could go between the garage and the back lawn which was fenced in. The garage was not heated, but there was a dog bed in the garage which he could use when he wished. But then the weather got really cold and the garage was pretty uncomfortable for him.

I started letting him out for a while in the morning and then again in the evening, shutting him in the laundry room where he had a warm bed, food, and water the rest of the time. This seemed to suit the dog all right and all was well.

One morning as we were taking our dogs for their morning walk, we stopped over at the neighbor's house to let him out while we went around the block with our two. Marty held our two dogs at their back gate while I let their dog out into the back lawn. He came around to see what our dogs were up to and sniffed noses with one of ours. Just then, our terrier gave a lunge and a roar at the gate where the neighbor dog was standing.

He suddenly stood absolutely rigid, completely stiff-legged, and fell over sideways, as rigid as a board. Marty and I and both of our dogs just stood and stared, totally amazed at this. Our dogs stared at the suddenly rigid dog lying on his side while Marty and I thought quickly, "What on earth can we tell our neighbors when they return? That we killed their dog? What kind of a lie can I think of that they will believe?"

I then picked up the stiff body and carried it into the garage. I laid him gently in his bed and stood thinking. Then I noticed that he moved a little. As I watched, in less than thirty seconds the dog seemed to relax, got to his feet and started out into the back lawn again.

We watched as he walked along the fence, ignoring our two dogs, sniffing here and there as though nothing had happened. Our two dogs, Marty, and I watched him without comment as he wandered off into the back part of the lawn. Then we continued on our walk with our dogs.

When we got back from our walk, I went over alone and let the dog back into his laundry room and warm bed. He ate his breakfast as though this was the sort of thing he did every day and everything seemed normal. We concluded that this was his defense mechanism — shock. If so, it certainly worked well.

I wanted to ask the neighbors when they returned if this had ever happened before, but I couldn't think of a way to do it without telling them that we had nearly killed their dog.

One Sunday morning our pastor was trying to explain the difference between predestination and foreknowledge, illustrating his explanation with a demonstration. He called a group of children to the front of the church and told them that the difference was whether God could control a person's decision by making them choose one thing over another, which would eliminate free will, a form of predestination, or whether God simply knew ahead of time what the decision would be. He selected one little girl, Charlene, who was about eleven and asked her to step out into the hall for a minute and wait until he called her back in.

As soon as she was out of the sanctuary, the pastor told the other children that when Charlene came back in he would offer her a choice between a nice peach in one hand or a bag of M&M candies in the other. He then asked the children which Charlene would choose. All but one of the children said, "The candy" knowing what they would choose. One little girl said, "I don't think so". All the others laughed at her and the pastor said, "Now, we know what Charlene will choose. That is foreknowledge. But we won't tell her what to choose."

He then called Charlene back in from the hall and offered her the choice of a peach or M&M candy. Charlene, without any hesitation, said, "I'll take the peach."

The congregation laughed and the pastor looked extremely embarrassed. When the laughter died down, the one little girl who had said, "I don't think so" spoke again. "I told you so", she said. This caused even more laughter.

The problem with the illustration was that the little girl who knew what the choice would be had a little more knowledge about Charlene's likes and dislikes than the pastor did. She had been a good buddy of Charlene's for several years and knew that Charlene didn't care much for candy and sweets but she did like fruit.

So much for inadequate foreknowledge.

More Quips and Quotes

Only men who are not interested in women are interested in women's clothes. Men who like women never notice what they wear.

Anatole France

A word fitly spoken is like apples of gold in pictures of silver.
Proverbs 25:11

Taxi! Taxi!

Almost anyone
(futilely) on a rainy day in
New York City

Every word of God is pure: He is a shield unto them that put their trust in Him. Add thou not to His words, lest He reprove thee, and thou be found a liar.
Proverbs 30: 5-6

The pictures on this page were drawn by Charles Dana Gibson about 100 years ago.

Do not rob the poor, because he is poor, or crush the afflicted at the gate; for the Lord will plead their cause and despoil the life of those who despoil them.

Proverbs 22: 22-23

[It might be pointed out that it is a waste of time to rob the poor anyway; they don't have much to steal. Rob the rich.]

A word processor is an aid to those who must eat their words.

Anonymous

User stupidity is an essential characteristic for a good documenter of software.

Tom Wyant

You can imagine my embarrassment when I killed the wrong guy.

attributed to Joe Valachi

This drawing is by F. H. Townsend and was published in *Punch* in 1909. Townsend was editor of *Punch* for a number of years and contributed many drawings to the magazine. He and Charles Dana Gibson were contemporaries.

Joe Valachi was an informer against the Mafia, for whom he had worked for many years. He was in prison on a life sentence for murder, the sentence having been reduced from death because he had informed on other members of the mob. He was later told that the mob had paid a certain enforcer who was in the same prison with Joe a fee for killing Joe. Because he knew the enforcer slightly, Joe decided to take action first and one day in the prison yard he cornered the man and stabbed him to death. Only then did Joe discover that the man he had killed was not the enforcer but merely a prisoner who looked very much like the enforcer. Joe was dreadfully embarrassed that he had made such a mistake.

Don't be so depressed, Robert. You're not obsolete just because your computer is obsolete.

As he came forth from his mother's womb, naked shall he return to go as he came, and shall take nothing of his labor, which he may carry away in his hand.

Ecclesiastes 5:15

Chocolate is Poison

Chocolate is poison to dogs. How many times have you heard this? I heard it all my life until I was about fifty years old. Maybe it is true for certain dogs that are allergic to chocolate.

When my family and I moved to Virginia we bought a puppy to help our two daughters' loneliness in a new home. We already had a six year old terrier but Marty and I thought that a puppy would help the girls. So we bought a Standard Schnauzer puppy about four months old.

The girls remembered the cute and cuddly puppy that our older dog had been when we got her. Pooka, as we named the new puppy, was truly a mischeivous spirit in animal form, the definition of pooka. Pooka was not what the girls expected. Pooka may have been cute, if you define cute as a thirty pound chunk of rough and raucus shaggy bundle of energy, but she wasn't cuddly. Pooka was about two thirds grown, on her way to a normal adult weight of forty five pounds, had legs like tree trunks, prick ears, a short tail, and boundless energy.

We got Pooka in July. About Christmas time that year, she had attained her full growth and was a full member of the family. She had adapted well and got along very well with the older dog in the family and with all the people.

That year, along with the other gifts under the tree was a two pound box of chocolate mints, the sort of candy one sees served after dinner at a fine restaurant. The box was long and slender and the chocolates were thin wafers of mint cream covered generously with rich chocolate.

The morning after Christmas we discovered that we had forgotten and left the box of candy under the tree and now it was just a few pieces of cardboard and candy wrappers. Pooka had found it and devoured the whole box of candy plus about half the wrapping. Two full pounds of chocolate candy, about the equivalent weight ratio as if an adult person had consumed about eight pounds of chocolate candy in one sitting. Enough to make one sick at least.

If Pooka suffered any ill effects from the candy we couldn't notice it. She ate a normal breakfast and seemed to feel fine all day. As to long term bad effects, we couldn't be sure, but she lived for more than fifteen years after that and never seemed to have any problems. So much for chocolate being poison to dogs.

Pooka in her winter coat   Pooka in her summer coat

Book Five
Olio

(No, it's not a cookbook.)

The author and his lifelong traveling companion.

My dictionary defines "olio" thus:
1. A heavily spiced stew of meat, vegetables, and chickpeas.
2. (a) A mixture or medley, a hodgepodge. (b) A collection of various or artistic
   works or musical pieces; miscellany.
I use the second meaning for this part of the book and I hope it is spiced to suit
you

Of all the things I have lost, I miss my memory the most.

Pat Anderson.

My wife and I have a good working relationship. I start a sentence and she
finishes it.

Anonymous

The restaurant says that if you recover you can have a free dinner next time.

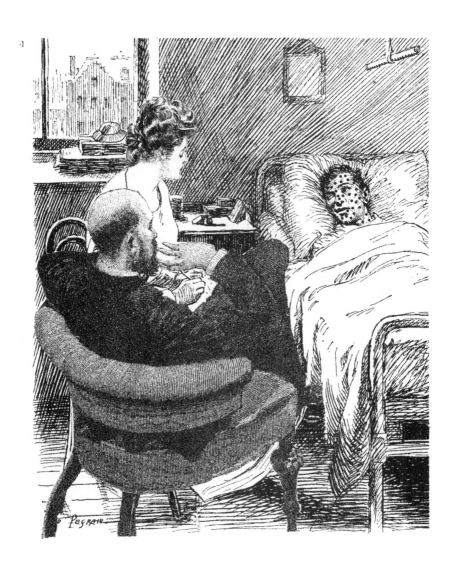

Visitor: **I knew a man had that once. Poor chap
never did get over it.**

Natural Laws

The following are natural laws which are usually phrased in slightly different words.

Schizophrenia sure beats dining alone.
Unknown

The difference between genius and stupidity is that genius has its limits.
Unknown

Never attribute to malice that which can be adequately explained by stupidity.
Ernie Doczy

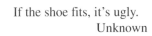

If the shoe fits, it's ugly.
Unknown

Cleanliness is next to impossible.
Unknown

The Ninety-Ninety Rule

The first 90% of a project takes 90% of the time. The last 10% of the project takes the other 90%.

If the facts do not conform to the theory, they must be discarded.

True wealth is not so much having talent, industry, and a bit of luck, so much as it is having a lot of money.

Laws of Thermodynamics

There are three laws of thermodynamics which are unbreakable, contrary to the beliefs of those journalists who from time to time tout some new perpetual motion machine. These laws can be stated in formal manner or in somewhat less formal phrasing, as follows:

- Heat always runs downhill. (Heat energy always moves from the hotter to the cooler body.)
- You can't get something for nothing. (You cannot get more energy out of a system than you put into it.)
- You can't even do that well. (Because of entropy, you can't get quite as much energy out of a system as you put into it.)

I have heard of a fourth law of thermodynamics which says that everything takes longer and costs more.

Research finds new fast way to correct bunions without surgery

Here are two examples of what happens when advertising copy writers don't review the work of the artists.

Ernie Doczy

No! I can't be bothered with any crazy engineer. I've got a battle to fight.

This is the fairgrounds of the Jackson County Fair in West Virginia ca. 1927. The photographer is unknown and the print shown here is actual size of the print I have. The only identification on the print is "Bollinger's Studio" embossed in the lower right margin of the print. The date cannot be much earlier than 1927, a few of the cars appear to be about 1926 or 27 models and I can identify only one car that might be a 1928 Model A Ford. All the others appear to be older than that.

This must have been the first year or so for the "new" fairgrounds. Prior to about 1926 the fair was held in the large open field belonging to Carroll Greene in Kenna, WV, my wife's uncle. It was just across the road from his home and was used for a number of years for the local fair. Some dissatisfaction was expressed the last year it was held there because of the congestion and difficulty of finding a place to park. If there were as many cars at the Kenna location as there are in this picture, I can certainly understand the complaints. It is a large open field, but not as large as the one in this picture.

Notice the airplane in the center of the race track infield. Many times during the 1920's, "barnstorming" pilots would come to gatherings of this type and offer airplane rides of five or ten minutes in their open cockpit biplanes. This practice continued up into the 1930's and I can remember seeing a plane in a large open field near my home when I was very small. The pilots tried to find a field that was reasonably flat, reasonably smooth, and reasonably clear of trees at the ends. It would be nice if the length of the field ran east and west, the prevailing winds being from the west, but the pilots weren't too choosy. The planes were pretty forgiving, having large wheels on the landing gear and fairly soft springing on the undercarriage.

The fares were probably about a dollar a minute for rides, pretty steep rates considering the cost of living at the time. Rates for plane rental today are not a great deal more than that and even instruction time is not much more. Consider that the cost of nearly everything is about fifteen times as much now as it was then, either the cost of flights was extraordinarily high then, or it is a real bargain today.

Notice the predominance of Model T Fords in the picture. There are a few other makes which I cannot identify and there appears to be one Model A Ford coupe which came out in late 1927. Most of the Model T's seem to be open touring cars with the cloth top, one of which seems to have been removed. At least it is put down but I can't see it folded up at the rear of the car so I guess that it has been removed.

Those tops, as I have heard my Dad tell it, were very prone to cracking if they were put up and down much so most people left them up all the time. Plenty of air came in from the open sides anyway. There were side curtains available to cut down on the air or rain coming in, but they were far from completely water or air proof. The gas tank on the touring car was under the front seat. The gravity feed for fuel necessitated backing up steep grades, but reverse gear was stronger than even low forward gear anyway. A bit slow though, but hey, it was better than nothing.

<u>Hustling Paw Tucker</u>

Paw Jumps to Conclusions

Paw gives
some advice
on economy

Paw uses all the tricks to postpone the evil hour.

A rose by any other name would smell as sweet.

Maw and the north wind make up Paw's mind.

A farm problem that's hard to let go of.

Paw's not slipping — it's just the heat.

At least he didn't forget the groceries.

This one had to have been drawn during World War II. Note the reference to tire rationing It was probably early in the war because Paw was unused to riding a horse. Later in the war it wouldn't have seemed so odd.

For variety, Paw gets a bucket of berries instead of milk.

Maybe Bossie likes the new milkmaid.

Spring
time is
painting
time.

Paw does his Christmas shopping.

Paw's on a diet — but what kind?

That's what he gets for cheating on Santa Claus.

Paw would rather eat than talk.

This was one of the very last that Caroline drew, some twentytwo years after Ray died.

**Mr. Bell says he feels much better since he
quit taking those pills you gave him.**

Another Traveler's Tale

A couple in Ohio had occasion to fly out of the Columbus airport on a commercial flight and planned to leave their car in the multi-story parking garage at the airport. They arrived rather close to flight time and hurried as they left the car with the luggage. Briefly they noted the location of the car by spotting a sign nearby with a large figure five on it.

They had a pleasant trip and returned refreshed after a few days vacation. As they took their bags into the garage, the husband said, "Where did we leave the car, do you remember?"

"Oh yes," the wife replied, "On level five."

They rode the elevator to level five and began looking for the car without success. After looking for a while, the husband said, "Are you sure it was level five we were on? Did you see the sign?"

"Oh, yes," said his wife,"The sign had a big five on it — there's one right over there."

The husband said, "That sign says 'Speed Limit 5 MPH.' and they are all over the garage."

"Oops," said his wife.

They went to the security guard and explained the problem. The guard was very understanding. He got the golf cart that he used to patrol the garage and they rode with him up and down the aisles until they found their car.

I've been pondering on one of life's great mysteries. Where did the first seedless orange come from?

Charming Personalities

This picture has always fascinated me. I have had it for at least 40 years or more and have told all kinds of stories about it. I don't even remember where or how I got it, but I probably bought it at a novelty store somewhere. It also is probably posed because I find it incredible that four real moonshiners would pose willingly for a photographer. They do look authentic though.

Doesn't the one on the right look friendly? And the one second from the right looks a bit thick. I knew a man like the one on the left; he was in my platoon in basic training. He was sent home after basic training because the army considered him "inept". He could strip an M1 rifle down to the tiniest screw and put it back together again with no trouble and he qualified as expert on the rifle range, but he couldn't get his uniform correct to save his soul. He was the only man I ever knew who could put on his ammunition belt backwards, inside out, twisted, and up-side-down, all at the same time. I wondered at the time if he was really stupid or just smart enough to know how to get out of the army.

Culture Shock

In 1760, an Englishman named Wright arrived in Savannah, Georgia, to take over his duties as Colonial Governor. He had been given the choice of either Georgia or Nova Scotia by the Royal Commissioners in London, and because Mr. Wright did not like cold weather, he chose Georgia. He arrived there in August.

He thought he would die! He took to carrying a large umbrella around all the time as a sun shade and he hung a thermometer from it to show to anyone who expressed any interest just how hot it was and tell them how miserable he was.

In 1782, the control of the colonies passed to the new United States and former Colonial Governor Wright was looking for another job. He was offered and accepted Nova Scotia. He arrived there in February. After twenty-two years in Savannah, he thought he would die!

Famous last words: "Hey, guys! Watch this!"

Bumper sticker seen in Maryland:

SUPPORT SEARCH & RESCUE
 GET LOST

Even a fool, when he holdeth his peace, is counted wise: and he that shutteth his lips is esteemed a man of understanding.

Proverbs 17:28

A man with a black eye was explaining to a friend how he got the shiner.

"I was talking to a guy in a bar last night and I'm a little hard of hearing. He said, "Shut up!" and I thought he said "Stand up.""

Model T Ford

The Model T in the picture was a bit different from most cars of that day. The T had an unusual door arrangement. There was a door **behind** the front seats on the right side. I don't remember if there was a door on the driver's side, but I know that if there was, it was in the same position as the one on the right. In general, Henry didn't hold with a door for the driver on anything but coupes. The front seats on this model had a narrow space between them for the driver and front seat passenger to get into their seats, much like some airplanes today.

The windows lowered about as much as is shown in the picture; they did **not** wind down and I don't remember if there was a half-open position. Note how the windshield is split horizontally and is hinged at the top to open; so much for safety. It was not safety glass either and just as on the touring cars and coupes, the top half opened outward to admit a blast of air and bugs. The visor was covered with the same "leatherette" material as the roof. The battery box on the running board held a six (?) volt "hot-shot" battery, a dry cell battery to be used only for starting when the car was cold. As soon as it was running, the driver switched the ignition key to the magneto position and the magneto took over for the spark. There was no generator. When the car was warm, a person could crank the engine fast enough for the magneto to provide enough spark to start the car. Sometimes, when the car was warm, if you switched the key to the "hot-shot" position, the engine would start without having to be cranked.

Note the funny door handle that looks like a stirrup and the rounded rear window. It didn't have much of a heater but the closed car was sure better than a touring car in the winter.

One of the neighbors had a closed Model T which had glass windows but the top was cloth, typical of all cars until the middle 1930's. He was blasting stumps of trees out of his pasture one day and used perhaps a little too much dynamite. The ground around Stoney Creek was full of rocks and gravel that had been gouged out of Lake Erie in the last ice age and one of the large rocks flew through the air and came down right through the roof of his Model T.

The winters in Stoney Creek could get pretty cold and T's were notorious for hard starting in cold weather. To compound the problem, the lubrication system for T's did not include an oil pump; the bearings were lubricated by what was called a splash system. This used a small spoon on the connecting rod that dipped into the oil in the pan on every revolution and splashed oil on the bearings.

The oil had a fairly high viscosity, no multigrade oils in those days, and when it was cold a man could stand on the crank and the engine wouldn't turn over. Farmers, at least, would soak corncobs in kerosene and light them under the oil pan to warm the oil before trying to start the car in cold weather. One of my friends from childhood told me about the time his older brothers lit the corncobs under the car one morning and then went to milk the cows while the engine warmed up enough to start. They took a little too long and the wooden floor boards of the car caught on fire. The floor boards were pretty easy to remove though so I suppose they saved the car by simply pulling the boards out and dousing them.

Henry Ford was very clever at saving money in the manufacture of his cars. He bought some of the parts for the cars from outside vendors and insisted that the parts be shipped in wooden boxes. The boards used for the boxes were cut and shaped so that the boxes, when empty, could be easily dismantled and the boards used without any further modification as floor boards for the Model T.

The old story about Henry saying that a Ford buyer could have any color he wanted as long as it was black is true for several years as far as it goes, but there was a good sound economic reason for it. Until about 1923 when duPont came out with what they called Dulux lacquer, only black paint was durable enough to suit Henry and dried fast enough that the Ford painters could keep up with the production line.

When other colors would dry as fast and last as long as the black, Ford cars could be obtained from the factory in several colors. The fenders and running boards on all Fords were always painted black when they left the factory, no matter what color the rest of the car was until about 1933.

Up until about the mid 1920's, Ford used unusually narrow tires with only a three inch cross section. This made very narrow ruts in soft dirt but it also allowed the wheels to drop into very narrow ruts in the road or pavement. This could lead to some interesting developments.

For example, Walter Lewis carried the mail for a number of years in the country north of Centerburg, Ohio. He used a horse and buggy for quite a long time but eventually graduated to the use of a Model T Ford touring car.

One lovely summer afternoon he asked his wife Katie if she would like to take a ride and he would show her some of the areas where he delivered the mail. Katie was not too sure about the new "Contraption", as she called it but she agreed to go.

His regular mail route was up State Route 314 and into the surrounding areas. Just north of Centerburg at the water tower, the railroad crossed Rt. 314 at a very oblique angle. It was a rather rough railroad crossing and full of ruts so it was advisable to cross at a leisurely speed. When Uncle Walter hit it at a pretty good clip, the narrow tires hit the tracks at an oblique angle. The Ford spun side- wise and started going down the track bumping violently at every cross tie.

Katie was screaming for Walter to do something—what, neither she nor he was sure! Suddenly a steam engine pulling a passenger train appeared and Walter yelled "Jump!" Katie opened the door, looked down and refused to jump. Walter gave her a shove and out she went, rolling down the bank along the track into the thistles and nettles that grew there. She smashed her favorite hat and tore its veil beyond redemption.

Walter jumped from the driver's side in time to avoid being run down, and after the train passed, he yelled for Katie in a sheer panic. She yelled back, "I'll never ride in that car again"

This actually was stating the obvious. There was very little left of the car after the train took it down the track several hundred feet, scattering pieces all along the way. Neither Walter nor Katie was hurt—scratches and bruises—but Katie's dignity suffered for some time. Walter loved to tease Katie and repeated the whole story for years, each time enhanced a little. Katie bemoaned the loss of her favorite hat and riding veil but she could never stop Walter from telling and retelling the story.

I had occasion one time to send a facetious question to a friend in Spain. I asked him what the Spanish call gasoline, given that the English call it petrol and the French call it essence, a rather romantic name for a prosaic material.

He sent a reply via email:

The Spanish name for gasoline is "gasolina". The feminine gender and the price (comparable with 24 carats gold) guarantee romanticism.

Interesting enough is that "gasoleo" means diesel and this actually puts in trouble non Spanish speaking people when they land in a gas station (you better don't know for experience what happens when you pump diesel into the tank of your gasoline car).

Actually what happens is that, provided you had about a half tank of gasoline in the tank already, you get a lot of smoke and a fair amount of "ping" as the diesel fuel mixed with gasoline burns in your engine. It doesn't do permanent damage as a rule but it is embarrassing as you drive along trailed by a smoke screen for miles and miles and miles. If your tank was nearly empty when you pumped in diesel fuel, the car may be reluctant to start at all.

Gratitude

"You hear what the weather forecast was just now on the radio, Otty?" his wife asked as she put his breakfast on the table.

"Nah," he replied, "I never listen to what them radio boys have to say."

"Well," his wife went on, "He says that there's a lot of rain comin' in the next few days and them beans need harvestin'. They'll be in the mud if you don't git 'em off pretty quick."

Otto's soy beans were ready for harvest. Most of the leaves had fallen off the stems and the bean pods were dry and ready to combine. [The word "combine" is a verb meaning to harvest with a combine, a noun, and pronouned "CAHM bine" in Ohio farm communities.] Otto had arranged for a custom harvester to come in later in the week with his machine to harvest the crop, but now his wife's concerns about rain began to worry him. If it did rain, a lot of the beans would be down in the muddy field and he would be likely to lose about half his crop. If, to top it off, the rain continued for a week or so, which was possible that time of year, the ground might be too wet to get machinery in the field until the ground froze. In that case, most of the beans would be lost.

Now Otto had a problem. The custom harvester was busy with other fields and couldn't get around any earlier than he had promised. Otto didn't have a combine of his own and everyone who did was either busy with it in their own fields or else doing custom work for others. It was right in the busiest time of harvest with both corn and soy beans ripe about the same time.

Otto Kuhn lived next door to Hank Sherman and could watch what Hank was doing in his fields. This morning he had noticed that Hank was out in his corn field harvesting his corn. Hank did have a harvester, one that could be converted from a corn picker to a grain combine in a matter of a few minutes. Hank was busy just now harvesting corn and had started early in the morning in order to get the corn in so he could start on his own soy beans. Farmers are pretty busy at harvest time.

Otto went over to Hank in the corn field and stopped him.

"Corn's pretty good this year, ain't it?" Otto opened the conversation. No courteous farmer began negotiations by stating his business first off. The amenities had to be observed.

"Not bad," Hank replied non committally, shutting off the machine and climbing down to see what Otto wanted. Otto was not noted for idle chit chat and he must want something or he wouldn't be there.

After some idle comments about crop yields and the weather, Otto got to the point. "How about switching your machine over to the combine and comin' over to do my beans?"

"Ain't you got Sam Harris' man comin' over Friday?" Hank asked.

"Well, yeah," Otto replied, "But the forecast is fer lots of rain and I'm scared the beans'll go down an' I'll lose half of 'em if I wait any longer."

"What about my corn?" Hank said, "An' I've got beans to harvest too."

"Well, the corn will stand better than the beans will an' yer bean fields drain better'n mine an' they ain't as ripe as mine anyway."

"Well, OK," Hank said, "I'll be over shortly. I gotta switch head on the machine to the combine so it'll be a hour or so."

"I sure appreciate it," Otto said and headed for home.

Hank came over and harvested Otto's soy beans, finishing the next day. The weather turned cloudy and rain threatened but held off until Hank got his corn and beans both in the granary and corn crib. Otto sold his beans immediately because the price was pretty good and he didn't have enough storage space for his whole crop. Things looked well and both farmers were happy.

Then a day or two later heavy rains set in for the whole midwest, ruining soy bean harvests for many farmers. The rains came just after Otto would have had his beans harvested by the custom harvester, so he didn't really need to have bothered Hank. However, immediately afterward, the prices went up considerably because of the poor harvests elsewhere. Otto was not happy watching the prices go up so precipitously because he had already sold his crop. Hank on the other hand, partly because he had postponed his own harvest, benefited greatly by the price increase.

Otto saw Hank at the feed store a few days later.

"Thanks a whole lot fer nuthin'," was his greeting to Hank. "If you hadn't been in such a damn hurry to harvest my beans I'd a got a whole lot more fer 'em. Why din't you wait till yers was done first?"

"Hey, man," Hank replied, "You was the one wanted 'em done right away. What are you mad about anyway? I just did what you asked."

"Well, it's yer fault that I got robbed by sellin' 'em so soon. If I had just waited a couple of days, they would've brought a lot more. Next time, don't be in sich a hurry."

The following year, Otto got the custom harvester to do his soy beans, but the windfall that he had missed never happened again. He didn't forgive Hank for several years, actually not until he wanted something again.

Friends say that I'm only fooling myself, but that's good enough for me.

Unknown

Satan to a new arrival in Hell: "The trouble with all you liberals is that you believe that you are the best people down here, when the truth of the matter is that you are merely the most numerous."

Unknown

Put it there, my man! You look like you might have the minimum daily allowance of intelligence. Tell me where I can find a book to help me gain self confidence.

Books and Authors

Word Games by Anna Graham
Voice of the People by Rankine Phyle
Ancient Styles and Mores by Dinah Sauers
Current Wedding Customs by Marian Haste
Statistics and Poll Results by N. A. Kerate
Apathy and Slow Motion by Lee Tharjick
Cryptography Made Easy by Rosetta Stone
Lucky Chances by Sarah Anne Dippity
Tough Love by Martin Nette
The Italian Cook Book compiled by Minny Stroney
Driving the Back Roads by N. X. Sessable
Driving the Interstate Highways by Beryl A. Long
Crime and Injustice by Molly Factor
Sleeping Well by Katy Tonnick
Sheep, Wool, and Shepherds by Lana Lynn

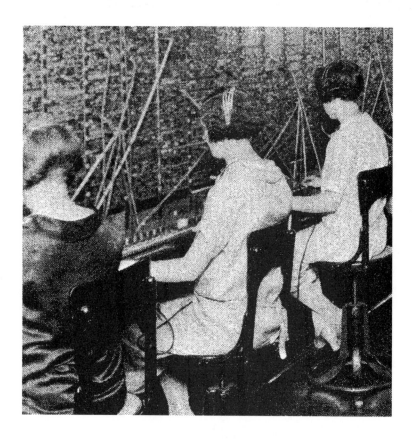

Operator: Of course you may call Santa Clara if you wish to, sir, but he's not going to like it.

A rock group asked the mayor for permission to hold a concert in the city park. The mayor said, "Only if you promise to clean it up."

The leader of the group replied, "That's OK. We don't mind it the way it is."

In 1985 I was living in Columbia, Maryland, at the time that the Grateful Dead rock group held a concert there. The next morning on my way to work, I drove through the area where the Deadheads had spent the night. I never saw so much trash in my life. In the evening as I drove home, the trash was all gone. The city had cleaned up most of it and the rest had gone home.

Practical Advice and Comments

Not everything good smells good.

REB

If you travel on the *Titanic*, why **not** go first class?

Unknown

Your car is on its way down, Mr. Morris

The bloke wot said 'is coffee tasted funny left wivout paying.

I bet yer'd like ter know wot 'appened to them chops on the way 'ere from the market. Drawings by F. H. Townsend, ca. 1904

1931 Dusenberg (Probably)

This is the kind of automobile my family would have had if they could have afforded it. All automobile sales were so bad in 1931 that only a few were manufactured. At the time, a new Ford or Chevrolet could be had for about $600 or $700. This doozy could be had for several thousand dollars, about five or six years income for my parents at the time. But is surely is pretty, isn't it.

In 1931 my parents had a 1924 Model T Ford touring car but they had it in the buggy shed on blocks to keep the load off the tires. For several years they couldn't afford the expense of licence tags and gasoline to keep the car running, so they stored it until times got better. My father walked to the nearest store when necessary for a few grocery items like salt which couldn't come from the farm. Meat, vegetables, flour, corn meal, and fruit came from the farm and garden. Occasionally, one or another of the neighbors or relatives would give us a ride to town or church.

In a couple of years, money was available to get the Ford back on the road and my father bought a closed coupe body for the Model T. He then removed the old touring car body and replaced it with the closed coupe body. That made the car marginally better winter transportation. There was no heater but at least most of the wind could be shut out of the coupe when moving along the road at a brisk twenty-five miles per hour. It was necessary to drain the radiator of the Model T when leaving it for more than an hour in the winter. Otherwise the radiator would freeze because few people we knew used antifreeze in their cars. In town, when leaving the car for a short time, a blanket would be placed over the radiator to keep it warmer for a while. When it was really cold, the blanket was left draped over the radiator because the wind through the radiator could freeze it even when driving along. Some motorists used kerosene in the radiator instead of water, a rather dangerous practice but probably not much more dangerous than the alcohol antifreeze in general use. Either one could be very flammable if the radiator or hoses leaked.

**Your dinner will be a little skimpy tonight. The
dog ate most of it before I could stop him.**

We had a visiting dog one time. Our daughter-in-law, before she and our son
were married, had two dogs but was supposed to have no more than one dog in the
apartment where she was living as their house was being built. So we kept one of
the dogs at our house for a few months. We already had two small dogs so one
more was no bother.

The visitor was a labrador retreiver, a very nice placid dog, but one that was
considerably larger than our two terriers. Marty was accustomed to having food in
preparation sitting on the kitchen counter without concern; our dogs couldn't reach
that high. The visitor could though.

One day, Marty left a large bowl of spaghetti and one of sauce on the edge of
the kitchen counter while she left the room for a minute. As soon as her back was
turned, the visitor pulled the bowls onto the floor and all three dogs had an Italian
dinner. They did a good job of cleaning up the bowl and the floor, but we had
something else for dinner that evening.

Irish Coffee

Irish coffee: a delicious blend of coffee and Irish whiskey. It provides every nutritional need for the human body, fat, sugar, caffeine, and alcohol. The only important food missing is chocolate. This lack can be remedied by replacing the whiskey with Bailey's Irish Cream.

REB

Sometimes on March 17, non-Irish people add green food coloring to Irish coffee, thus making an otherwise delightful beverage into an absolutely vile looking liquid.

A Irish Expression

The very lovely and talented Irish lady, Anna McGoldrick, tells of an embarrassing event in her career when she used an expression which would be readily understood by another Irish person, but not necessarily by someone else.

Anna was singing at a concert in Los Angeles, California. As she left the stage, a woman who had been watching from the wings complimented Anna profusely on her performance. She also said that at the same concert bill the previous year, a young singer had done quite poorly and was obviously inexperienced. Anna happened to know the young singer, who later went on to become one of the leading sopranos at London's Sadler's Wells Opera Company, but at this point in her career was a bit nervous and uncertain.

The very elegantly dressed and coiffured woman, who was an attorney/agent in show business, praised Anna for her stage presence, her beautiful voice, and her proven ability to use it well. At the same time, the woman was very critical of the young singer for her somewhat disappointing stage manner. Anna, seeking to soften the criticism a bit and explain why the young singer was still not up to her potential, said, "Ah, well, the old dog for the hard road...", whereupon any Irish person would know the rest of the expression is "...and the pup for the path." This, of course, means simply that the old dog knows the ways of traffic well enough to be comfortable on the hard road (main highway) while the pup is safe on the path until it has learned how to handle itself in traffic. In other words, experience helps.

Unfortunately, the woman talking to Anna had never heard the expression and took immediate offense. She apparently thought that Anna had responded to compliments with an insult. "I'll have you know I'm only fifty years old!" she exclaimed. Anna found that the more she tried to explain the expression the worse the situation got. Anna decided that it is best to use Irish sayings with Irish people but not with just anyone.

Doctor: So what is your trouble?
Patient: I can't pee any more.
Doctor: So how old are you?
Patient: 97
Doctor: Aaah, ye've peed enuff!

Murphy and Sullivan had a rather long convivial night of it and made pretty heavy going on the way home. The next day, Murphy saw Sullivan and noticed that Sullivan's hands were bandaged. Murphy said, "What happened to your hands after I left you last night?"

"Ah, I was getting along fine going down the High Street till I got to me own street. No trouble at all at all. Then as I was turning into me own street, some fool stepped on me fingers."

Sod the garden! I'm off to the pub!

This is a caption that fails to amuse Americans, but does get a laugh from British or Irish. The term "sod" means "apply grass turf" to Americans, but has the additional meaning of "commit the act of sodomy" in British or Irish slang.

In the same way, the following story doesn't mean a thing to an American. A Police Constable stopped an Irish motorist and asked, "Are you fully licenced?" "Indeed I am!" replied the motorist. "Oh, thanks be to God and all his angels!" said the policeman. "I'll have a gin and tonic."

The term "fully licenced" in Britain and Ireland means that a restaurant or pub owner is licensed to sell all alcoholic beverages, including spirits as well as beer and ale.

An Irishman is not drunk as long as he still has a blade of grass to hang onto.
Unknown, sometimes attributed to Dylan Thomas

She: You feel OK? That chicken sure smelled funny when I cooked it!

An Answered Prayer

A man was stranded on a desert island in the South Pacific. After struggling ashore and exploring the small island he found that there was an old hut on the island that was still somewhat serviceable and that there was a supply of fresh water not too far away. By diligent searching he found enough crabs and shell fish along the shore and some fruit and coconut palms to provide some vegetable supplement to his diet. But things were difficult.

He prayed to the Lord to save him from this island every day but as the days wore on, he became very discouraged. His prayers became more desperate.

One day as he was returning to his hut after searching for food as far from the hut as he could get on the island, he discovered the hut in flames. The thunderstorm that had passed by had apparently set the house on fire with lightning. The man was devastated and railed against God.

"Why have you done this to me?" he cried, "I was in bad shape enough before but now you have taken my only shelter."

Just before it got dark, the man saw a small freighter approaching his island. As it neared, the man began waving his arms and shouting. The freighter captain sent a small boat ashore to rescue him and when the man reached the ship he asked, "How on earth did you find me? I've been here for weeks and there were no ships passing by."

"Oh, as we were going by, just over the horizon, I saw smoke. I knew that there was supposed to be nothing over here, so I decided to investigate. You were lucky to have lit a fire just when you did."

First invader: Every day since we've been in England it has rained and rained, but today it's just drippy.
Second invader: Yeah, but where are all the people?
Squad leader: Hey, old man, where is everyone?
Old Timer: Oh, on a nice day like this, they all go to the beach.

Music always sets a romantic mood. Can't you imagine the scene where there is candlelight and wine, a beautiful woman and a young man having dinner. Doesn't it really complete the scene when he says, "After dinner we can listen to music; I have my concertina."

Unknown

A gentleman is one who can play the concertina but doesn't.

Unknown

Lackey: Senator, there's a man outside who wants to know what to do with your old campaign posters.

Senator: Why, those are collector's items!

Well, what did he say?

Put them out by the street for the trash collector.

Religious Conversion

When Ole moved up north he discovered that he was the only Lutheran in his whole new little town of all Roman Catholics. That was OK, but the neighbors had a problem with Ole's habit of

barbecuing venison every Friday evening. Because they couldn't eat meat on Friday, the tempting aroma was getting to them.

Hoping that they could say something to stop this, the neighbors got together to go over and talk to Ole. They eventually persuaded Ole to join their church.

The big day came and Ole knelt for the priest to bless him. The priest put his hand on Ole's head, sprinkled some incense and holy water over Ole's head and said, "You were born a Lutheran, you were raised a Lutheran, and now you are a Catholic."

Ole was happy and the neighbors were happy. But the next Friday evening at suppertime, the familiar odor of grilled venison steaks wafted over the neighborhood from Ole's back yard. The neighbors went to talk to him about this but as they approached Ole's back fence they heard him say, "You were born a whitetail, you were raised a whitetail, and now," he said as he sprinkled barbecue sauce on the steaks, "You are a walleye."

Unknown

One sign of getting older is when you start forgetting things that happened. Another sign is when you remember things that never happened.

REB

The University of Virginia contains the cream of Virginia — rich and thick.

paraphrased from Samuel Beckett

I don't care much for alcohol as such, but all of the drinks that taste really good seem to contain alcohol.

REB

The Customer is Always Wrong

Customer: Your sign is wrong.
Shopkeeper: The sign is right! <u>You</u> are wrong!

You can get more with a kind word and a gun than you can with just a kind word.

Attributed to Al Capone

I prefer rogues to imbeciles because they sometimes take a rest.

Alexander Dumas

Neglected Childhood

I was a neglected child because both of my parents were artists. My mother never baked cookies the way a proper mother should for her children. If I asked for a cookie she would draw or paint a picture of one for me. She painted in oils when she wasn't drawing with pen and ink and she could make very realistic looking cookies.

One winter day when I was about five or six, too young to go to school yet, I asked for cookies one day and wasn't satisfied with the drawing I received. Mom was busy at her drawing board so I decided to bake my own cookies. I had learned enough about reading that I thought I could handle a recipe book, so I started in.

The first lot of sugar cookies was about to come out of the oven — we had a wood-burning cook stove that had a pretty tricky oven, but the stove was kept hot all winter — when Mom came out of her study to see what the strange odor coming from the kitchen was. She took the cookies out of the oven, tasted one, and said, "What did you put in these cookies?"

"Just what the recipe called for," I replied.

"Show me the ingredients," Mom said. So I showed her the sugar, butter, eggs, milk, flour, baking powder, vanilla, except when I showed her the vanilla bottle she realized that I had not read the label carefully.

The bottle of vanilla looked a great deal like the bottle of liniment that was kept in the same cabinet. Liniment does add a sort of piquancy to cookies. Vanilla is better.

Mom threw out the batch that I had mixed up and told me to start over. Then she went back to her drawing board. She never baked again that I recall until I grew up and left home. Any baking that was done, I did it.

Well then, read it yourself! It says "Five pounds of flour, five pounds of sugar, quart of milk, a dozen eggs, a bottle of vanilla, and don't forget anything!

Bloody Nuisance

In the 1930's, as in ages past, a regular farm chore was butchering animals for the family's meat supply. Every boy growing up on a farm was accustomed to this chore as soon as the weather got cold enough that the meat wouldn't spoil before it could be preserved by one means or another. How any farm boy could then grow up fainting at even the thought of blood is beyond my comprehension, but one of my school classmates did just that. Just the mention of blood would cause Richard Hall to pass out cold.

All of the classmates and most of the teachers were aware of this quirk of Richard's and were kind enough never to say "blood" in his presence or mention anything that would even evoke the thought of blood. That is, until in eighth grade a new math teacher came to our school.

Mr. Harris was a new graduate of Ohio State University and this was his first year of teaching. He taught eighth grade math among other things, and was quite enthusiastic about his work. He liked to liven up his classes by recounting adventures he had experienced in college; math is a pretty dull subject otherwise.

One day he told about a prank he and some of his fraternity brothers had pulled one evening on one of the brothers who was out on a date. They had found a male mannequin, dressed it in pajamas and put it in the brother's bed. Then they messed up the room to look as though a struggle had taken place and drove a knife into the dummy's chest. Then they poured catsup all over it to look like blood.

Richard was seated near the back of the classroom and was paying attention to the story. He was doing fine until Mr. Harris got to the word "blood" whereupon Richard's eyes rolled upward, his face paled, and he slid sideways out of his chair to the floor. Mr. Harris's mouth dropped open in shock, but two of the boys in the class picked Richard up and half carried, half dragged him out to the corridor to the water fountain. By this time, Richard had recovered enough to get a drink and return to his seat.

Mr. Harris then said, "Now, where was I? Oh, yes, we poured catsup all over the dummy to look like blood..." There went Richard again onto the floor. This time the two boys simply picked Richard up and set him back in his seat and supported him there for a few seconds until he was able to sit there on his own.

Mr. Harris, somewhat shaken but still determined to continue his class said, "As I was saying, we poured catsup all over to look like blood..." and there went Richard onto the floor a third time.

As the two boys picked Richard up yet again, one boy said, "Mr. Harris, for God's sake please stop saying 'blood'. We're getting tired of picking Richard up." At the sound of "blood", Richard passed out a fourth time.

That pretty much put an end to Mr. Harris's story and he continued with the math lesson for the day. He never again used the word "blood" in Richard's hearing and I suspect that if Mr. Harris is still alive, he remembers that day in class.

Welsh Nicknames

There are many Evans, Jones, Hughs, Williams, and Thomas names in Wales so the Welsh use imaginative nicknames to distinguish one from another in conversation. Here are some examples: ("Dai" is a short form of the name "David")

Dai Loco:	An engine driver (locomotive engineer)
Georgie One Ball:	Obvious
Evans the Death:	An undertaker
Barry Central Eating:	Has one tooth in front, close to centrally located
Dai Eighteen Months:	Has one whole ear and one half ear
Will Population:	Has twelve children
Davy Eleven Waistcoats:	Dressed against winter's chill
Dai Mikado:	Once sang in a Gilbert and Sullivan opera
Jack the Bomb:	Was in an army ordnance bomb squad
Willy Bingo:	Owns a bingo hall
Dai Quiet Wedding:	Wore sneakers to his own wedding
Horizontal Harry:	Was a boxer who often lost
Dai Upper Crust:	Once shook hands with a royal family member
Ned Bakerloo:	Got lost once in London's underground
Mrs. Dai Double Yolk	An egg merchant's wife who had twins
Toni Titanic	Weighed 280 lbs.
Jones the Filth	A newsagent who received some pornographic literature by mistake

Told by a Welsh friend who chooses to remain anonymous

The difference between Heaven and Hell is that in Heaven the French are the cooks, the English are the policemen, the Germans are the mechanics, the Italians are the lovers and the Swiss are the organizers. In Hell it is just the opposite, the French are the mechanics, the English are the cooks, the Germans are the policemen, the Italians are the organizers, and the Swiss are the lovers.

Unknown

You'll have to eat in the kitchen. Your steak is stuck to the grill.

I have a niece who does wonderful things with leftovers. She throws them out. She figures why waste time and refrigerator space when that is what will be done with them eventually anyway and rightfully so.

REB

Let others praise ancient times; I am glad I was born in these.

Ovid (ca. 1 a.d.)

I have learned how to spell hors d'oeuvres, which grates on many peoples' nerves.

Unknown

Chop: A piece of leather, skillfully attached to a bone and administered to patients at restaurants.

Ambrose Bierce

Tea, not tree! I ordered a small tea!

One must be specific when ordering anything. You usually get what you ask for, but it may not be exactly what you want.

A mouse had been having trouble with cats chasing it. The mouse had heard that the owl was a pretty wise old bird so the mouse decided to consult the owl about his problem. The mouse thought he had better call the owl on the phone because he had also heard that it was safer for a mouse not to get too close to an owl.

He told the owl his problem and the owl gave him some good advice.

"All you need to do is change yourself into a dog and you can chase the cats instead of them always chasing you," was the owl's advice.

"Sounds good to me," said the mouse. "Now how do I do that?"

"Look, son," said the owl. "I'm an idea man. You'll have to work out the details for yourself."

This advice is about as good as what one gets from most motivational speakers who get good money at seminars and retreats. Their advice sounds good until you get out of the seminar and try to put their ideas into practice.

Mimi O'Graf, the Irish Printer

Oh come now! Surely you must know if you have hospitalization insurance!

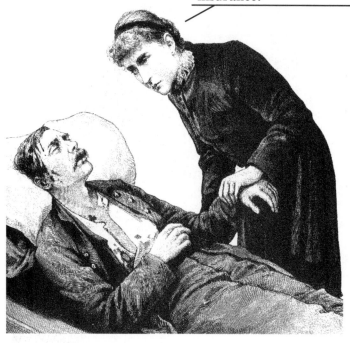

I have always been puzzled to hear of accident or murder victims so badly mutilated that they have to be identified by their dental records. What I can't figure out is, if they have no idea who it is, how do they know who the victim's dentist is?

Unknown

Now, remember. Tell Mr. Bell to take one pill every night at bedtime and one each morning just before he wakes up.

Tiny objects, when dropped, run and hide.

Murphy's Third Law

There is an updraft over wastebaskets.

Murphy's Law of Aerodynamics

Grub first, then ethics.

Politician's Credo

If you think it is tough now, just wait.

Optimist's Forecast

No, no, that's just an alligator that's got him. A crocodile has a much longer and narrower snout and is inclined to be dangerous!

But I don't know how to spell hydrochlorothiazide/triamterene!

The Technical Writer Proofreader's Nightmare
(Before spell checker systems)

A burglar broke into a house and was flashing his light around looking for something of value. Just as he spotted some beautiful candlesticks and reached for them he heard a loud voice say, "Jesus is watching you." The burglar stopped reaching and flashed his light all around the room but didn't see anyone. So he reached again for the candlesticks only to hear the voice again, "Jesus is watching you."

This time when he flashed his light around he saw a parrot in a cage in the corner of the room so he said to the parrot, "Did you say that?"

"Yes," said the parrot, "Jesus is watching you."

"Aah, what do you know?" said the burglar, "Who are you anyway?"

"I'm Moses," said the parrot.

This time the burglar laughed and said, "Aah, what crazy people would name a parrot Moses?"

The parrot replied, "The same crazy people who named the rottweiler Jesus."

I said STEAK, not snake, you idiot! I ordered rare steak!

A Safety Lesson

On the surface Joe Tomko was a rude, crude, foul mouthed, sneaky, dishonest, insensitive bully, but deep down in his heart he was just plain rotten. Joe had injured his left foot many years before and walked with a limp, not that he needed to, the pain having been long forgotten, but from force of habit.

Joe was a shop supervisor in a firm manufacturing telephone equipment. Joe managed a shop molding plastic parts and was responsible for the quantity and quality of product produced by his machines and people. He was not responsible for the design and specifications of the parts he molded. Mike Svoboda was the Product Engineer and had that responsibility.

One morning Joe was informed by the inspector of his parts that one batch of parts did not meet the requirements and would need to be scrapped. Joe immediately called Mike to inform him.

"Mike, you got a problem," Joe stated, somewhat inaccurately because the problem most likely lay in Joe's territory but Joe didn't like to take the blame for any problem that could be laid at someone else's door.

When Mike came into the shop, Joe began a tirade about the poor engineering support that Mike provided, losing his temper in the process. Joe's temper was not connected very strongly anyway and was easily lost. At the conclusion of the tirade, to which Mike has listened patiently and calmly, Joe said, "Mike, you got your safety shoes on?" and brought his heel down sharply on Mike's toes.

The company was very safety conscious and one of the hard and fast rules was that no street shoes were to be worn in the shop. All shoes must have steel cap over the toes to protect the foot from falling objects. The penalty for being caught without safety shoes was one day off without pay, regardless of the rank of the person. One couldn't tell by looking at the outside of the shoes if they were safety type or street shoes.

Mike never flinched. He calmly said, "Yes, I do. Do you?" and stamped hard on Joes right foot. Joe was not wearing safety toe shoes.

Joe's face paled, partly from the pain and partly from the realization that if Mike chose to report Joe's violation of a company saftety rule, Joe would have a day off without pay. Joe muttered something about Mike trying to see what the problem with the parts was and hobbled over to his desk, trying to limp on both feet at the same time.

The machine operator who had been standing by waiting for his boss to finish chewing Mike out, said, "You gonna report him?"

Mike said, "For what? I can't tell by looking whether he has safety shoes or not. Let's look at those parts and see if we can figure out what's wrong."

**Hmmm, my ad isn't having the effect I had hoped for.
I wonder if the newspaper misprinted my hours.
Nope, they got it right: 6 a.m. until noon.**

Druggist: Ah, uh…, if you're going to wait for this prescription, please don't touch anything.

My dog can lick anyone.

Unknown

Headline: Suicidal twin kills sister by mistake.

Unknown

Mr. Bell was employed by me for a brief time. I can confidently say that anyone would be lucky to get him to work for them.

From a letter of recommendation to a prospective employer

Falklands Islands Folly

The Falklands are located some 300 miles off the southern coast of Argentina and inhabited in 1966 by penquins, a few sheep, some 2300 farmers and fishermen, and not a whole lot else. [1995 population was about 4700.] The climate is something like Britain's except the Falklands are colder and more drizzly. They were originally settled by the British in 1833 but have been claimed ever since that date by Argentina, which calls the islands the Malvinas, which means something like bad wine. The ownership has been debated before the OAS and the UN and they are even featured in postage stamps put out by both countries. Every Argentine schoolboy has been brought up on the slogan, "The Malvinas are Argentina's."

In 1966, sixteen years before the Argentine army decided to invade the Falkland Islands, a group of zealots from Argentina jumped the gun. Led by a blonde playwright, eighteen members of the Movimiento Nueva Argentina climbed aboard a DC4, a commercial airplane scheduled to go from Buenos Aires to Rio Gallegos in southern Argentina.

Shortly before the plane was scheduled to land, the group pulled out pistols and submachine guns and ordered the pilot to change course for Port Stanley, the capital of the Falklands. This was a really well thought out plan, led by a real organizer, Maria Cristina Verrier, a cross between a glamor girl and James Bond. If all went well, they would land about dawn, surprise the British Governor and police chief in their beds, and take control without firing a shot.

Then plans fell apart. First, the flight to the Falklands took longer than they had planned and then they discovered that there was no airstrip on the islands. So the frightened pilot had to do his best to set the plane down on a race track. Fortunately, there were no races scheduled that day. When the shaken conspirators left the plane, they found themselves surrounded by curious islanders, none of whom spoke enough Spanish to understand that they had been conquered by the victorious Argentines. Then the invaders discovered that the Governor was off the islands.

The natives were very hospitable. They took the plane's 23 non-conspirators into their homes and their feelings were hurt when Maria Cristina and her group refused to be welcomed and chose to stay on the plane. The last straw for the conspirators came when the island's small police force politely informed them that it was against the law anyway to arrest the police chief or to capture public buildings. Very much disappointed, the conspirators gave up and accepted beds in Port Stanley residents' homes.

News of the invasion shocked all of Argentina. The country's Peronist labor unions called for an all-out mobilization in preparation for the invasion of the Falklands. A gang of hoodlums invaded the British consulate in Rosario and burned a portrait of Queen Victoria. In Buenos Aires, eight shots were fired at the shuttered windows of the British embassy, where Prince Philip had just arrived for a three-week goodwill visit.

Too sour, old boy?

To calm the uproar, President Juan Carlos Ongania issued an announcement declaring that, although the Malvinas were the rightful property of Argentina, the government would permit no violence to enforce its claims. So saying, he declared the conspirators to be under arrest and sent a ship to pick up the DC4's stranded passengers and invasion force. There was no need to apologize to the citizens of the Falklands; the attempted invasion had given them something to talk about for sixteen years.

It was on April 2,1982 that Argentina did begin the ill advised attempt to capture the Falklands, an invasion that lasted until June 14, the same year. The reason it lasted so long was that it took the British aircraft carriers until May 21 to get from England to the Falklands. They are a long way from the United Kingdom's main island. So the invaders had to wait. There wasn't much else to do on the islands anyway except chase sheep and annoy the natives.

If you are going to do it, do it big.

REB

A: Have your eyes ever been checked?
B: No, doctor, they've always been blue.
Anonymous

A few years ago I was getting some new glasses fitted and the technician said, "Did you know that you have one ear lower than the other?" Of course I did, so I just mumbled something like, "Uh-huh" and let it go at that. Then the technician went into the other room and the optometrist came in to check the fit on my glasses.

He looked at them and then said, "That's odd. Did you know you have one ear higher than the other?" I said, "Oh? That really *is* odd! Your technician said that one ear was *lower* than the other." He looked at me strangely for a second and then said, "Excuse me a minute," and then went in the next room where I could hear him saying something in a low voice to the technician. Then I heard her laugh and he came back in where I was and completed the fitting.

I don't think he ever figured out that I was kidding him. That is part of the fun of teasing someone — keeping a straight face. As someone once said, it is easier to pretend to be serious than it is to pretend to be witty.

The Devil is in the Details

There is always some little detail that will screw up the best laid plans, some little item that one overlooks.

When I was still living on the farm and trying to earn my money on a job in town, I had to get up and milk the cows before leaving for work. The usual routine was for me to shower, shave, eat breakfast, milk the cows, change clothes and hurry to work. Any interruption in that routine made a hash of the whole schedule.

One morning I discovered that one of the cows needed a medicated salve rubbed on her udder to heal an irritation. A large container of salve was in the house so I carried the milk to the house, found the salve and then considered how to transport enough to the barn for the treatment without carrying the whole container. I don't know why it was so important not to carry the whole container and then bring it back, but I must have had a reason.

I looked around for a disposable container to carry the salve to the barn and my eye lit on a crust of toast left over from breakfast. "Why not?" I said to myself. So I dabbed a bit of salve on the toast and hurried back to the barn carrying the toast and salve.

At the barn, I had to set the toast down for a minute while I got the cow back into the stall so that I could treat her. When I then turned to pick up the toast, I saw the cat carrying it away. I don't know if the salve made the toast taste better or worse for the cat; I never tried salve on toast. But the toast and salve were both gone now.

I had to make a second trip to the house for more salve. This time I carried the whole container and then put it back after use. The cat didn't seem any the worse for the salve. Maybe it liked it, I don't know. But I was late for work that day.

Hey! Last night I prayed to you for patience! What's the delay?

Cheaper by the Carton

Dick Tate was a stingy man. In addition to having acquaintances make fun of his name from the time he was in kindergarten, he also had experienced people trying to take advantage of his good nature all of his life. As a result, he had become extremely sensitive to anyone trying to get the better of him in any dealings, financial or otherwise. As an adult he wouldn't give anyone anything, not even the benefit of the doubt.

Dick worked in the same engineering office that I did at the time. He rode to and from work in a carpool with three other men and always seemed to get a slight edge on his share of the rides. The agreement was that each man would drive one day a week and every fourth Friday. The other men always managed to do their shares of driving but Dick always had an excuse on his Friday to drive and one of the other men would always fill in for him. This was more of a source of amusement to the other men, but it was deadly serious for Dick; it saved him a few dollars a year in gasoline.

The engineering office was isolated from the other buildings for the company and had no cafeteria. Also, before the day of the ubiquitous vending machines, there were no soft drink or snack machines in the building. As a result, the employees had set up a refrigerator for soft drinks in the cloakroom by the stairs. They also had installed a cupboard with cigarettes, candy, and snacks by the refrigerator. All of the items were purchased on the honor system with a box beside the cupboard for money. One purchased what one wanted and left the money in the box, making change if necessary. The system worked well and there was quite a selection of goodies to choose from.

Dick Tate kept the concession stand stocked with goodies and took care of the money. He was suspicious and grasping but he was honest. He made a little profit on the items because he bought candy bars by the box, drinks by the case, and cigarettes by the carton and sold at normal retail prices. It was a convenience for the employees and no one begrudged Dick the little profit he made.

One of the other engineers liked to give people what he called "the mental hotfoot", practical jokes that caused puzzlement and perhaps frustration, but no physical harm. Because he may still be alive and might feel obligated to play one of his jokes on me, I will use the name Jerry Mander for him because that is not his real name.

Jerry decided one day to give Dick a hard time. Jerry normally bought cigarettes from the grocery store by the carton, paying the regular retail price. At the time, cigarettes could be purchased for about $1.60 a carton. Dick charged 20¢ a pack for cigarettes from the cupboard, the price most retail sales places charged. Obviously, Dick made about four cents a pack profit, no big deal.

Jerry approached Dick one morning and offered to sell him three cartons of cigarettes for $1.52 each. Dick, of course, jumped at the bargain; he had been paying what everyone else did and this saved him a few cents on each carton. He wasn't one to look a gift horse in the mouth.

After Jerry had done this every week or two, Dick began to question him on where he could get cigarettes at such a low price. Jerry wouldn't tell him. Dick couldn't imagine anyone selling anything unless there was a profit in it, so therefore Jerry must know of a place that sold cigarettes for less than $1.52 a carton. The puzzle really bothered him.

Dick came around to me one day wondering if I knew where Jerry was getting the cigarettes for such a low price. I knew because Jerry had shared his joke with me, but I pretended I didn't.

Dick went to other engineers in the place asking them if they knew where Jerry could buy cheap cigarettes, but if they knew, they didn't tell Dick. This obviously bothered Dick. The puzzle went on for months. I went into the army about a year later and Dick still didn't know at that time that Jerry was pulling his leg. I never heard out if he ever did find out.

A Helpful Suggestion

Above all, don't be afraid, George! They can sense fear, you know!

A Word in Private
IF YOU ARE DULL YOURSELVES, DON'T HAVE YOUR DINNERS TOO LONG.

The cartoon above was originally published in 1901 and the one below in 1894 by Life publishing company. Both were by Charles Dana Gibson and were subsequently printed in The Gibson Book II by Charles Scribner's Sons in 1907.

GULLEM AT THE ADVICE OF HIS PHYSICIAN TAKES OUT-OF-DOOR EXERCISE.

Another Helpful Suggestion

Would it be advisable to back up?

An Encouraging Word

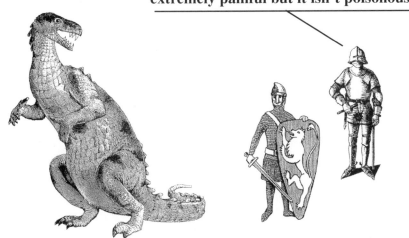

This picture appeared in an advertisement for a hearing aid service. I have reprinted it here with permission from GNResound, the manufacturer of digital hearing aids. I can empathize with Grandpa because my hearing is no longer as sharp as it used to be. Of course, neither are any of my other faculties. But I hope I would have smelled smoke before my granddaughter had to notify me with a note even if I didn't hear the commotion.

A Fiery Letter

June 6, 1974

SCRIPTO, INC.
423 Houston Street N.E.
Atlanta, Georgia, 30302
Dear Sir:

Having decided many years ago that being fundamental is not always the easiest way to camp, I have progressed to magnesium pack frames, nylon packs, freeze-dried trail foods, feather-light tents, butane stoves, and the like. In this headlong plunge into "modern" camping, it occurred to me that since dew makes matchheads mushy and rain, perspiration or water in the canoe makes matches disintegrate, I should provide myself with a handy-dandy, foolproof method of producing a flame. First I bought a non-refillable lighter named Butane Match but the fuel supply was not visible and it pooped out unexpectedly right in the middle of a camp-out. Fortunately the spark could be used to light the butane stove and the resultant WHOOSH vaporized only about 25% of the hair on the back of my hand.

I solved the problem by buying a 99¢ Scripto (made in Japan), visible fuel supply, adjustable flame butane lighter. But, alas! I only introduced a new set of problems. First, the flame cannot be adjusted long (or strong) enough to clear the thumb when the lighter is tilted over to ignite butane stoves, campfires, or pipes. Second, the head of the lighter supports combustion! (Can this be Scripto's ecological masterpiece — a self-consuming lighter?) Instinctively, I immediately smothered the flame with my thumb. Shame! Shame, Scripto! You must share in the guilt of contributing to the delinquency of a minor. Can you imagine the shock on the faces of seventeen Scouts and five adults when their leader put his thumb in a puddle of melted sticky plastic? My deleted expletives actually took the bark off several trees.

I took the lighter to Eckerds (a drug store chain) in hopes of exchanging it for a pipe lighter or something more suitable to my purposes, but all they had in stock was more of the same and one named Cricket which is no better suited. I, therefore, hand my problem over to you — I would like to trade you this lighter. Please look around your sample room, or whatever, and see if you have something more suited to my needs — actually the Butane Match (you probably don't make it), rechargeable, with visible fuel supply would be perfect. I have no further use, having quit smoking 3 years ago, for the flammable lighter so you may have it back if you want it.

Actually the first of this letter is in a lighter (get it?) vein, but since I, too, am in industry, I am well aware of the increasing emphasis (and authority) given to both OSHA and to governmental consumer groups which hold that manufacturer's responsibilities extend ad infinitum. It is possible, therefore, that an event which I consider to be a humorous anecdote could be parlayed into a massive product recall program, or some equally obnoxious activity. At least, now, you are aware that the lighter will burn.

So now the problems are yours. You have to — (1) decide whether or not I deserve a new and different lighter, and (2) decide what to do about the "made in Japan" flammable lighter. Good luck to me in (1) and good luck to you in (2).

Yours truly,

A. P. SYKES, JR.
2015 Woodland Avenue
Burlington, NC, 27215

Visitor: **I hope it's not contagious**

We will now begin boarding the aircraft at the rear of the cabin. Those seated in rows fifty-five to sixty may now begin boarding. Rows fifty-five to sixty only.

**...and I'm pleased to report that our sales have tripled since we
changed the directions from "Use sparingly" to "Apply liberally."**

Unless constantly nurtured, nothing is as short-lived as a good customer.
                                                                Unknown

A recent news item on our local radio station concerned a citizen who had
recently been interviewed by the roving reporter at the Federal Courthouse. Mr. X
said that he was hoping to become a neutralized citizen that day and that he had
been for some years an osteopathetic physician.

Policeman: **"Where did you get that bag?"**
Bill Sikes (indignately) : **"There you are! Fine thing, in a free
country, that a man can't have a quiet hundred up without the
Police interfering!"**

Times Haven't Changed

This cartoon was published by Frank Townsend in 1906 and shows what suspicious minds the police had. The modern policemen have just such nasty suspicious minds, as is indicated by an event that happened in 1999 on a major highway in England.

The southern part of England had been having a rash of robberies of automatic teller machines (ATM's). The robbers would drive up to a machine in the wee small hours with a fork lift truck, smash into the wall where the machine was located, and tear it out of the wall. Then they would drive away with the machine on the fork lift to some isolated spot where they could smash the machine open at leisure.

On one occasion the police, having suspicious minds, stopped a fork lift truck driving along a major highway in Dorset, far from any village or town, carrying an ATM on the lift. It aroused their suspicions when the police noticed that the ATM had bits of masonry and mortar stuck to the outside of it. They arrested the driver without having any reports of stolen ATM's, thus indicating how little times have changed since Townsend drew his cartoon nearly a hundred years ago.

Lost in Tok

One of the towns in Alaska is named Tok. It used to be Tokyo until 1941 when the town leaders decided that Tok was better. It is still pronounced "Toke" and it is still a small town, of about 1000 year round population. Its main distinctions are that it is at the major cross roads in Alaska and it has an airport.

The two major highways in Alaska are Alaska Route 1 and Alaska Route 2 If you drive into Alaska on Route 2 from Canada, the Alaska Highway, about 120 miles into Alaska you enter Tok. If you turn left onto Route 1, in another 400 miles or so you will enter Anchorage. If you continue straight on Route 2 at Tok, in another 320 miles or so you will enter Fairbanks. There are not many opportunities to get off those routes, so your chances of getting lost are nil if you stay on the paved road.

One day about five in the afternoon a man entered the Tourist Information office in Tok and asked the lady at the desk, "Where is this?"

The lady replied, "Tok."

"Where is Tok?" he then asked.

"Here." she replied.

"But where is Tok?" he asked again.

"Right here. This is beautiful downtown Tok," she answered.

"Tok what?" he then asked.

"Tok, Alaska."

"Alaska?! Alaska! Are you **sure** it's Alaska?"

"Yes, it's Alaska. Where did you think it was?" the lady said. "You came into Alaska from Canada about 120 miles down the road." (She had seen the direction he came from and there isn't anywhere else that direction.)

He didn't answer the question. He just said, "But I didn't intend to come to Alaska. I was headed for Arizona."

He left the Tourist Information office muttering incredulously, "Alaska, Alaska."

He got in a new Dodge camper truck with Oregon plates on it and drove away, headed toward Fairbanks. He appeared to be alone so presumably he didn't have anyone along to ask him where he thought he was going.

If he had left Oregon on Interstate 84 headed east, the logical route to Arizona would be to go to Interstate 15 in Utah and turn right. If he turned left on Interstate 15 instead of right, he conceivably could end up in Alaska if he kept going north long enough and made the correct turns. It isn't easy but it could be done.

That is carrying not stopping to ask directions to extremes. One would think the scenery he was passing through would have tipped him off that something just wasn't right. Alaska doesn't look like Arizona at all although both are sparsely populated.

Druggist: Uh, I never could read your doctor's
writing. What are your symptoms?

Editor's Diary

Thursday, July 26, 2001

I just finished my supper of two slices of chewy rye bread spread generously with cream cheese. I topped that off with a banana. After that sumptous feast, I am ready to relax and write a bit in my journal. Well, actually to whine a bit. Perhaps this will make useful material for my autobiography if I ever get around to writing one.

I spent the better part of today playing in the traffic. I had to go all the way downtown to Capitol Mac to get the new Epson scanner I thought I needed. There is always something else needed when you have a computer.

I stopped on the first trip out to leave my old printer's toner cartridge for a refill and then stopped again on the way back home to pick it up. All the running around in traffic pretty well killed the morning.

After lunch I discovered that the cable included to hook up the scanner was the wrong cable for my computer, so back downtown again to get the correct one. Connecting any peripheral device to a computer always requires something you didn't get when you bought the item.

On the way I stopped at the office supply store and bought a ream of extra good paper for the fax machine. The paper I had been using, the same as for the printers, was of a little too heavy a quality for the fax machine and about two of every three sheets fed through it jammed. Never on a fax I was sending but only on incoming faxes. Then I would have to unjam it and try again. Fortunately the fax machine remembers what it is supposed to print so it just does it again when I put paper back in. Often it jams again. Frustration. Maybe it will like the thinner paper; I hope so.

Then I went to the cleaners to drop off a suit that needs cleaning and pressing. He has gone out of business since I was there last, so I had to take the suit to a different cleaner. It will probably be OK.

On the way home I went by the post office to see if anyone remembered my address and had sent me something. There was nothing but some junk mail in the box but I had to stop to find that out.

Then when I finally did get the scanner operating, I discovered that I can't see any improvement in quality over what I was getting with the old one. It turned out that I didn't need a new scanner after all, but now I have two. I thought that the poor quality of some of the graphics in this book was due to my old scanner having given up on doing a good job, but it seems that the problems were due to the skill of the operator, me. Ah well, I probably can use the new one too. I certainly am not going to admit that I was mistaken and return an item that there is nothing wrong with. So I'll keep it anyway and have two scanners, one 8 1/2 by 11, the new one, and one 8 1/2 by 14, the old one. The new one has a few bells and whistles the old one doesn't have which I may find useful. I hate and detest having to take something back when there is nothing wrong with it, just a mistake on my part. I hate to admit I was wrong.

Friday, July 27, 2001

Today I went to see my optometrist first thing in the morning. He is so slow he gets on my nerves, but he is so thorough and careful that I keep going back. About 15 years ago, I had a problem one evening that made me fear I had a detached retina so I went to see this man first thing in the morning without an appointment. He looked and looked and then sent me to an opthamologist who put me in the eye hospital immediately for laser and cryogenic treatment that day. The opthamologist at first looked and looked and finally said, "Ah! That could have been missed easily." That is when I decided I could overlook the optometrist's slow ways. He is thorough.

It is now late afternoon and I haven't been able to see properly for hours because of the pupils being dilated. Ah well, this is a slow time anyway in the publishing business.

I have the two scanners sitting side by side on my reference table. Just to be certain that one is as good as the other, I scanned two similar photos at the same 600 dots per inch, left both images untouched in PhotoShop® and then moved both onto one document in PageMaker® to print them one above the other to see if I could see any difference. I couldn't. So it just looks like I have an expensive hobby, but at least it is cheaper than a boat.

While I was at the optometrist, the plumbers came and replaced our water heater. I don't need new glasses but the money I would have spent on glasses went for the water heater. I guess we saved some; I don't think the water heater was as expensive as new glasses would have been. The pressure at the showers and faucets had dropped to a trickle because a pipe inside the old water heater disintegrated into small chunks of white plastic which went all through and clogged all the pipes in the house. The replacement took care of part of the problem, but the pressure is still pretty low because it will take months for all the particles in the system which are clogging the lines to dissolve or whatever they do.

There is always something expensive when you have a house. Our grandparents didn't have this kind of problem; they had Indians lurking in the woods behind the house instead so that every trip to the "bathroom" was an adventure. I prefer low water pressure.

A few years ago, Marty and I stopped to visit her Uncle Pete who lived in a small village just off the Interstate highway we take to visit relatives in Ohio. Uncle Pete was nearly ninety and in pretty shaky health, but in good spirits. I asked him how he was doing and he said, "Well, pretty good, I guess. But I've quit buying green bananas."

He figured that he might not live long enough for them to ripen and he didn't want to waste the money. I can't help but wonder if I have been buying green bananas by starting a business at my age. I may not live long enough for it to become profitable. But at least it keeps me off the streets and out of the pool hall as one of my old classmates pointed out. Maybe I'll write a book telling all the mistakes I have made in starting a publishing business and help some other poor soul avoid those mistakes. Maybe such a book would sell and make me some money. Maybe it isn't just a hobby after all.

More Traveler's Tales

We have had some interesting experiences with rental cars in England. Safety and luxury features often appear on European cars before they do on American cars and sometimes they are confusing or puzzling to a driver who is not used to them. For example, VW introduced a safety feature on their cars in England before it was used in American cars, an interlock to prevent your pulling the gear selector out of Park unless you had your foot on the brake. (This feature now is on some American cars but not others, which shows that some designers think it necessary and others don't.)

We were stopped on a narrow street in the residential part of Oakhampton, Devon, one day because the trash collection truck was blocking the street as the men picked up trash at various houses. It would move a few houses and stop again. We couldn't get around until it reached an intersection, so we waited. The street happened to be level, a rarity in Britain, so there was no need for me to use the parking brake or foot brake to prevent rolling. I just put the selector in Park and shut off the engine while waiting. Petrol (gasoline) is expensive in England, more than four times what it is in the United States, so one doesn't waste it.

When the truck moved on, I started the engine but couldn't put the selector out of Park. I fiddled with it and cursed it and then it moved to Drive as I wished. This happened every time the truck stopped and we had to wait. I never did figure out the combination. Actually, I stepped on the brake without giving it any thought as I was struggling with the gear selector; then it worked. I never figured that out but Marty got out the owner's manual and read it a day or two later and told me what the combination was. The cursing really had no effect, in spite of what I thought.

The other feature was one that VW had for at least one year. I think they dropped it after one year.

Most British cars have had a feature that American cars finally got around to. When the driver's door is locked, either with a key or the remote control, all the doors are locked and when the driver's door is unlocked, all doors are unlocked. Convenient. Then VW added a little icing on the cake. They fixed it so that the alarm system was activated whenever the driver's door was locked either with a key or the remote control. All doors locked and alarm set all in one motion. Terrific! Really convenient. Now most cars with alarms have that feature. Except that VW made the alarm sensitive to the car being rocked or jostled in addition to sounding off if a door was opened.

We arrived at a B&B the first day in England and settled in for the night. Our room was at the back of the house, a very nice room, and the car was pulled up next to and facing the front of the house, just outside the host's bedroom. The night was a bit windy and the gusts of wind were strong enough to rock the car. Enough in fact to set off the alarm which sounded loudly for a full minute every time it happened. And it happened several times that night.

We didn't hear it but the host mentioned it the next morning at breakfast. Because we were in the country, we didn't really need the alarm, so I looked in the owner's manual to see how to lock the car without setting the alarm. There was a procedure described for doing just that, except that it didn't work. There must have been a way to do it, but the manual writer and the car manufacturer weren't singing from the same song sheet. We never did figure that one out but occasionally I could manage it by trial and error, never consistently though. What worked one time, didn't work the next. We just left the car unlocked most of the time at night, or we parked it facing away from the B&B and as far away as possible when we were in an area where there might be a need to lock the car.

We could tell if the alarm was set or not when the door was locked because there was a little red light that blinked if the alarm was on. Sometimes I could lock the door without the little light coming on, most times I couldn't. The next year, VW didn't have that feature. The alarm could be set only with the remote control, not the key. So then it was easy to lock the car without the alarm. They also apparently fixed the alarm so that wind gusts wouldn't trip it. We never had that problem after that one year.

The things one learns when traveling. No wonder they say that travel is educational.

This is a bangers race in England The racers are amateurs and get together on Sunday afternoons at a more or less natural amphitheater in the South Downs of England. The track is dirt, which in this part of England is mostly chalk so it makes a good, smooth, but dusty track.

Many of the races are between skilled amateur race drivers in good sport cars and the race is quite serious and quite good. The race in the picture is what they call a bangers race. In it, the object is to finish first no matter what, and there are no rules other than to stay within the confines of the track and go completely around the course each lap. If someone is in the way, it is perfectly within the rules to knock him away. Often a car gets turned over and rolls into the infield such as it is. In that case the pit crew and other volunteers rush into the infield and try to right the car, usually successfully. If it can still run, and it usually can, it then gets back in the race and continues to compete.

The favorite cars for such races are Ford Escorts or Austin Minis. Austin Minis were first on the market in 1959 and are incredibly small and incredibly fast. They have tiny wheels on the corners and are remarkably stable, so they are ideal for racing. They have seats for four adults and were a very popular "first" car for young people in England. In 2000 they were still being made and sold, having changed very little from the original design.

One comment by an automobile critic when the Mini first came out was, "If God had intended cars to go this fast, He'd have given them bigger wheels." The first few years of the design, Minis were imported into the United States, but were never very popular because they are even smaller than the well known VW "bug". But the ones that were brought in were fast and surprised many American sport car aficionados by running away with prizes at sport car rallies. It looks like a small family car, but its performance is amazing.

I remember driving down an English motorway one time at about 90 mph and being passed by a Mini with four or five football fans on their way to a game. It went by me without a bit of problem with banners for their favorite team blowing to tatters out the windows.

We can no longer bring Minis into the States sad to say. They will not meet our emissions standards.

A 1959 Austin Mini. The ones in the bangers races don't look quite this good.

Brighten Your Smile!

Before   **After**

Teeth can be lengthened to even them up.

Teeth can be widened to close gaps.

Teeth can be whitened as much as fourteen shades of white, without harsh chemicals.

All work done while you wait.

Windsor Orthodontic Clinic
Four Chairs —No Waiting

Tom's Tire Shop

Do you fix flats?

We can repair almost any tire damage. If we can't fix it, we will tell you what you can do with it.

Tom's Tire Shop is ready to help you get back on the road. Open most days from nine to noon.

Floyd and Cecil's Diagnostic Service

Bring us your hard to solve problems

Cecil wanted me to ask you if you know where your owner's manual might be

Al's Auto Repair Shop

Bring your car to us and you'll never go anywhere else.

Now watch what happens when I turn on the…

Bernie's Body Shop

We'll save you a bundle

Well, at least we'll save a bundle on gas the next few weeks.

Phil's Fuel Injector Service

If we can't find the problem we'll tell you where to go.

We found your problem. It's dog hair in the fuel system.

Worley's Wrinkle Cream

Where you get what you ask for

Monday

I'd like a cream for wrinkles.

Tuesday

Perhaps I should have been more specific.

Attend the Church of your choice on Sunday

We've got room for just one more today. Which of you is the more humble?

An Answered Prayer

A six-year-old girl came crying to her mother. Her brother was setting a trap in the back yard to catch a squirrel and the little girl was very upset about it. Her mother suggested that the girl go back into the family room and pray to God to keep any creatures from getting caught in the trap.

Ten minutes later the mother noticed that the little girl was contentedly playing in the family room, apparently without a care in the world. So the mother asked her, "Did you pray to God to keep the animals out of the trap."

"Oh yes," replied the girl, "And he answered my prayer right away. He told me to go out and kick that trap all to pieces. So I did."

Pray as though it is up to God. Work as though it is up to you.

Thomas Aquinas

When all else fails, seek divine help

My man is afraid that your engine computer has been possessed by an evil demon, Mr. Bell. He suggests you contact a priest.

Ed's Experts
Automotive Specialists

If we can't find the problem, we'll guarantee our work

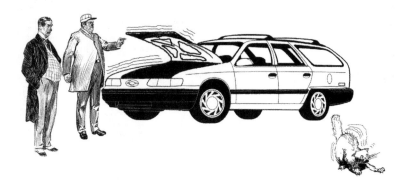

See that cat, Mr. Davis? That means you either have a bad vacuum leak or your power steering pump is shot.

Ernie Doczy

At the time that Ernie Doczy drew this cartoon, which was used in a presentation to one of the government commissions, the liberals were doing everything they could to destroy the Bell System. The main cause of their concern was that American Telephone and Telegraph had customarily overcharged business long distance calls in order to subsidize local private telephone service. The result was that competing telephone companies could not get any local customers because they couldn't reduce their rates low enough to compete and still make money.

The tactics used to break up the company included placing so many restrictions and red tape in the way of doing business that the company had to increase rates to make a profit. Then the competitors could get into the long distance business, because they found that the real money was not in local business but in long distance service so they never bothered trying to get into local service.

Shortly afterward the government broke up the Bell System and local rates went up to reflect real costs and long distance rates came down.

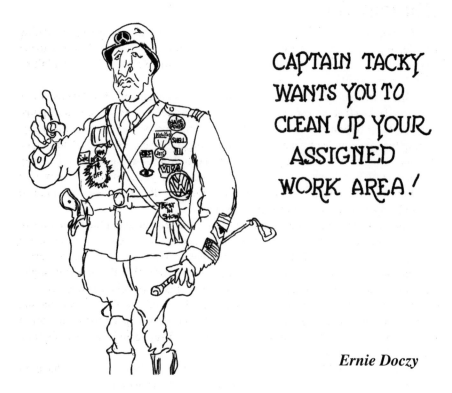

CAPTAIN TACKY WANTS YOU TO CLEAN UP YOUR ASSIGNED WORK AREA!

Ernie Doczy

When Ernie drew this cartoon, the company, Western Electric at that time, had a management team that believed it was important that the office area, which was never seen by visitors, should be neat and tidy at all times.

A decree came down that all desks were to be cleared every evening before going home. Nothing was to be on the desk after hours, all books, papers, drawings, telephones, everything was to be shut in closed cabinets when we were not there. The cabinets did not have to be locked; it was not a security problem. They merely had to look neat when no one was there.

Each evening after working hours a committee of management types would tour the engineering and administrative offices awarding points for neatness. The result of this campaign was that the last fifteen minutes or so of every day were spent picking up work and neatly hiding it away in desk drawers and cabinets and the first fifteen minutes or so of every morning were spent getting the material out of the drawers and cabinets in preparation for work.

Ernie posted this cartoon on the bulletin board and some of the upper management people found it offensive rather than amusing. He had to remove it the next day but I persuaded him to give it to me. I have saved it for about twenty years.

This is the company that eventually became Lucent.

Student Days

One of the real benefits of attending college is the acquaintance of interesting people. Even though much time is spent on academic pursuits, one has time to get to know lots of other people, most of whom are a little weird or they wouldn't be there in the first place.

One of my early acquaintances at Purdue was a man named Jim Adams. I was working days and attending evening classes at Purdue's extension in Indianapolis. Jim was from Indianapolis and was also attending Purdue's extension in that city, getting his first couple of years in by going to night classes. He worked during the day and lived with his parents in the north end of town, saving his money to pay for his last two or three years on campus in West Lafayette, Indiana. Jim was an excellent student and was getting very good grades in all of his classes, planning to obtain his degree in Mechanical Engineering.

Both of us moved to the campus in West Lafayette at about the same time to attend classes full time for the last three years and get our degrees. I was married and had a family so I lived in the married student area in one of the converted army barracks that were so common on campuses after World War II. Jim, still single, lived in one of the dormitories on campus but we had some classes together.

Shortly after starting classes on campus, Jim told me that he was having difficulty meeting expenses and would probably need to drop out for a semester or two to work full time and save some more money. I suggested that he apply for a scholarship, as I had done, which would help.

"Oh, they wouldn't let me have a scholarship," Jim replied. "I have an automobile and have made too much money when I was working."

"What do you have to lose by asking?" was my answer to that.

So Jim went over to the scholarship office and talked to the people there. He ended up with a much better scholarship than I had obtained, one that paid most of his school and living expenses. He had excellent grades and met the needs requirements, even though he had an automobile which he thought would disqualify him. I wasn't doing too badly with a scholarship, but I didn't have as good a grade index, so I didn't get quite as good a scholarship as he did.

Jim was a quiet, scholarly type, who studied regularly and didn't attract much attention. Another student who lived near me in the married student area was a very different type. This chap didn't attract favorable attention, at least not from me, because he drove a new Ford hardtop with loud dual exhaust pipes. He had two radio antennas, both with fox tails dangling from them and liked to sit at a traffic light with one foot on the brake and the other tapping the accelerator, racing the engine a bit. When the light would change he would release the brake and take off with tires squealing, drag racing with any other driver who would accept the challenge. He almost always had a stub of a cigar stuck in the side of his mouth and was, in my opinion, rather brash in his manners. Not my type of guy at all.

Joe Mechem was a bit older than most of his classmates. He was probably in his early thirties and had spent several years in the army before coming home to Lafayette and getting a job with a manufacturing plant, the largest employer in the area. He had completed his apprenticeship and was now a master machinist, working full time at night and going to Purdue in the day time. He was married and had four children, and lived not far from me in the married student area.

Joe's personal appearance didn't do much to endear him to me either. He had a rather low forehead and a short and stocky build. He looked like my idea of a truck driver. During my first year on campus, I didn't happen to have any classes with him, which suited me fine.

At the beginning of the second year on campus, Jim and I found ourselves in the same electrical engineering course which included a couple of lab sessions a week. Lab assignments were set up in teams of three students at a bench position and Jim and I discovered that we were teamed with Joe. This was not to the liking of either of us, but neither had ever had a class with him.

At the first lab session we were instructed to put together the specified device and test it. We were cautioned that the power connections were not to be made until the instructor had inspected the setup to be sure that we would not electrocute ourselves, burn down the building, or cause any other disaster. Joe, as was his habit with lab classes we learned, showed up after the initial instruction lecture, about 15 minutes late. Jim and I had set up most of the wire and equipment, following the diagram shown in the lab manual. We were nearly finished and Joe glanced at the setup and the diagram in the manual, grabbed a couple of wires and connected them and then reached toward the power connections.

"Wait a minute," both Jim and I exclaimed. "The instructor said for us to have him check the setup before we connect any power."

"Oh?" Joe replied, "Well, let's see."

He quickly glanced over the setup, took a quick look at the diagram in the manual, and said, "Looks OK to me."

He then connected the power and we finished the experiment in a few minutes. We spent a total of perhaps thirty minutes in a two hour lab session and got everything done satisfactorily. Even the instructor was surprised.

This turned out to be a typical lab session in that class. Jim and I would arrive on time and do about half or so of the preparation for the experiment.. Joe would show up about fifteen minutes late, glance at the diagram, complete the setup in a few minutes, turn on the power and we would be out of the lab in less than an hour every time. Fastest worker in the lab I ever saw.

As we got to know Joe better, we found that he was going to school on full GI Bill benefits, having spent over four years in the army. He was working as a master machinist working at least a forty hour week at the factory, every day from three o'clock in the afternoon until eleven thirty at night. He was carrying not just a full load of credit hours — he was on the accelerated schedule to complete the five normal years of study in four years or less, going summer sessions as well as regular semesters. His point average was nearly perfect so his grades obviously didn't suffer much from his activities. I think the only courses he didn't have a perfect score were a few of the nontechnical electives where he might have gotten a B.

I asked Joe once when on earth he studied. He told me that his work often could be done by setting up a machine in the first hour or so of his work shift and then let it work automatically for several hours while he just watched to make sure that nothing unpleasant happened. He could study at that time, sitting by his machine.

He didn't have a scholarship, other than his GI Bill, because he was making so much money on his full time job. Scholarships were and are granted about as much on need as on scholastic performance.

His financial status caused him a problem when it came close to graduation time. Most of the engineering students interviewed recruiters and were offered jobs about the middle of the senior year. As May approached and there were only a couple of weeks left before graduation, Joe had not received an offer although he had interviewed with several company recruiters. He was already making more money that the starting salaries for newly graduated engineers. He was seriously considering staying at Purdue and getting a graduate degree, which would probably have compounded his problem.

Just before graduation, the company he was working for gave him an offer that was satisfactory. They planned to send him to one of their foreign operations to supervise part of the work at that location. He got a generous salary plus travel and moving expenses for his family and promises to pay all of the expenses for return to Lafayette with his family annually for vacations.

I have had no contact with these two characters since graduation. I wonder what has become of them.

One of the lessons I learned at Purdue was not to judge anyone by appearances, especially first impressions.

Ernie Doczy Quotations

On this day in 1945, the first all white Dalmation was spotted.

On this day in 1973 a new drink was invented, the tequila mockingbird.

Book Review Section: Lincoln, the Man, the Car, and the Tunnel
                                                    by Noah Vale
                        Hail, Hail, the Gang's All Queer
                                                    by Anita Bryant

Mr. Eubeedee: "Yes, I've changed a good bit since then, Mrs. Jones."
"And for the better, I trust."
"They used to call me a Wild Youth, you remember, but now—"
"Now?"
"Now they call me an Old Reprobate."

This cartoon by Charles Dana Gibson was first published in 1904. I don't think it is very funny; it hits too close to home for my liking.

If you like this book, watch for some of the present and future releases from Penrith Publications:

Traveling the South Pacific, Without Reservations by Evangeline Brunes. This is a description of the author's experience, traveling alone through the South Seas, without reservations and on a very limited budget. Best of all, she tells how any reader can do the same, avoiding the expensive tourist places, enjoying the scenery and meeting the real people.

Released October 2001.

Buying Green Bananas by Robert E. Bell and Evangeline Brunes. This sometimes hilarious and often informative description of how three people, all over seventy years of age, formed a new company to publish books. The learning experiences of this group, about as well matched in ambition, ability, and personality as Stan Laurel and Oliver Hardy, will entertain as well as help the reader start a business without getting into lot of the problems that this group experienced.

Planned release date is October 2002 (if they live that long).

Penrith Publications, LLC
7340 Penrith Drive, Mechanicsville, VA, 23116, USA
(866) 746-8150 Fax: (804) 746-8190
email: penrithpub@aol.com

Copies of this book can be obtained from your local bookstore. If they don't
have it, the bookstore can order it from Baker and Taylor, Inc. or from Quality
Books, Inc. You can order it directly if you wish from:

> Book Passage
> 51 Tamal Vista Blvd.
> Corte Madera, CA, 94925
> 1-800-999-7909

Penrith Publications, LLC

7340 Penrith Drive, Mechanicsville, VA, 23116, USA
(866) 746-8150 Fax: (804) 746-8190
email: penrithpub@aol.com

A completely satisfied customer